FROM THE LIBRARY OF
Charles Stark

The University of Chicago Publications
in Religious Education

Edited by

W. C. BOWER   EDWIN E. AUBREY

W. C. GRAHAM

GREAT MEN OF THE CHRISTIAN CHURCH

THE UNIVERSITY OF CHICAGO PRESS
CHICAGO, ILLINOIS

—

THE BAKER & TAYLOR COMPANY
NEW YORK

THE CAMBRIDGE UNIVERSITY PRESS
LONDON

THE MARUZEN-KABUSHIKI-KAISHA
TOKYO, OSAKA, KYOTO, FUKUOKA, SENDAI

THE COMMERCIAL PRESS, LIMITED
SHANGHAI

GREAT MEN OF THE CHRISTIAN CHURCH

By
WILLISTON WALKER
Late Professor in Yale University

THE UNIVERSITY OF CHICAGO PRESS
CHICAGO, ILLINOIS

COPYRIGHT 1908 BY THE UNIVERSITY OF CHICAGO
ALL RIGHTS RESERVED. PUBLISHED DECEMBER 1908
TENTH IMPRESSION SEPTEMBER 1938

COMPOSED AND PRINTED BY THE UNIVERSITY OF CHICAGO PRESS
CHICAGO, ILLINOIS, U.S.A.

EDITORS' PREFACE

The development in the field of religious education has made it plain that there can be no hard-and-fast curriculum for the Sunday school or for other agencies by which morals and religion are to be taught children and youth. Each group of pupils must be carefully studied with reference to its own needs. It is far more important to develop the religious interest and activity of a class than to insist upon the precise sequence of textbooks in an elaborate course of study. The "Constructive Studies Series" attempts to meet the needs of the teacher without too precise adherence to any predetermined curriculum. Its various textbooks have been prepared to give pupils of different ages and development both a knowledge of the Christian religion and also inspiration and direction in the development of character. Especially do they seek to stimulate the self-activity of the pupils. In the nature of the case a textbook will be somewhat formal and didactic. The skilled teacher, however, will place emphasis where the needs of the class demand, and will develop discussion of social problems which grow out of the material of study. To this end, the series which at the beginning was primarily concerned with biblical material and the biography of Christian leaders is constantly being enriched by the addition of volumes dealing with educational projects, the use of pageantry, drama, the discussion of social and international questions.

Without the prescription of a course of study in Christian biography at any point in the curriculum, it will be entirely natural that a group of students will be interested to know something about the great personalities who have appeared through the Christian centuries. When that interest is developed this textbook will be available as a guide.

AUTHOR'S PREFACE

This brief series of biographies is designed for the reader or student without technical training in church history. For this reason considerable attention has been paid to the general condition of the church or of religious thought in the periods in which the leaders here described did their work, in order that the reader may appreciate their relations to their times. The number of biographies might well have been increased and the selection may easily be criticized; but the writer believes that none have been chosen who were not really representative men, and his aim has been to illustrate the manifold variety of Christian service, life, and experience.

In mentioning additional reading the aim has been to present a few only of the most accessible works in the English language. Questions have been appended to facilitate review or to aid possible instructors who have made no special study of church history.

YALE UNIVERSITY
May 1, 1908

CONTENTS

	PAGE
JUSTIN MARTYR	1
TERTULLIAN	21
ATHANASIUS	41
AUGUSTINE	63
PATRICK	85
BENEDICT	101
HILDEBRAND	117
GODFREY	139
FRANCIS	157
THOMAS AQUINAS	175
JOHN WICLIF	195
MARTIN LUTHER	215
JOHN CALVIN	235
JOHN KNOX	253
IGNATIUS LOYOLA	271
GEORGE FOX	285
NICOLAUS LUDWIG VON ZINZENDORF	301
JOHN WESLEY	319
JONATHAN EDWARDS	339
HORACE BUSHNELL	355
INDEX	371

JUSTIN MARTYR

I
JUSTIN MARTYR

To pass from the time of the Pauline epistles to the middle of the second century is to come into a very different world of thought. The old battle which the Apostle to the Gentiles had bravely fought against the imposition of a legalistic Jewish yoke upon heathen converts had become well-nigh forgotten ancient history. The destruction of Jerusalem (A. D. 70) and the rapid growth of churches on Gentile soil had shifted the center of gravity of the Christian population, so that the vast majority of disciples were now of heathen antecedents. Of all parts of the Roman Empire, Asia Minor was that in which the church was now most strongly represented. Syria, northward of Palestine, Macedonia, and Greece were only in less degree its home. Probably it was already growing strong in Egypt. A close-knit, extensive, influential, Greek-speaking congregation was to be found in Rome, and a group of small assemblies existed in the Rhone Valley of what is now France. Probably, but less certainly, the church was already well represented in the old Carthaginian region of Africa; but, in general, the Latin portion of the Empire was as yet little reached by the gospel.

Christians, though rapidly growing in numbers, were still chiefly from the lower classes of the population and of slight social influence. They were knit to one another by a common belief in God and Christ; a confidence in a divine revelation contained in the Old Testament and continued through men of the gospel age and subsequent times by the ever-working Spirit of God; a morality relatively high as compared with that of surrounding heathenism; and a confident hope that the present evil world was speedily to pass away, and the Kingdom of God to be established in its stead. As sojourners separated from the world they owed each other aid, and developed a noble Christian benevolence.

Yet, though the Christianity of the middle of the second century had possessed itself fully of Paul's freedom from Jewish ceremonialism, it was far from being Pauline. It did not consciously reject him; but it was unable to grasp his more spiritual conceptions of sin and grace and the significance of Christ's death. Paul had been only one, if the greatest, of the missionaries by whom Christianity had been preached. To ordinary disciples of heathen antecedents Christ seemed primarily the revealer of the one true God whom heathenism had but dimly known, and the proclaimer of a new and purer law of right living. God, through Christ, had revealed his nature and purposes, and had given new commandments which were to be fulfilled by chaste living and upright conduct. "Keep the commandments of the Lord, and thou shalt be well-pleasing to God, and shalt be enrolled among the number of them that keep his commandments,"[1] said Hermas, writing at Rome between 130 and 140; but he added with an utterly un-Pauline feeling of the possibility of works of supererogation: "but if thou do any good thing outside the commandment of God, thou shalt win for thyself more exceeding glory." "Fasting is better than prayer, but almsgiving than both," said a preacher to his hearers a few years later, probably in Corinth or Rome.[2]

These changing conceptions of the Christian life were not the chief perils, however, which Christianity was encountering. It had come into no world empty of thought. As we do now, that age attempted to interpret the gospel message in the light of its own science and its own conceptions. It had its own philosophies and its own religions with their secrets for those initiated into their mysteries. The result was a number of interpretations of Christianity, called in general "Knowledge" ($\gamma\nu\hat{\omega}\sigma\iota\varsigma$), the thought being that those who possessed this inner and deeper understanding knew the real essence of the gospel much better than the ordinary believer. Gnosticism had its beginnings before the later books of the New Testament were written. The Pastoral

[1] *Similitudes*, v: 3.

[2] The Sermon erroneously called II Clement, chap. 16.

Epistles and the Johannine literature, whenever composed, contain clear references to it.[1] Its full systems did not, however, develop their power till the second quarter of the second century. Gnosticism had many forms, but its essential feature was that it made the God of the Old Testament a relatively weak and imperfect being. It taught that the perfect and hitherto unknown God, far abler and better than the God of the Old Testament, sent Christ to reveal himself and to give men the knowledge by which they can be brought from the kingdom of evil to that of light. Since most Gnostics regarded this physical world as evil, any real incarnation was unthinkable, and Christ's death can have been in appearance only. If his body was more than a ghostly deception, then Jesus was a man indwelt by the divine Christ only from his baptism to shortly before his expiring agony on the cross.

This thinking, though urged by men of great ability, denied the historic continuity of Christianity with the Old Testament revelation, it rejected a real incarnation, and it changed Christianity from a historic faith to a higher form of knowledge for the initiated, explanatory of the origin and nature of the universe. This Gnostic crisis was the most severe through which the church had yet passed; and its dangers were doubly increased when essentially Gnostic views of the Old Testament and of the

[1] E. g., I Tim. 1:4; 6:20; II Tim. 3:6–8; I John 4:2, 3.

inferior character of the God therein revealed, though by no means all the Gnostic positions, were advocated by a man of deep religious spirit, in some respects the first church reformer of history, Marcion. Having come from Asia Minor to Rome about 140, he broke with the Roman church in 144, charging it, not wholly groundlessly, with having perverted Paul's Gospel to a new Jewish legalism. To him Paul was the only genuine apostle; and he gathered a little collection of sacred writings, including ten of Paul's epistles and the Gospel of Luke, but shorn of all passages intimating that the God of the Old Testament was identical with Him whom Christ revealed. All the rest of the apostles and of our New Testament writings he rejected. It was indeed true that the church of his day was un-Pauline; but his Paulinism was of a type which Paul himself would have been the first to discredit.

To the Gnostics the party in the church representing historic Christianity replied by gathering a collection of authoritative writings, the major part of our New Testament; by the preparation of creeds, of which that at the basis of what we wrongly call the "Apostles" is the earliest; and, especially, by appealing to the teaching handed down in the churches founded by the apostles, and guaranteed by the continuity of their officers. Out of this struggle the rigid, doctrinally conservative, legalistic church of the third century—the "Old Catholic" church—came.

To these perils from within were added the dangers which sprang from popular hatred, due to heathen misunderstanding and jealousy, and to the occasional active hostility of the Roman government, which viewed the new religion as unpatriotic and stubborn because of the unwillingness of its adherents to conform to the worship prescribed by the state. Its feeling was much that which would animate many among us should any considerable party now refuse to honor the flag. To the unthinking, because they refused to join in the worship which the state required, the Christians seemed at once atheistic and unpatriotic. Popular superstition, because of their refusal to share in heathen festivals and their worship by themselves, charged them with practices of revolting immorality. The Jews, also, though politically insignificant, were critical of Christianity; and, existing as they did in every large Roman community, their objections had to be met. These conditions determined Justin's work. He would defend Christianity against its heathen opponents, its Jewish critics, and its enemies within its own household. Hence the threefold battle which he fought.

Justin, in whom is to be seen one of the most characteristic Christian figures, as well as one of the most useful Christian writers, of the second century, was a native of Flavia Neapolis, near the older Shechem, in ancient Samaria. Though thus born

JUSTIN MARTYR

within the bounds of Palestine, and speaking of himself as a Samaritan, he was uncircumcised and doubtless of heathen origin and training. It was not till after his conversion that he became familiar with the Old Testament. Of the date of his birth nothing certain is known; but it must have been not far from the year 100. From early youth he was evidently studious, and he gives, in his *Dialogue with Trypho*,[1] a picturesque account of his search for a satisfactory philosophy. His first initiation was through a Stoic, but when he sought knowledge of God this instructor told him it was needless. He then turned to the Aristotelians, but the promptness with which the teacher sought his fee made him doubt the genuineness of such interested claims. A Pythagorean next was sought, but this philosopher insisted on extensive preliminary acquaintance with music, astronomy, and geometry. Discouraged thus, Justin now turned with hope to a Platonist, and found real satisfaction in this most spiritual of ancient philosophies. He must have made no little progress in his new studies, for he now adopted the philosopher's cloak as his distinctive garb—a dress which he thenceforth always wore. Yet, even while a Platonist, the constancy with which Christians met death impressed him, and led him to doubt the crimes with which they were popularly charged. It was through the gateway of his beloved philosophy

[1] Chap. ii.

that Justin was to be brought, however, into the Christian fold. As he tells the story, a chance meeting with an old man, as he walked by the sea, probably near Ephesus, resulted in a discussion in which his adviser turned his attention to the prophets as "men more ancient than all those who are esteemed philosophers, both righteous and beloved of God, who spoke by the Divine Spirit, and foretold events which would take place, and which are now taking place. .... Their writings are still extant."[1] The effect upon the inquirer was immediate and powerful. "Straightway," he records, "a flame was kindled in my soul; and a love of the prophets, and of those men who are friends of Christ, possessed me; and .... I found this philosophy alone to be safe and profitable. Thus, and for this reason, I am a philosopher."[2]

This conversion, whether the exact circumstances narrated are historic or are the product of Justin's literary skill, took place, we may conjecture, before A. D. 135, and therefore before he had reached middle life.[3] Its fundamental experience was in entire harmony with Justin's previous philosophic

[1] *Dialogue*, chap. vii.

[2] *Ibid.*, chap. viii.

[3] In his *Dialogue* he pictures his conversion as having occurred, possibly some considerable time, before his meeting with the Jew, Trypho, who is represented as "having escaped from the war lately carried on" in Judea, i. e., Bar Cochba's rebellion, 132–35.

training. Its central feature was not, as with Paul, a profound sense of sin, and of new life through union with Christ, but rather a conviction that God had spoken through the prophets and revealed truth in Christ, and in this message alone was to be found the true philosophy of conduct and life and the real explanation of the world here and hereafter. To him the Old Testament was always the Book of books; but primarily because it foretold the Christ that was to come. For these truths he was willing to suffer; and to teach them became henceforth his employment. Just where he lived and labored it is, in general, impossible to say; but he was in Rome soon after the year 150, and it was there that he was later to meet his death.

It was at Rome, not improbably in 152 or 153, and certainly within the four or five years immediately subsequent to 150, that Justin wrote his noteworthy defense of Christianity against its heathen opponents which placed him first among Christian "apologists." This earnest appeal for justice—the *Apology*[1]—is addressed to the emperor, Antoninus Pius (138–161), and his adopted sons, Marcus Aurelius and Lucius Verus. In direct and manly fashion he calls upon these rulers to ascertain whether Christians are really guilty of the charges popularly laid against

[1] The so-called First and Second *Apologies* are really one. They may be found, in English translation in, *The Ante-Nicene Fathers*, I, 163–93.

them and not to condemn them on the mere name. The Christians are accused of atheism, but they disown only the old gods, whose existence Justin does not deny, but whom he regards as wicked demons.

We confess that we are atheists, so far as gods of this sort are concerned, but not with respect to the most true God, the Father of righteousness and temperance and the other virtues, who is free from all impurity.

They are charged with disloyalty to the Roman state; but that is due to a misunderstanding of the nature of the kingdom that Christians seek.

When you hear that we look for a kingdom you suppose, without making any inquiry, that we speak of a human kingdom; whereas we speak of that which is with God.

Christians are not disloyal. On the contrary their principles make them the best of citizens.

More than all other men we are your helpers and allies in promoting peace, seeing that we hold this view, that it is alike impossible for the wicked, the covetous, the conspirator, and for the virtuous, to escape the notice of God, and that each man goes to everlasting punishment or salvation according to the value of his actions.

Christians worship God, Justin declares, rationally; not by destroying the good things he has given by useless sacrifices, but offering

thanks by invocations and hymns for our creation, and for all the means of health, and for the various qualities of the different kinds of things, and for the changes of the seasons; and to present before Him petitions for our existing again in incorruption through faith in Him. Our teacher of these things is Jesus Christ, who also was born for this purpose, and was crucified under Pontius Pilate, procurator of Judea, in the times of Tiberius Caesar; and that we reasonably worship Him, having learned that He is the son of the true God Himself, and holding Him in the second place, and the prophetic Spirit in the third, we will prove.

The last quotation shows that Justin's view of Christ had not developed the form which we are accustomed to connect with the doctrine of the Trinity, judged by the standards of the fourth and fifth centuries. He has a doctrine of the Trinity, but it is relatively unthought-out. Yet his view of Christ is lofty indeed. It sees in him the divine activity always manifest in the world, the constant outflowing of the wisdom of God, or we might say, the intelligence of God in action. Taking up the "Logos" doctrine of the Stoic philosophers, so akin in many respects to that of the Fourth Gospel, and so easily combined with the conception of the divine "Wisdom," set forth, for example in Proverbs,[1] Justin taught that the divine intelligence had been always at work, not merely in creation and in the revelation of God to an Abraham or a Moses, but illuminating a Socrates or a Heraclitus, and the source of all good everywhere. In Jesus, this divine Wisdom was fully revealed. It, or to reflect Justin's view we should say He, "took shape, and became man, and was called Jesus Christ."

[1] Prov. 8:22-31.

In speaking of Justin's conversion, mention was made of the importance which he attached to the prophets and to the fulfilment of their utterances. They were men "through whom the prophetic Spirit published beforehand things that were to come to pass." It was therefore natural that a large part of his *Apology* and of his *Dialogue with Trypho* was devoted to an exposition of such of their utterances as he believed bore on the life and significance of Christ; but he went much farther. Like Jewish writers before him, he looked upon the philosophers of Greece, especially his honored Plato, as having borrowed much from Moses. In Christianity was that true philosophy which all the philosophers, in so far as they have seen truth at all, have dimly perceived. The Jews, in his opinion, had special ordinances, such as the Sabbath, circumcision, and abstinence from unclean meats, given them on account of the peculiar "hardness of their hearts;" but Christ has now established "another covenant and another law." He has revealed God and God's will to men; has overcome the demons who deceived men and delighted in their sins, whom Justin identifies with the old gods; and has appointed baptism as the rite effecting the remission of offenses. Christ's work is, in Justin's estimation, essentially that of a Revealer and Lawgiver, though he is not without some appreciation of the saving significance of his life and death and declares that "we trust in the blood of salvation." This redeeming aspect of Christ's work remains, however, relatively undeveloped.

Thus Justin defended Christianity against its heathen and its Jewish critics. He also replied to its foes of its own household, but his writings against Marcion are lost. His attitude may, however, be surmised from his declaration that "the devils put forward Marcion of Pontus." The contest with Gnosticism was, indeed, strenuous; but charity toward those deemed "heretics" was never one of the virtues of the early church.

A most interesting glimpse is afforded in Justin's *Apology* of the yet simple worship of the Roman church in the middle of the second century. Admission to its membership was by faith, repentance, an upright life, and baptism, though in Justin's view faith is primarily an acceptance of Christ's teachings rather than as with Paul a new personal relationship.

As many as are persuaded and believe that what we teach and say is true, and undertake to be able to live accordingly, are instructed to pray and to entreat God with fasting, for the remission of their sins that are past, we praying and fasting with them. Then they are brought by us where there is water, and are regenerated in the same manner in which we were ourselves regenerated.

He who was baptized was counted fully of the church and shared in its worship. On Sunday the congregations gathered in city or country; the "memoirs of the apostles," i. e., the gospels, or "the writings of the prophets" were read. Then the "president," for Justin avoids technical terms for church officers, "verbally instructed," that is, preached a sermon. Next, all rose and prayed standing, the "president" doubtless leading, and the people responding "Amen." Prayer ended, they "saluted one another with a kiss." Bread and wine mingled with water were next brought to the "president," probably by the deacons; and after "prayers and thanksgivings" offered by him, the Lord's Supper was administered to those present, and the consecrated elements were taken by the deacons to the absent. The service closed with a collection, from which the necessities of widows, orphans, the ill, prisoners, and strangers were relieved; for "the wealthy among us help the needy, and we always keep together." A pleasing picture, surely, of the simple worship and mutual helpfulness of what it must be remembered were still close-knit little congregations, regarding themselves as separate from the world, and all too unjustly looked upon by it as misanthropic, unpatriotic, atheistical, and guilty of secret crimes.

Justin himself was to receive the crown of martyrdom. After the composition of his *Apology* he left Rome, but of his journeys we know nothing, and he was back in the city where he was to die during the governorship of its "prefect," Junius Rusticus, that is between 163 and 167, in the early part of the reign

JUSTIN MARTYR

of Marcus Aurelius. The account of his trial gives an interesting picture of the examination of a company of Christians at the bar of Roman justice.[1] In form, as in all ancient procedure, it was much like an examination in a modern police court, the judge questioning and sentencing the prisoners. Justin was brought before Rusticus, with six other Christians, one a woman, whom the judge evidently regarded as his disciples.

Rusticus the prefect said to Justin, "Obey the gods at once, and submit to the Kings." Justin said, "To obey the commandments of our Saviour, Jesus Christ, is worthy neither of blame nor of condemnation." Rusticus the prefect said, "What kind of doctrines do you profess?" Justin said, "I have endeavored to learn all doctrines; but I have acquiesced at last in the true doctrines, namely of the Christians, even though they do not please those who hold false opinions." Rusticus the prefect said, "Are those the doctrines that please you, you utterly wretched man?" Justin said, "Yes, since I adhere to them with orthodoxy."[2]

Justin then tried to explain Christianity; but the judge soon cut him short.

Rusticus the prefect said, "Tell me where you assemble, or into what place do you collect your followers?" Justin said, "I live above one Martinus, at the Timiotinian Bath; and during the whole time (and I am now living in Rome for the second time) I am unaware of any other meeting than his."

[1] Its genuineness, formerly doubted, is now generally admitted. See Harnack, *Geschichte der altchrist. Litteratur, Chronologie*, I, 282.

[2] *The Ante-Nicene Fathers*, I, 305, 306.

Whether this was literally so may be doubted, but Justin was not unnaturally anxious to prevent persecution extending to his fellow-Christians.[1]

Rusticus said, "Are you not then a Christian?" Justin said, "Yes, I am a Christian."

Thus satisfied of the guilt of the prisoner, the judge turned to his six fellow-accused, and tried to make several of them acknowledge themselves Justin's disciples. They all promptly owned themselves Christians, but gave evasive answers as to Justin's share in their conversion, doubtless wishing to shield him. But the judge was disposed to overlook the past provided the prisoners would now yield full obedience. Here came, as in most early Christian trials, the real test of steadfastness; and a terrible test it was. A pinch of incense cast on the fire burning on the altar before the bench would have freed them; but it would, in the opinion of the time, have been a denial of Christ.

The prefect says to Justin, "Hearken, you who are called learned, and think that you know true doctrines; if you are scourged and beheaded, do you believe you will ascend into heaven?" Justin said, "I hope that, if I endure these things, I shall have His gifts. For I know that, to all who have thus lived, there abides the divine favor until the completion of the whole world." Rusticus the prefect said, "Do you suppose, then, that you will ascend into heaven to receive some recom-

[1] Possibly Justin meant that his was the only "school" where Christianity was taught in Rome. See Harnack, *Die Mission und Ausbreitung des Christentums*, p. 260.

pense?" Justin said, "I do not suppose it, but I know and am fully persuaded of it." Rusticus the prefect said, "Let us, then, now come to the matter in hand, and which presses. Having come together, offer sacrifice with one accord to the gods." Justin said, "No right-thinking person falls away from piety to impiety." Rusticus the prefect said, "Unless ye obey, ye shall be mercilessly punished." Justin said, "Through prayer we can be saved on account of our Lord Jesus Christ, even when we have been punished, because this shall become to us salvation and confidence at the more fearful and universal judgment-seat of our Lord and Saviour." Thus also said the other martyrs: "Do what you will, for we are Christians, and do not sacrifice to idols." Rusticus the prefect pronounced sentence, saying, "Let those who have refused to sacrifice to the gods and to yield to the command of the emperor be scourged, and led away to suffer the punishment of decapitation, according to the laws."

So died, a martyr for his faith, one of the most deserving of the Christian leaders of the second century.

QUESTIONS

1. What was the state of Christianity in the middle of the second century? Its geographical extent? Its external enemies?

2. How far was this Christianity Pauline?

3. Gnosticism, its nature and dangers? How was it met?

4. The circumstances of Justin's life? His conversion? His chief writings?

5. Against what charges and how does he defend the Christians?

6. Justin's view of Christ?

7. His valuation of the Old Testament? His opinion of the old gods?

8. How does he describe the terms of admission to the church? Its services?

9. The circumstances of Justin's trial and death.

ADDITIONAL READING

F. W. Farrar, *Lives of the Fathers* (New York, 1889), I, 93-117.

Philip Schaff, *History of the Christian Church* (New York, 1889), II, 710-26

TERTULLIAN

II
TERTULLIAN

The general tendencies characteristic of the church in the days of Justin continued to show their force during the half-century that followed his martyrdom. At his death the Gnostic movement, against which he struggled, was at its height. It continued to engage the opposing strength of the ablest champions of what was beginning to call itself the "Catholic," that is "Universal," church, in distinction from all "heretical" bodies. That name goes back indeed to Ignatius of Antioch, and the opening years of the second century; but was used by him as a designation of the ideal communion of all Christians, as we now speak of the "invisible" church. But, by the close of the second century, it was becoming the designation of the visible, close-knit body, spreading throughout the Roman Empire, and representing historic Christianity over against the more recent speculations of Gnosticism. Its emphasis on the succession of its officers as guaranteeing the continuity of its faith, its insistence on testing purity of doctrine by creeds, and its recognition of a collection of authoritative New Testament books, were the chief means by which it fought the "heretics;" but these characteristics tended rapidly to bind Christianity with fixed forms of worship, of doctrine, and of organization, to legalize and externalize it, and were therefore producing that compactly organized, rigid form of the church which has been well called by modern scholars the "Old Catholic," to distinguish it from the later Greek and Roman Catholic churches, which in so many ways resembled it.

Yet it would be wrong to look upon this development as wholly an evil. No organization less compact and united could probably have conquered the Roman Empire. It is difficult, moreover, to see in what other ways the Gnostics could have been overcome. What could a Christian of the second century answer to their claims to a new and profound knowledge of Christianity, but that their views were not contained in the writings of apostles and Evangelists, and had never been taught by the responsible officers of the churches which the apostles founded? The result of this reply was, however, twofold. It emphasized the feeling that the bishops, who had become well-nigh universal by the middle of the second century, by reason of their position as heads of important churches, were guardians of the faith handed down from the apostles; and it specially increased the prestige, as fountains of pure doctrine, of those churches in which the apostles themselves had labored. There, certainly, it was easy to think, men would know what the apostles had taught, and by them error could be detected and resisted. Of these apostolic churches there were many in the eastern half of the Empire; but the West claimed only one—that of Rome—rendered doubly influential by its position in the capital of the Empire and its numerous congregation. Hence we find the anti-heretical champions of the latter half of the second century urging the necessity of agreement in doctrine with Rome. Not that they recognized in the Roman church any legislative authority; but because Christian truth had there been handed down since Paul; and Peter also (so men of the closing quarter of the second century firmly, and probably truly, believed), had there taught and suffered.

Conspicuous among these champions was Irenaeus, the ablest theologian of the second century. While recent discussion has been much divided as to the epoch of his birth,[1] he was evidently a native of Asia Minor, and in youth a hearer of the martyr, Polycarp of Smyrna, who, in turn, had listened to the apostle John. How much Irenaeus received from Polycarp may well be questioned, but he undoubtedly represented and transmitted the Asia Minor type of theology, of which the Johannine Gospel and epistles are the highest productions. His work was not to be, however, in his native region. About 154 he visited Rome; and, before 177, was

[1] Zahn puts it about 115; Harnack, 135-142. Polycarp suffered February 23, 155.

26   GREAT MEN OF THE CHRISTIAN CHURCH

a presbyter in the far-off Christian outpost of Lyons in what is now France. In the year last mentioned a severe persecution of that congregation began. Its aged bishop, Pothinus, suffered martyrdom; and to the office thus made vacant Irenaeus succeeded, holding it till his death, soon after 190. Here in the closing years of his bishopric, 181–89, he wrote his chief work, *Against Heresies*. To him the New Testament is fully as authoritative as the Old, and the tradition handed down in churches of apostolic foundation is its proper interpreter. Scripture and tradition alike, he urged, give no countenance to the Gnosticism which he elaborately described and refuted. But he had his own clear central theologic thought of the work of Christ. He is the most original theologian since Paul. God made man in his own image and like himself immortal; but Adam broke this union and destroyed in large part God's work, man becoming mortal thereby. In Christ the work so interrupted has been restored; mortality becomes immortal; and hence he is the head of a redeemed humanity.[1] It is interesting to note also, that in Irenaeus we find the earliest clear intimation of the prevalence of infant baptism;[2] and that his own anticipation, like that of the apostolic age, placed the coming of Christ to reign over a redeemed earth near at hand. In Irenaeus Gnosticism had its most

[1] Book III, 18, 1.
[2] Book II, 22, 4.

able opponent, and the forming "Old Catholic" church one of its most gifted defenders.

Irenaeus belonged to two epochs. In him the traditional theology of the early church as illustrated in such a doctrine as that of Christ's speedy second coming was combined with the newer emphasis on creed, organization, and orderly succession—thoughts which logically involved the expectation of a slow and long-protracted growth of the church. In most minds the millennial anticipation was growing dim, and close-knit order, regular succession, and agreement with generally recognized creeds were becoming the tests of the true church, rather than that immediate, enthusiastic confidence in the leadership of the Spirit and his inspiration of "spirit-filled" men which had marked the apostolic age[1] and persisted in ever-weakening measure into the second century. It was natural, however, that a reaction in favor of the older views should manifest itself, and such a revival of the earlier faith in the direct and present special inspiration of Christians by the Spirit appeared in an exaggerated form in Montanism.

Soon after the middle of the second century, possibly in 157, Montanus, who is said to have been a recently Christianized priest of Cybele, began his teaching in Phrygia, in Asia Minor. With him as a prophet were soon joined two prophetesses, Prisca and Maximilla, the latter of whom survived her

[1] E. g., I Cor. 12:4–11.

associates and died in 179. To their thinking the promise of Christ that "the Spirit of Truth"[1] should come was fulfilled in their utterances. They affirmed the immediately approaching end of the world; and declared that, as a preparation, all Christians should lead lives of peculiar asceticism. Paul had recommended abstinence from marriage for the same reason,[2] but the ascetic spirit had been steadily rising since his time, and Montanus went much farther. He commended virginity as specially pleasing to God, condemned a second marriage as unlawful, and greatly multiplied and increased the strenuousness of fasts. Martyrdom was not to be avoided by flight, but sought as an honor to Christ. These views won widespread following, and were soon represented, not only in Asia Minor, but in the western portions of the Empire, where their ascetic rather than their prophetic aspects won most approval.

Such was the situation in the church when Quintus Septimius Florens Tertullianus began his noteworthy activity as a writer on Christian themes. Born in the ancient Carthage, probably between the years 150 and 155, he was the son of a centurion in Roman service, and was educated in the excellent schools of that flourishing capital of Roman North Africa as a heathen. Here and at Rome he studied

[1] John 16:13.
[2] I Cor. 7:7, 24-40.

rhetoric and philosophy, and gained considerable acquaintance with law, though the extent of his legal knowledge has probably been usually exaggerated. Of passionate, fiery nature, intense in all that he did, his life as a heathen attorney in Carthage, or possibly also in Rome, was not unspotted; and on his conversion to Christianity, an event which occurred in one of the years from about 185 to 195, he manifested at once a Puritan severity. He was chosen a presbyter at some uncertain date, but probably not long after his conversion. He never rose to higher rank in the ministry. In 202 or 203, during the reign of Septimius Severus, a wave of persecution swept over the North African church, and it is probable that in connection with its strenuous sifting of the disciples there Tertullian became acquainted with the courage and enthusiasm of the Montanists. Their asceticism attracted him. By 206-8, he had attached himself to them wholly and had broken with the "Old Catholic" church, which from now onward he unsparingly condemned. All of his later writings show him as a convinced Montanist; but, if a tradition preserved by Augustine is to be trusted, he separated in old age from even these associates and founded a little sect of his own. Certainly so-called Tertullianists were to be found in Carthage nearly two centuries subsequent to his death, which took place not long after the year 222. Great as his services to theology, especially to that of Latin Christendom, were to be, this Montanism, so congenial to his enthusiastic and Puritanic temperament, has robbed him of the fame that would otherwise have been his. Without this "heresy," he would undoubtedly have lived in Christian tradition as "Saint" Tertullian. Yet his asceticism went little farther than that which the "Catholic" church was to praise within two centuries of his death; while his faith in the prophetic claims of Montanism was hardly more than an exaggeration of that belief in the guidance of the Holy Spirit which had been universal in the church of the apostolic age.

Tertullian's chief fame is as a writer. Though he used Greek freely and wrote in that language treatises that are now lost, North Africa was a Latin-speaking land, and Latin was the vehicle which he preferred. By its use he became "the father of church Latinity." He stamped the impress of his own thought and usage permanently on the language. Nervous, vigorous, often strained and far-fetched in his speech, he is always the passionate advocate of his cause. Tertullian was never dull. He was often unfair to opponents, not always consistent with himself, but always readable and effective. His force was that of a mighty, passionate personality, who felt strongly and wrote at a white heat.

Tertullian's tracts, about thirty of which have survived, naturally fall into three great groups, the earliest, written before 202, which show no Montanist leanings, those of his transition period, and those after his breach with the "Old Catholic" church and full acceptance of Montanism. His vehement invective, always marked, rises to its greatest heights as he feels himself the representative of a small and rejected Christian party.

Tertullian's writings embrace a great variety of themes. He defended his conceptions of Christianity against Marcion, Praxeas, and other "heretics." He exhorted his readers to modesty in apparel and conduct. He warned against the theater, second marriages, or flight in persecution. He encouraged martyrs. He discussed the soul, baptism, penance, patience, prayer, idolatry, the resurrection. The whole round of Christian life and doctrine interested him.

To Tertullian's thinking Christianity is a great divine foolishness, wiser than the merely human wisdom of the deepest philosophies, but in no way to be squared with them. "Away with all attempts to produce a mottled Christianity of Stoic, Platonic, and dialectic composition. We want no curious disputation after possessing Christ Jesus, no inquisition after enjoying the gospel. With our faith we desire no further belief."[1] This was the direct contradiction, not merely of the Gnostic position, but of the influential school of theology then beginning in Alexandria, of which Origen was to be the most

[1] *Prescription*, chap. vii.

brilliant teacher. That school viewed philosophy as the handmaid of a true theology, and sought to unite the two in a great intellectual explanation of Christian truth. Christianity, in Tertullian's teaching, demands a complete change of life. Christ "preached the new law and the new promise of the kingdom of heaven."[1] This Christian inheritance is the possession solely, Tertullian argues, of the orthodox church. In his *Prescription against Heretics*, written between 198 and 203, and therefore before he became a Montanist, he denies to the "heretics" any right in the Scriptures, or any share in true Christian tradition, and appeals to the churches founded by the apostles as the depositaries and guardians of the truth. That truth once possessed, it is merely idle curiosity to inquire farther. "You must 'seek' until you 'find,' and believe when you have found; nor have you anything further to do but to keep what you have believed."[2] The principle he here enunciates is one of mighty influence in the church till the Reformation broke its fetters. It makes it the prime duty of the Christian to accept unquestioningly the faith which the church transmits to him.

Tertullian has, however, a keener sense of the depths of human sinfulness, and of the need of divine grace for man's rescue than any writer had possessed

[1] *Prescription*, chap. xiii.
[2] *Ibid.*, chap. ix.

since Paul. Christianity is above all a revelation of salvation; and this primacy of the great doctrines of sin and grace he was to impress on the Latin portion of Christendom to a degree never paralleled in the East, and that may be said to have influenced ultimately all Latin and Reformation thought. But though profoundly conscious of the reality and depravity of sin, Tertullian lays great weight on works in his doctrine of salvation. We are "competitors for salvation in earning the favor of God;"[1] by public confession, by "mortification of our flesh and spirit," we "make satisfaction for our former sins."[2] These merits flow chiefly from confession, self-humiliation, and voluntary ascetic practices. All this is un-Pauline enough; but it moved in a direction that aroused few protests till the Reformation epoch.

The means for the forgiveness of sins is the divinely instituted rite of baptism, by which "we are set free into eternal life." It can be received but once, though a martyr's death constitutes for him an exceptional and effective second baptism; and hence so precious a remedy for sin is not to be lightly used. To Tertullian's thinking, children and the unmarried should postpone it, because not yet fixed in character.[3] This delay of baptism, in order that its benefit might extinguish as large an amount of one's total accumulation of sins as possible, was nothing

[1] *Repentance*, chap. **vi.**   [2] *Baptism*, chap. **xx.**
[3] *Ibid., passim.*

peculiar to Tertullian, and had a curious illustration, to mention a single instance, in the case, a century later, of the emperor Constantine, who postponed the rite till his last illness.

But sins are committed after baptism; and the attitude of the church toward those of a heinous nature was changing in Tertullian's time, and with it the conception of what the church itself is. From New Testament days the church had been looked upon as a company of actual disciples of Christ— as "saints," though still imperfect—and some sins were so bad as to bar out the sinner from it forever.[1] Murder, apostasy, and adultery were looked upon as such offenses; and Tertullian clearly states the distinction between venial and deadly sins which was thus implied.[2] For severe sins, not of the unforgivable category, however, God had provided a remedy through public confession, which Tertullian calls a "second reserve of aid against hell"[3]— baptism being the first; but, like baptism, it was to be used once only; it was the last hope. Whether the church had any hope to offer to grievous sinners, or to those who had exhausted their repentance, was in dispute in Tertullian's time. He himself seems in his earlier period to have inclined to the milder view that God might have some mercy even

[1] I John 5:16; Hebrews 6:4–6; 10:26.
[2] *Modesty*, chap. ii.
[3] *Repentance*, chap. xii.

for great offenses;[1] but his Montanistic rigor in later life disposed him to the earlier severity. Tertullian's final tract, *On Modesty*, was a biting reproof to Bishop Calixtus of Rome (217/8–222/3) who by his own fiat had declared his willingness to treat adultery and fornication as forgivable sins, after which the repentant offender could be restored to church fellowship.

This high-handed act of the Bishop of Rome was but the logical outcome of the feeling that had been growing in the church that the officers of the congregation—above all its bishop—were its organs in judging and pronouncing censure and restoration. In Pauline times the right of the whole congregation, it came naturally to be exercised through the executive officers. But Calixtus' removal of these offenses from the list of the unforgivable implied a change in the original theory of the church itself—it is no longer viewed as a household of "saints," but as an agency for salvation. Calixtus himself likened it to Noah's Ark, full of clean and unclean beasts. The two conceptions of the church have persisted, and today divide Christendom. Those bodies which insist on conscious Christian discipleship as the condition of membership represent the older view; while those communions, which, like the state churches, reckon all who have been baptized as of their membership, and require no profession of a

[1] *Ibid.*, chap. viii; written between 198 and 203.

"change of heart," stand essentially on the inclusive basis which Calixtus expressed. Conservatives, like the Montanist Tertullian, might protest; but Calixtus undoubtedly, rather than he, represented the tendency of the times. His theory of the church explains how after the attitude of the Roman government had been changed, a century later, to one of favor to Christianity, the population was swept by the thousand into at least nominal membership in the church.

In one very important theological doctrine Tertullian coined and gave significance to many of the later phrases employed in its discussion—that of the Trinity. The word itself he brought into its present use. Such terms as one "substance," in which the Father, Son, and Spirit alike share, as well as the clear distinction between the divine and the human in Christ—who, to him, is God and man, joined in one person without confusion—he wrought out, largely by the light afforded by Stoic philosophy, for, in spite of his contempt for philosophy, he made use of it when he chose. His late treatise *Against Praxeas*, written between 213 and 218, was the clearest exposition of the "Logos" Christology that had yet appeared, and not only gave a fixed content to many of the Latin terms he employed, but in many respects anticipated the Nicene decision of a century later in its formulation of the doctrine of the Trinity.

Possibly the best illustration, however, of Tertullian's fiery nature, his mastery of invective, and no less of the revolt of the Christians of his day from the brutalizing public spectacles by which the heathen population was amused and degraded, and of their confidence in the coming triumph of the Kingdom of God, may be drawn from a pastoral denunciation, written before he became a Montanist. The amusements of his day in the theater were often grossly licentious, while those of the gladiatorial amphitheater were cruel in the extreme. Both appealed to the crudest and lowest passions of human nature. Neither was, in Tertullian's judgment, fit for Christian eyes. But he went much farther than mere criticism. He was evidently goaded by heathen taunts. Over against the temporary spectacles of the present he placed the vivid realities of a day of judgment, already discerned by faith. It is, harshly and unsympathetically indeed, an exhibition of that "other-worldliness" with which these despised Christians comforted themselves amid the sensuality, cruelty, and hostility about them. It speaks the fierce longing, natural to the human heart, for a day of vengeance on their enemies.

What[1] a spectacle is that fast-approaching advent of our Lord, now owned by all, now highly exalted, now a triumphant One! What that exultation of the angelic hosts! What the glory of the rising saints! What the kingdom of the just

[1] *De spectaculis*, chap. xxx

thereafter! What the city New Jerusalem! Yes, and there are other sights: that last day of judgment, with its everlasting issues; that day unlooked for by the nations, the theme of their derision, when the world hoary with age and all its many products shall be consumed in one great flame! How vast a spectacle then bursts upon the eye! What then excites my admiration? What my derision? Which sight gives me joy? Which rouses me to exultation?—as I see so many illustrious monarchs, whose reception into the heavens was publicly announced,[1] groaning now in the lowest darkness with great Jove himself, and those, too, who bore witness of their exaltation; governors of provinces, too, who persecuted the Christian name, in fires more fierce than those with which in the days of their pride they raged against the followers of Christ. What world's wise men besides, the very philosophers . . . now covered with shame before the poor deluded ones, as one fire consumes them! Poets, also, trembling not before the judgment-seat of Rhadamanthus or Minos, but of the unexpected Christ! I shall have a better opportunity then of hearing the tragedians, louder-voiced in their own calamity; of viewing the play-actors, much more "dissolute" in the dissolving flame; of looking upon the charioteer, all glowing in his chariot of fire; of beholding the wrestlers, not in their gymnasia, but tossing in the fiery billows; unless even then I shall not care to attend to such ministers of sin, in my eager wish rather to fix a gaze insatiable on those whose fury vented itself against the Lord. "This," I shall say, ... "This is He whom you purchased from Judas! This is He whom you struck with reed and fist, whom you contemptuously spat upon, to whom you gave gall and vinegar to drink!" . . . . What quaestor or priest in his munificence[2] will bestow on you the favor of seeing and exulting in such things as these?

[1] Alluding to the deification of deceased emperors.

[2] I. e., givers of public gladiatorial and theatrical shows.

And yet even now we in a measure have them by faith in the picturings of imagination.

There is much more of the joy of future triumph than of Christian charity in this vivid picture; but it shows us the strength of the hope in which Tertullian walked and did his strenuous work.

QUESTIONS

1. What were the general tendencies manifest in the church at the close of the second century?

2. Were they wholly an evil?

3. What value was placed on the churches founded by the apostles? Why?

4. What was the significance of Irenaeus?

5. What reaction did Montanism represent? Why was it natural? Its exaggerations?

6. What was Tertullian's career?

7. What was Tertullian's significance in the development of a Latin Christian literature? The characteristics of his style? His writings?

8. What was Tertullian's conception of the relations of Christianity to philosophy?

9. How far should a Christian seek truth? Where can he find it?

10. What emphasis does Tertullian lay on sin and grace?

11. What was the value attached to baptism in his day?

12. What two theories of the church were then in contest?

13. What was Tertullian's contribution to the doctrine of the Trinity?

14. How did he triumph over present ills in the hope of the coming of Christ in judgment?

ADDITIONAL READING

F. W. Farrar, *Lives of the Fathers* (New York, 1889), I, 118-84.

Philip Schaff, *History of the Christian Church* (New York, 1889), II, 818-34.

A. H. Newman, *A Manual of Church History* (Philadelphia, 1900), I, 257-65.

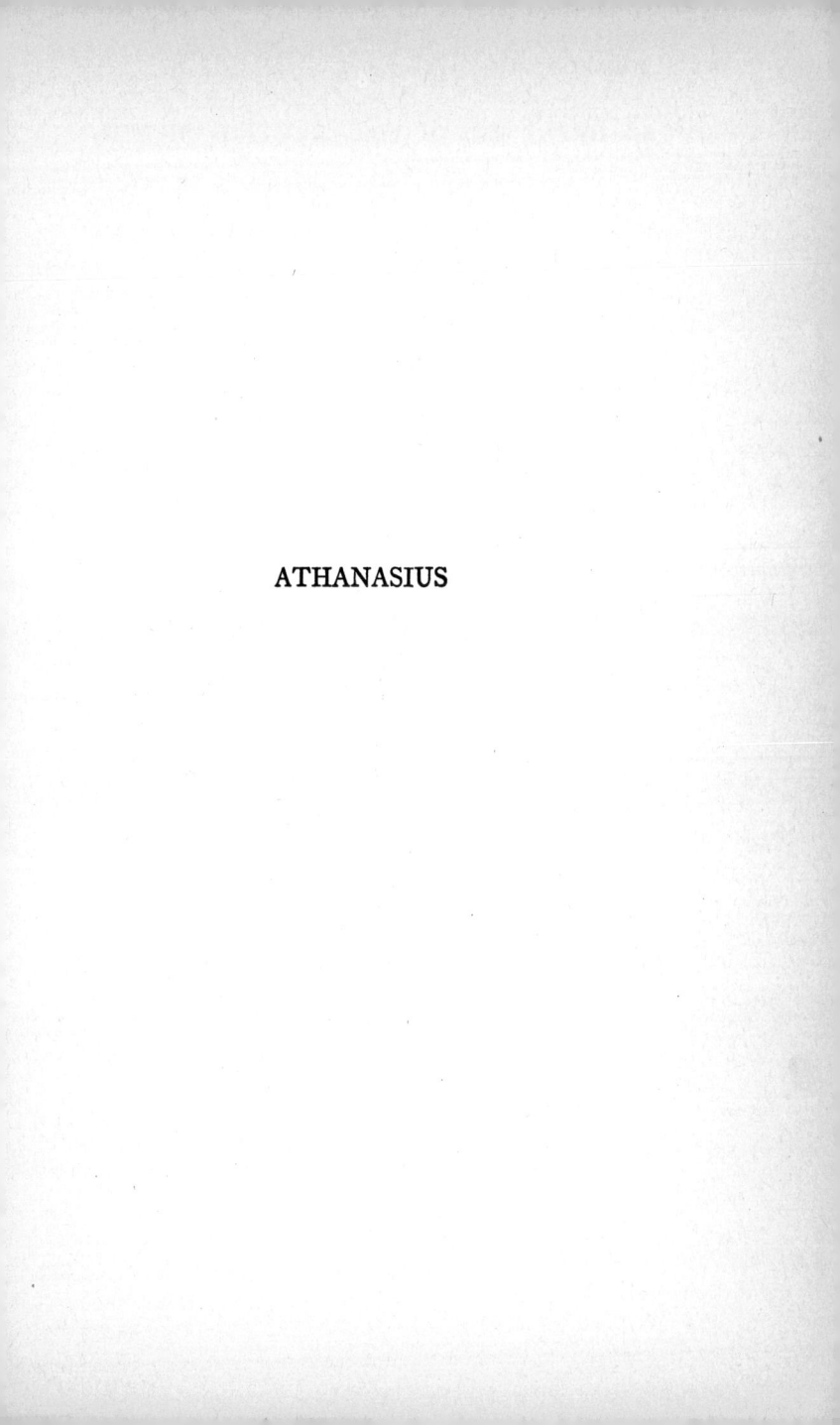

ATHANASIUS

III
ATHANASIUS

The epoch from the death of Tertullian to the rise into prominence of Athanasius—practically a century—was one of tremendous changes in the Christian church. It had to pass through the two greatest persecutions which it experienced, that under Decius, 250, which was renewed from 257 to 260 by Valerian, and that begun in 303 by Diocletian. These persecutions were what none had been before. They were systematic, extensive, and persistent attempts to crush out Christianity by men of principle who were convinced that the evils from which the Empire suffered were due to the refusal of Christians to worship the old gods under whom these persecutors believed that Rome had grown great. They involved many martyrdoms. They led to thousands of denials of the faith. When those who in their terror had abjured their faith sought readmission to the church, great divisions arose as to the course to be pursued. A considerable party, the Novatian at Rome after the Decian persecution, and that of the Donatists in Africa after that of Diocletian, would, in accordance with the older rigor, bar them from the church; but the majority in each instance favored their readmission, if repentant, and thus a second class of offenses was removed from the list of unforgivable sins.[1]

In spite of these fearful trials, however, the church grew mightily, especially as it was favored by almost absolute peace between the persecutions. By the close of the third century it was vastly more numerous than in the days of Tertullian. Moreover, Christianity, in the third century, was extending rapidly into the higher classes of society. It was gaining intensively as well as extensively; at the same time its exclusiveness was breaking down; and it was, undoubtedly, making many compromises with the world that the first or even the second century would have rejected. Though average Christian morality was less exacting, the ascetic life was increasingly looked upon as the ideal, and a double standard of Christian living was growing up that was to have influence for centuries—in fact in some branches of the church to the present day. While the requirements binding on the ordinary Christian were comparatively low, he who would lead the holier life must be much more strenuous. The way was thus preparing for demands upon the clergy not required of the ordinary believer, and for the rise of monasticism, the rapid spread of which was to be such a feature of the fourth century. The combined influence of heathen worship and of Old

[1] The first was that of unchastity under Calixtus. See *ante*, p. 35.

Testament example had changed the conception of the ministry into a priesthood; and, by the middle of the third century, the Lord's Supper was looked upon, well-nigh universally, as a sacrifice made by the priest to God—the mass. It had become, at least a century earlier than that, the central and most sacred part of the service. By the middle of the third century, also, the importance always attached to the great churches of the capital cities, especially those of apostolic association, was giving them a metropolitan authority over their districts. This was notably the case with Rome, Antioch, and Alexandria, whose bishops were regarded as the chief men in the Christian church. To such a writer as Cyprian, bishop of Carthage from 248 or 249 to his martyrdom in 258, salvation outside the visible church is impossible, and that church is built on the unity of its bishops, of whom the highest in honor is the bishop of Rome. The church was thus a close-knit, visible *imperium in imperio*.

During the third century, also, theology took on a notable development, especially in the school of Alexandria, under Clement of Alexandria, who flourished in the last decade of the second century and the first years of the third; and especially under his great pupil, Origen, who labored as a teacher and even more as a writer from 203 to his death in 251. In Origen the oriental church had its greatest theologian, and Christianity as a whole one of its profoundest interpreters. In absolute opposition to Tertullian he viewed philosophy as a true guide in the development and systematizing of the simple elements of the popular creed which embodied the Christian revelation; and by its means he constructed an immense edifice of speculation which profoundly influenced subsequent thought and may be said to have completed the union of Christian truth with the best that the ancient Greek civilization had to offer into one intellectually imposing system. It was a marvelous interpretation of Christianity in the light of the knowledge of that epoch; but the process has to be repeated with every advance of knowledge, and Origen's work was so fully the creation of his own age that its value is relatively slight for our own. It dominated the theological thought of the oriental church in the centuries that immediately succeeded him, however; though the lesser men who followed him were inclined to judge him more heretical than orthodox.

Greatest of all external changes in the fortunes of Christianity were its recognition by the state, the consequent cessation of all serious opposition, and the positive and powerful aid of the imperial government which came to it in the second decade of the fourth century. The proportion of Christians to the total population of the Empire is impossible of estimation. They were very unequally distributed in its various provinces. But in the central provinces which possessed political leadership the church was undoubtedly very strong, and the persecution begun by Diocletian not only failed to crush it, but showed by the popular apathy that the old opposition to Christianity had largely vanished. The church was a political force which a clever politician, especially one in some degree of sympathy with its principles, could use in a struggle to obtain mastery of the Roman world. Such a far-sighted politician was Constantine, and his victory over his rival Maxentius, just outside of Rome in October, 312, to which he had marched as a Christian champion, and with soldiers bearing the symbol of the cross, was followed at the beginning of 313 by the publication at Milan, of a joint edict by Constantine and Licinius, the ruler of a large part of the East and then Constantine's supporter. By this edict universal toleration was granted. It was no exclusive establishment of Christianity, but it granted to Christians full rights; and the hearty personal support which Christians received from Constantine made Christianity practically the most favored religion. By 324 Constantine was sole ruler of the Empire. His legislation constantly favored the church, and its numbers now grew enormously with the incoming, not merely of genuine converts, but of that great class which always desires to be on the winning side. To Constantine's statesman-like mind the support of Christianity seems to have appeared the completion of the great process of unification which had been working for centuries in the Empire. It had long had one law, one citizenship, and, in theory at least, one ruler. It was but a further step in the same direction that it should have one religion.

This unity was at once threatened by a serious dispute in the church itself, the focus of which was Alexandria, the largest city of Egypt, though the roots of the quarrel were ancient, and its ramifications widespread. It had to do with the most fundamental problem of Christianity—the nature of Christ himself. The first disciples had recognized in Christ a revelation of God, without asking much about his relations to the Father. Matthew's Gospel records his declaration that "no man knoweth the Son but the Father; neither knoweth any man the Father save the Son."[1] The three earliest evangelists show that His claim to forgive sins was regarded by those who heard him as an exercise of divine authority.[2] Luke shows that he held himself superior to the most sacred parts of that Jewish law which his contemporaries believed to be God-given.[3] Paul views prayer to Him as a universal Christian practice.[4] But the need of explanation of his divinity was early felt; and the New Testament presents three interpretations, not necessarily mutually exclu-

[1] Matt. 11:27.
[2] Matt. 9:2, 3; Mark 2:5–7; Luke 5:20–24.
[3] Luke 6:5.   [4] I Cor. 1:2

ATHANASIUS

sive, but still explanations of the *how* of the great fact which the early disciples experienced—his endowment with the divine Spirit,[1] his virgin birth,[2] and his pre-existence.[3] These were not philosophical interpretations, however, and the second century was busy with its speculations. Gnosticism, as we have seen, had its theories. In the church itself, the "Logos" Christology, which looked upon Christ as the personal embodiment of the divine activity in the world, flowing out from God, one with him, yet in some real sense distinct from the Father—the "Word"—had the largest following. There were, however, not a few in the second and third centuries who rejected the Logos Christology, and were called "Monarchians." Of these some insisted that there was no real distinction between Christ and the Father, and that the Father suffered on the cross. Such was Sabellius, who flourished at Rome from about 215, and taught that the Father, Son, and Spirit were but various forms in which the one God had manifested himself. Other Monarchians viewed Christ simply as one peculiarly filled with the Spirit of God, and hence Son of God by adoption. But, thanks to the work of Tertullian, of Novatian at Rome (*ca.* 251), and of the Roman bishop, Dionysius, (*ca.* 260), the Logos doctrine, and

[1] E. g., Mark 1:9–12.
[2] E. g., Matt. 1:18–25; Luke 1:34, 35.
[3] E. g., John 1:1; Col. 1:15–17.

the conception that Father, Son, and Spirit, while one in substance, were yet distinct in person—a real Trinity—won practically complete control of the West. The East was not so united. It was far deeper and more speculative in its thought than the West, where the primary interests, as befitted the Latin spirit, were practical.

But within the victorious Logos Christology it was possible to hold at least two views as to Christ's relations to the Father, and out of these the great controversy was to come. One of them was championed by Arius, probably a Libian by birth, who had been trained in Antioch, and who when he comes to prominence in the controversy was well on in years, and in high repute as pastor of the church called Baucalis in the Egyptian capital, Alexandria. To Arius' thinking Christ is the highest of all created beings. The chief of all creatures, he is still a creature; and, as compared with God who made him, inferior, limited, and secondary. Though God's agent in creating the world, and therefore earlier than it, he was not eternal. "There was when he was not." In his birth on earth this secondary God took to himself merely a human body, of which he constituted the soul. Christ was, therefore, to Arius, neither fully God nor perfect man, but a being intermediate between the two. The view was essentially polytheistic, and asserted the existence of two Gods—one high, perfect, and remote, the other near, created, limited, and inferior.

These opinions were in opposition to those of Arius' ecclesiastical superior, Alexander, bishop of Alexandria from 311 to 326, who represented the other interpretation to which reference has been made. How fully Alexander had worked out his own views it is difficult to say; but it is plain that he emphasized the unity of Christ with the Father. Apparently Arius criticized his position publicly about 318; and, about 320, Alexander called a synod by which Arius was excommunicated. Far from accepting this condemnation, Arius found support, notably in Eusebius, bishop of Nicomedia, the ablest politician in the eastern episcopate, and in Palestine. The quarrel at once assumed large proportions, and Constantine, whose political ideals determined his religious policy, and whose prime thought was unity in church and state, found himself confronted by a bitter dispute in the church to which he had so recently given freedom. After trying in vain to bring Arius and Alexander to agreement through the agency of his ecclesiastical adviser, Hosius, bishop of Cordova in Spain, the puzzled emperor now called the first general council of the church to meet in Nicaea, near Constantinople, in May, 325. Local synods had been frequently held since the Montanist dispute raged in Asia Minor in the latter half of the second century; but now for the first time the whole church was invited—and invited by the head of the Roman Empire—to send its bishops for deliberation. About three hundred answered the call. Entertained at imperial expense, and enjoying the presence and largely the guidance of the emperor himself, it was indeed a splendid gathering, and it has lived in tradition as the most sacred of all the councils of the church.

Though professedly a deliberative body, the council was largely determined in its action by the emperor, probably less by his direct intervention, though that was exercised, than by the natural glamor of his presence in a body representative of a church which had so recently come forth from persecution largely through his aid. Constantine's policy was simple. He was no expert theologian. He wished peace and unity. He saw that the majority of the council, which was almost wholly from the eastern portion of the Empire, were unlearned men who had no definite convictions on the more difficult aspects of the question at issue, and therefore would be swayed by one or the other of the parties to which the question was vital, that of Arius and Eusebius of Nicomedia, or that of Alexander. His own training in the western portion of the Empire, and the views of his trusted friend, Bishop Hosius of Cordova, inclined him to the side of Alexander, which accorded with the feeling of the West generally. Constantine threw the weight of his influence against Arius, who was promptly condemned. The creed of the church of Caesarea in Palestine was adopted with the insertion of the anti-Arian declarations that Christ is "of the substance of the Father," "begotten not made, of one substance (ὁμοούσιον) with the Father." The Greek word just quoted became henceforth the battle-flag of the Nicene faith. The powerful influence of Constantine, coupled with threats of banishment, secured the signatures of all bishops save two; and the council dissolved, having, it was believed, given the desired peace to the church.

The majority at Nicaea had, however, been surprised and led rather than convinced. The real battle was after rather than at the council. The council was brief, the battle lasted more than half a century. Its hero was Athanasius, to whose efforts the permanent victory of the Nicene faith was primarily due. Born, probably in Alexandria, about 293, he became a deacon under Bishop Alexander, and that prelate's hearty supporter, possibly his amanuensis. He was present in Nicaea during the council, though of course, being not yet a bishop, he was not one of its official members. While his influence there, such as it was, was exercised in favor of the result reached, it was in no sense a deciding factor. But, with Athanasius' promotion to the see of Alexandria on the death of Alexander, in 326, his leadership became incontestible, and till his own demise, in 373, he was the foremost figure in the struggle. A thinker of clearness, rather than an original theologian, he adopted the Nicene decision as his own and was admirably fitted to represent a great party. His enthusiasm, his steadfastness of purpose, his unbending and high-minded resolution to yield nothing, made him the commanding leader of his century and a permanent force in the history of Christian thought.

Athanasius' impulse was far more religious than philosophical. To his thinking, Christ is the full manifestation of the one God, eternal, subordinate in office to the Father, yet forever one with him in nature. In the incarnation the one God was united with a perfect and complete manhood, so that Christ is at the same time fully God and fully man. There is no far-off God, remote from the world which he has made, but God himself has revealed himself in the incarnation to men.

These may seem remote matters of speculation; but in the existent state of Christian thought they were not. The ancient world was in real danger of putting God a great way off, of so emphasizing his transcendence as to separate him by a vast gulf from his creatures. That Arius did; and with many the Logos Christology, which makes Christ a divine agent of the one God, had that effect in spite of its assertion of Christ's divine character. To Athanasius the "Son" rather than the Logos or "Word" was always Christ's chief title. Only as God is shown to be active, sympathizing with man's need, sacrificing himself for man's sins, really uniting men to himself, present in his world, is a real salvation possible. So Athanasius conceived the matter; and he was right, however completely our modern age has discarded the philosophic garb of that time in which he clothed his thoughts. His fundamental contention is forever true. No intermediate being, however gifted, could really reveal God to men or effect that reconciliation and union of men with God by which alone salvation is possible.

Athanasius entered on his bishopric in 326. There was need for his firmness at once. The defeated party at Nicaea had an able leader in the politically skilful Eusebius of Nicomedia, who soon won favor with Constantine. To many of those who had belonged to the great undecided middle body of the council the result arrived at in Nicaea seemed one-sided and Sabellian. A reaction soon set in. By Eusebius' maneuvers the emperor was persuaded that Arius was not as bad as he had been painted. Constantine did not in any way become an Arian; but Arius now laid before him a brief and vague confession of faith that seemed to the untheological mind of the emperor not only orthodox but indicative of a willingness to end the dispute. What seemed enough to the emperor, Constantine naturally thought ought to satisfy Athanasius; and as Athanasius still opposed Arius' restoration, Constantine was at last persuaded by Eusebius of Nicomedia, though with difficulty, that, after all, Athanasius' obstinacy, and the tyranny with which he was falsely charged, were the roots of the quarrel, and that a period of exile would bring him to terms. So Constantine banished Athanasius to Trier, in Germany, late in 335; and so successful were Arius' friends that he was about to be restored to the church when he died in 336.

Constantine's own demise, in 337, found Athanasius still in exile, and that death brought a marked strengthening of the anti-Athanasian party. The great emperor had tried in an unsuccessful way to make peace. Of his sons, Constantius, who received the eastern portion of the Empire, was under the influence of Eusebius of Nicomedia, whom he made bishop of his capital, Constantinople, in 338. To Constantine II and to Constans came the rulership of the West, which the death of Constantine II, in 340, soon placed wholly in Constans' hands. Unlike his brother, Constantius, Constans favored Athanasius, and, like the region of which he was the ruler, supported the Nicene decision. The reign of the three emperors was begun, however, by the recall of all who had been banished by Constantine, and thus, before the end of 337, Athanasius was once more in friendly Alexandria. His peace was not long undisturbed, however. Early in 339, a synod of his enemies at Antioch ordered his deposition. He was driven by force from Alexandria, and fled to Rome, a new bishop was put in his place, and his second exile, which was to last till October, 346, was begun.

Then followed a period of great interest, not merely in the life of Athanasius, but of high importance in the development of the papacy as well as in the progress of the Nicene struggle. Both the Eusebian party and Athanasius appealed to Bishop Julius of Rome (337-52), an exceedingly skilful and statesman-like pontiff, who saw in the situation an opportunity not merely to aid the side which he believed right but to advance papal authority. By Julius, Athanasius was heartily welcomed and declared orthodox. The situation between Rome and Constantinople was strained in the extreme; but now the emperor Constans, largely at the insistence of the aged Hosius of Cordova, persuaded his brother Constantius to join with him in the summons of a new designedly general council, to meet in 343 at Sardica, now Sofia in Bulgaria. On its assembly it was evident that the western bishops, in sympathy with Nicene views, were in the majority, and the Eusebian party therefore withdrew in anger because Athanasius and his friends who were present were received in fellowship by that majority. On the departure of the Eusebians, the remaining bishops pronounced in favor of Athanasius, and, in a famous series of rules, authorized the Bishop of

Rome, when appealed to by bishops who deemed themselves unjustly deposed, to examine into the cases and cause them to be reopened. This was of course a party decision, unrecognized by the Eusebians, and favorable to Athanasius and his friends; but it became a precedent for many later papal claims.

Unfavorable as the situation seemed, a change came in Athanasius' favor, when, in 346, Constantius, moved by Constans' urgency, recalled him to Alexandria. The second exile was ended, and for ten years Athanasius was in possession of his bishopric. But his hardest trial was yet to come. The death of the friendly Constans in 350 left Constantius sole master of the Roman world, and with his exclusive rulership the anti-Nicene party which he favored was of course strengthened. By 355 the emperor and his ecclesiastical friends were so dominant in the West that at a great synod held in Milan in Italy Athanasius and his supporters were condemned by the western bishops there gathered; and those who then or soon after opposed this forced decision, like Bishop Liberius of Rome and other leaders of the West, were sent into exile. Soldiers were employed to seize Athanasius in Alexandria. He escaped with difficulty in February, 356, but he was now an Egyptian national hero, and in this third exile (356-62) found protection in defiance of the imperial power in the deserts of his native land.

Much of this protection came from the monks, for monasticism was growing rapidly in Egypt, and found in Athanasius its first eager supporter in high ecclesiastical position, and its earnest advocate.

The defeat of the Nicene party, of which Athanasius was the head, seemed now complete; but the anti-Nicene opposition was made up of very diverse elements, and with its victory it divided into factions. The old middle party of Eusebius, who had died in 341, now developed a conservative wing that, while not ready to say with the Nicene creed that Christ was of one substance with the Father, would yet approach it far enough to declare that they were of the same attributes ($ὁμοιούσιον$). Its radical wing, on the other hand, asserted the old Arian position that Christ was of other substance than the Father. Constantius tried to compromise by rejecting all forms of the word "substance" as unscriptural, and holding that Christ is "like" the Father, "in all things as the Scriptures teach," which was really avoiding the questions at issue; but the result was that the Athanasians and the conservative Eusebians came constantly nearer together, and the Athanasian cause was greatly strengthened by these divisions of its opponents.

In 361 the emperor Constantius died, and was succeeded by the last heathen that sat on the Roman throne, Julian, misnamed "the Apostate." Anxious to aid heathenism by increasing the quarrels of

Christians, Julian called home all banished bishops; and in 362, Athanasius was once more in Alexandria. But before the year was out, angered by Athanasius' opposition to heathenism, Julian sent him into his fourth exile, which lasted this time till 364, and was spent, as his third had been, under the protection of his Egyptian sympathizers.

On Julian's early death in 363, Christian emperors succeeded, though till the advent of Theodosius, in 379, they were, like Constantius, anti-Nicene in sympathies. But Athanasius' party constantly grew, aided as it was by powerful men of a younger generation, notably Basil the Great, Gregory of Nyssa, and Gregory of Nazianzen. A fifth exile came to the aged Athanasius for a few weeks, late in 365, when the emperor Valens banished all bishops whom Constantius had driven from their sees. But from 366 to his death on May 7, 373, at the age of about eighty, Athanasius remained in quiet possession of the bishopric which he had so long held, and from which he had been so often expelled. The full triumph of his cause he did not live to see. That was not to come till the Spanish-born emperor Theodosius put all the weight of imperial politics as firmly and as ruthlessly on the Nicene side, as ever Constantius had supported its opponents. But even his power could not have won the ground permanently for the Nicene cause had it not been for the long work of Athanasius. The courage, persistence, and conviction with which he had fought his battle won victory in the end. Whether Athanasius' spirit was always that of his Lord may well be doubted, but none can question his heroism, or the depth of the religious conviction which animated him in the long struggle. It is no less evident that the interference of the Christian emperors was a source of great evil to the church. In the existing state of the Empire that interference was unavoidable, but it made every theological question a political problem, it led to the use of very carnal weapons of controversy, and it turned Christian interest largely from matters of life and conduct to bitter wranglings over points of doctrine. Yet in the large retrospect we may be grateful that Athanasius did his work so well, and that the outcome of the struggle was what it was.

QUESTIONS

1. When were the great persecutions and what problems did they raise?

2. What changes in the conceptions of Christian life and worship took place in the third century?

3. Who was Origen and what was his significance?

4. How did Constantine come to embrace Christianity and what was the effect of his conversion?

5. With what great dispute was Constantine confronted?

6. What were some of the views regarding Christ's relation to the Father which had been previously held in the church?

7. Who was Arius, and what were his views?

8. How did Arius and Alexander of Alexandria differ?

9. What was the occasion and significance of the Council of Nicaea? Did it end the dispute?

10. What was the early history of Athanasius? Why did the controversy seem to him of great religious significance?

11. How did Eusebius of Nicomedia regard the result at Nicaea? What was the position and what the influence of the emperor Constantius?

12. How many times was Athanasius exiled? Some of the circumstances?

13. What was the significance of the Council of Sardica?

14. What was the outcome of the Nicene struggle? In how far and how did Athanasius contribute to the result?

ADDITIONAL READING

F. W. Farrar, *Lives of the Fathers* (New York, 1889), I, 331-425.

Philip Schaff, *History of the Christian Church* (New York, 1884), III, 616-88, 884-93.

H. M. Gwatkin, *The Arian Controversy* (New York, no date) ("Epochs of Church History" Series)

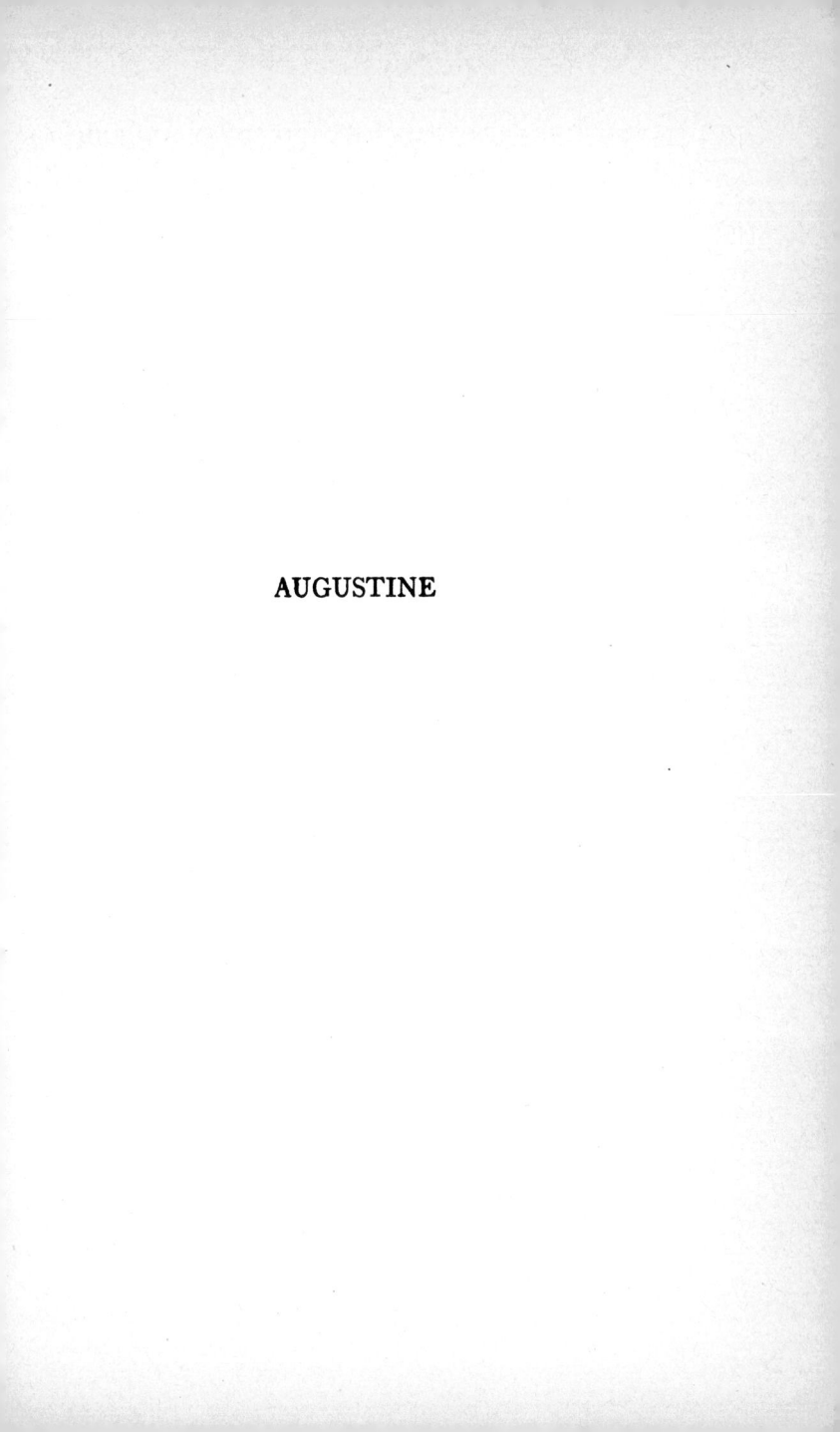

AUGUSTINE

IV
AUGUSTINE

The contests in which Athanasius was engaged, though arousing interest in the western portions of the Empire, and involving its leaders, were primarily eastern. The western mind was more practical, the eastern more speculative. In the East the discussions begun regarding the person of Christ long continued. The Nicene view of divinity united to humanity was everywhere accepted; but, granted that, the further question arose as to how the divine and the human were joined in Christ's person. As the result of the discussion of this problem in embittered quarrels, it was decreed by the Council in Chalcedon, near Constantinople, in 451, that Christ is "known in two natures, without confusion, without conversion, without severance, and without division," that is, that in the one person of Our Lord two complete natures, one human, the other divine, are united. Curiously enough, though interest in the debate was primarily eastern, the words of the Chalcedonian decision were borrowed almost wholly from a letter of the greatest of the early Roman bishops, Leo I (440–61).

With this decision the East exhausted about all that it had to contribute to the development of

Christian doctrine. That this was the case was largely due to its conception of the nature of salvation. As already pointed out in speaking of Irenaeus,[1] it viewed fallen man as having lost his unity with God, and as hence incapable of a joyful immortality. Only by the union of God with men was a true immortality possible for the Christian. Hence the stress which the East laid on the real union of God and man in Christ. Only by that union was spiritual death overcome and life and happy immortality brought to light. Emphasizing thus the victory over death as the prime thing in salvation, the East had little sense of sin and of its consequent guilt. The question of how guilty men might be made right with God had comparatively little interest for the East. Its problem was how mortal men might be made immortal.

To the western mind the problem of guilt was the more pressing. Its prime interest was how sinful men could be made righteous, and the consequences of their sins overcome. Hence the West showed an interest, never developed in the East, in the nature of man and the way of his reconciliation with God. This enabled the West to make a real advance in theology over the East, and gave its thinking a practical value, consonant with the legal and practical, but relatively unspeculative, western mind. It has its highest illustration in the greatest of western

[1] *Ante*, p. 26.

theologians—probably the greatest theologian of all the early church—Augustine.

Of all the leaders of the ancient church, we know Augustine most fully. Thanks to the facts recorded in his writings, especially in his *Confessions* and *Retractions*, and to a *Life* written by his intimate friend, Bishop Possidius of Calama, we are able to follow his spiritual development and his controversies in all their phases, to know the circumstances of his conversion, and to appreciate his relations to his age. We can give the exact dates of his birth and death—a definiteness of knowledge not to be attained regarding any other great character of the early church. We can follow most of his experiences and become acquainted with his friends and opponents.

Augustine was born on November 13, 354, under the reign of Constantius, in Tagaste, a little town in what was then the flourishing North African province of Numidia, in the region now known as Algeria. His father, Patricius, was an easy-going heathen of good position, but small property; his mother, Monnica, a Christian of eager ambition for her son, who had the highest reverence for her, although she was in his younger years of rather external and superficial piety. As he was a boy of promise, the family, in spite of its limited resources, was determined to give Augustine the best education that the time afforded, and, accordingly, he was sent to school first in the neighboring Madaura, and then in the

North African capital, Carthage, where Tertullian and Cyprian had labored. Here, in Carthage, if not earlier, he gave way to the sensual temptations which the age and heathen traditions pressed upon him; but though he paints his lapses in the most abhorrent colors in the pitiless self-condemnation of the *Confessions*, they did not wholly dominate him, and he acquired repute as a brilliant and earnest student. Here at Carthage, when about seventeen, he entered into a kind of partial marriage—a relation of concubinage then legal and not wholly condemned by the church, but severable at will—to which he remained faithful for the next fifteen years, and from which a son, Adeodatus, to whom he was devoted, was early born. Undoubtedly, however, sensuality was the form of temptation to which the youthful Augustine felt himself most exposed, and this defiling experience colored his later conceptions of the nature of sin, and marked the depth of the degradation from which he felt himself rescued by divine grace.

His higher nature, however, constantly asserted itself. A lost treatise of Cicero, the *Hortensius*, which came into his hands when in his nineteenth year, convinced him intellectually that truth must be the object of his search—a determination that was thenceforth masterful in his life. But the old temptations still assailed, and like Paul,[1] though in a

[1] Romans 7:14–24.

different way, he felt that two natures, a higher and a lower, were struggling in him with varying success for the mastery. In this contest he turned to the Bible; but as yet it did not speak to his heart. To the rhetorical taste of the young student its style seemed barbarous, and he now revolted from Christianity of which he had been thus far nominally an adherent.

The form of faith to which Augustine now turned was Manichaeanism, then widespread, in spite of persecution, in the Roman Empire, and one peculiarly appealing to a man like Augustine, who felt two tendencies at warfare within him. Mani, its founder, had taught in Persia, and had there met a martyr's death by crucifixion in 276 or 277. His system combined Zoroastrian, Hindu, Gnostic, and Christian elements; the fundamental basis being the thought that the universe is the scene of the eternal conflict of two powers, the one good, the other evil. Man, as we know him, is a mixed product, the spiritual part of his nature being made of the good element, the physical of the evil. His task is therefore to free the good in him from the evil; and this can be accomplished by prayer, but especially by abstinence from all the enjoyments of evil, riches, lust, wine, meats, handsome houses, and the like. The true spiritual Jesus, as with the Gnostics, had no material body, and died no real death. His purpose was to teach men the way from the kingdom of darkness to that of light. Like the Gnostics, the Manichaeans held that much of the New Testament is true, but they rejected all in it that seemed to imply Christ's real sufferings, and they discarded the Old Testament altogether. Their adherents were divided into two classes, the "perfect," who lived a strict life of ascetic self-denial, and the "hearers," who were still allowed to marry, to trade, and in many ways to conform to the world.

Augustine remained an eager Manichaean for nine years, from 374 to 383; but dissatisfaction with its teachings at last arose in his mind, especially under the influence of the most spiritual of the philosophical systems of the ancient world, that of neo-Platonism. As a Manichaean, however, he taught grammar in his native Tagaste, and rhetoric in Carthage, and though inwardly doubting the truth of this system, it was at the suggestion of Manichaean friends, that he removed to Rome in 383. Not long after his arrival in the capital he secured from the prefect, Symmachus, a professorship in the State University in Milan (384); and thither he was followed by his widowed mother, and some of his African friends, for his was always an attractive personality. He was now thirty years old, in established position in life, and with every prospect of worldly success; but he was more than ever deeply dissatisfied with his life. He separated from his faithful concubine that he might become

AUGUSTINE

betrothed to a young woman of wealth and position; but he could not master his sensual nature, and the conflict became increasingly distressing to him. With his residence in Milan, however, he came under the powerful preaching of Ambrose, whom he first heard as an illustration of pulpit eloquence, but whose message soon impressed his soul, and undoubtedly developed into noble fruitage his mother's spiritual life.

Ambrose was one of the most remarkable men of the age. The son of a high officer of the government, and himself destined for political life, he came to Milan as governor of northern Italy, probably in 373, and the next year, in spite of his want even of baptism, was chosen by the people of the city as their bishop. From the first he looked upon the call as that of God. No greater administrator, no more effective preacher, no more devoted pastor than he was to be found in that age. He dared to rebuke the great emperor, Theodosius, when that ruler sinned, yet with such evident honesty of purpose as not merely to bring the imperial offender to repentance but to secure his lasting friendship. To be brought in contact with such a man as Ambrose was of immense value to the inwardly distressed Augustine.

Yet the immediate occasion of Augustine's conversion seems to have been, as so often in Christian history, personal example. He consulted Simplicianus, a friend of Ambrose, who told him of the religious transformation of the rhetorician, Victorinus, by whose writings Augustine had been introduced to neo-Platonism. A fellow-African, Pontitianus, described the life of the Egyptian monks with its rejection of the temptations of the world. Augustine felt a burning sense of shame that these unlearned men could win spiritual battles in which he, with all his education, felt only defeat. His sense of sin and of his own powerlessness was profoundly stirred; and, as he walked in agony in his garden, he heard a child's voice saying, "Take and read." Instantly he picked up a New Testament, and the words on which his eyes fell were suited perhaps above all others to his mood: "Not in rioting and drunkenness, not in chambering and wantonness, not in strife and envying; but put ye on the Lord Jesus Christ, and make not provision for the flesh to fulfil the lusts thereof."[1] As Augustine himself recorded, "Instantly, as I reached the end of this sentence, it was as if the light of peace was poured into my heart, and all the shades of doubt faded away."[2]

On the eve of the following Easter, 387, Augustine, with his son, Adeodatus, and his friend, Alypius, was baptized by Ambrose in Milan. A few months later he set out for Africa, but on the journey his mother died in Ostia, and the narrative of her con-

[1] Romans 13:13, 14.
[2] *Confessions*, Book VIII, chap. xii.

versations and her death, as recorded by Augustine, is one of the noblest monuments of Christian experience.[1] By the autumn of 388, he was once more settled in Tagaste, and about this time the death of his son added to the grief already experienced in the loss of his mother. Of his experiences till his mother's death he wrote, between 397 and 400, a most remarkable description in his *Confessions*—an unsurpassed spiritual autobiography, in which he endeavored to show the greatness of the divine work by which he had been rescued from his sins and made one of the children of God.

Augustine had been greatly impressed, in connection with his conversion, with monasticism, and an opportunity came to him in 391 to share in founding a monastic establishment in Hippo, now Bona—a monastery that was not merely the first in that part of Africa, but served also as a ministerial training school. Here in Hippo, in 391, by popular insistence and against his will, Augustine was ordained a priest; and, in 395, on the wish of Bishop Valerius, he was chosen assistant bishop of that see. When he succeeded to the full bishopric of Hippo is unknown, but for thirty-five years, till his death on August 28, 430, during the siege of the city by the Vandals, he was practically its ecclesiastical head. As an administrator he was distinguished for his simplicity in food and dress, his encouragement of good morals and

[1] *Ibid.*, Book IX, chaps. x and xi.

education among the clergy, his advocacy of monasticism, and his abilities as a preacher. But his fame as a theologian was now widespread throughout the Empire, and was to be his most eminent claim to remembrance.

Augustine's abundant discussion touched most of the aspects of the theology and philosophy of his age. Beyond any other teacher of the ancient church, subsequent to the apostolic age, he influenced the religious thought of western Christendom not merely throughout the Middle Ages but even more powerfully at the Reformation when his conceptions of Christian truth largely determined the form in which the theology of that great revolt was cast. There were two distinct, and to some extent irreconcilable, aspects to his thinking, however, so that if he is the spiritual father of Protestant theology, the characteristic contentions of mediaeval Catholicism could also find in him their most powerful exponent. If his doctrines of grace, of sin, and of predestination largely furnished the ammunition of the reformers, his conceptions of the church, of the sacraments, and of monasticism were no less influential upon their Roman predecessors and opponents.

Augustine's chief contests were with his old associates the Manichaeans (388–405); against the Donatists, who, starting as a protest against easy treatment of those who had been unfaithful in the Diocletian persecution, divided all North Africa into warring factions, alike in all other beliefs, but each declaring the other no true church (393-420); against the Pelagians, of whom more will be said (412-428); and against the Arians, especially in his treatise on the *Trinity* of about 416. But as it is impossible to describe these contests in any detail in the space at command, but three important aspects of Augustine's thought will now be mentioned as illustrative of his profound influence on his own and subsequent ages.

Augustine worked out his doctrine of the church largely in his disputes with the Donatists. Orthodox as they were in belief, yet opposing the church of the Empire, he had to show to his own satisfaction that they were not a part of the true church. That only is the church, he held, which has faith, hope, and love; but love can only be the possession of the one visible and universal church. Hence not only could there be no real church but the one Catholic body; there is no salvation outside of it, for without all the three Christian virtues of faith, hope, and love none can be saved. The bonds which unite the church, the signs which distinguish it visibly, are the sacraments, which, though possessed by others, are of value only in the one Catholic church to which alone the name church rightly belongs. To the divine operation of the sacraments and the grace conferred by the Holy Spirit through them, the holiness of the church is due; and they are divinely placed in the charge of the properly ordained clergy. Hence the clergy are the indispensable element in the membership of the church. Yet while Augustine thus advocated views of the church which were to come to full development in mediaeval Roman Catholicism, his own conception of its membership or of the sacraments was not always clear. The bestowment of grace is not inseparably bound to the reception of the sacraments. He spoke of the visible church sometimes as a mixed company of good and bad; but he sometimes, also, approached the definition of the church as really the good only, whom God alone can distinguish in the visible body on earth—that is, he was not far at times from that conception of the invisible church as the only true church which was to spring into such power at the Reformation.

Augustine's conceptions of sin and grace grew largely out of his own experience, and were developed in their leading features before the Pelagian controversy, though that discussion brought them to full expression. The Apologists like Justin Martyr had emphasized man's freedom to do right or wrong, and that conception had prevailed, especially in the Greek-speaking portion of the church. Pelagius, a British, or less probably an Irish, monk, who had lived long in Rome, carried these thoughts to sharper expression. He denied that sin is inherited from Adam. Man still has freedom by nature to act righteously or sinfully. Nor is death a consequence of Adam's transgression. Adam, indeed, introduced sin into the world, his corrupting example spread it to his posterity. Almost all the human race have sinned; but it is possible not to sin, and some have not. God predestinates none, save in the sense that he foresees who will believe and who will reject his gracious influences. His forgiveness comes to all who exercise "faith alone;" and it is interesting to note that no one between Paul and Luther so emphasized "faith alone" as the condition of salvation as did Pelagius. But, once forgiven, man has power of himself to live a life pleasing to God, and Pelagius makes relatively little of the aid of the Holy Spirit. His ideal of the Christian life is rather the Stoic conception of ascetic self-control.

All this was contrary to the views which Augustine's experience had wrought in him. His sense of the depth of his sin was profound, and hence his conception of the greatness of salvation needed was correspondingly exalted. He felt that nothing less than irresistible divine power could have saved him from the slough of sin in which he was till his conversion, and only constantly inflowing divine grace could keep him in the Christian life, the essence of which is not Stoic self-control, but love for righteousness infused by the constant work of the Spirit of God. As Augustine studied the Scriptures, especially the Pauline epistles, he believed his experience confirmed.

In Augustine's view all that God has made is in itself good. The first man, Adam, was created a holy, happy, and harmoniously constituted being.

He had the possibility of not sinning, and, had he refused to sin, the practice of righteousness would have become a habit, and the possibility of not sinning would have become a moral impossibility to sin. Instead, Adam, who had free will, sinned, and ruin was the result. The harmony which kept the body subject to the soul was broken. The body asserted itself in passions, of which, to Augustine's thinking, the most characteristic is lust. His mental faculties were clouded. His vision of God lost. His power to do right gone. In a word, Adam died, spiritually; and soon physically. But he was not alone in his ruin. On the basis of a mistranslation of Romans 5:12, Augustine taught that all the race was in Adam and shared his fall. It all became a "mass of corruption," incapable of itself of any good act, and deserving, in each of its members from earliest infancy to old age, nothing but damnation.

Since man can now do nothing good himself, all impulse or power to do good must be the free gift of God, must be, that is, a "grace." Out of the mass of the fallen race God chooses some to receive grace, which comes to them from the work of Christ, through the church, and especially through its sacraments. All who receive baptism receive regenerating grace. Such grace is irresistible. It gives man back his freedom to serve God, though that service is imperfect even in the best, and is maintained only by the constant incoming of divine aid. Those to whom God does not send his grace are lost. Nor can any man be sure, even if he now enjoys God's grace, that he will be saved. Only he to whom God gives the added grace of perseverance, that is, who has divine aid to the end of his life, will be redeemed. Man, therefore, has no power or worthiness of himself; all his salvation is of God. The principal effect of grace, according to Augustine, is not, however, forgiveness of sins, though that is one of its consequences, but the building-up of a righteous character, through the infusion of love by the Holy Spirit. That character God rewards. He treats it as meritorious in us, though its creation is wholly his work.

About 410 Pelagius, with his disciple, Caelestius, came from Rome to North Africa. There Caelestius tried to secure ordination as a priest; but was rejected and his views condemned at a synod in Carthage, at which Augustine was not present, in 411. He then went to the East, whither Pelagius had preceded him, and where they had a fairly friendly reception. Augustine now came forth as their opponent in a strenuous literary warfare, reinforced by the efforts of his friends with other weapons. In 416 Pelagius was condemned by African synods in Carthage and Mileve, and Pope Innocent I approved the decision. His successor, Zosimus, at first looked leniently on Pelagius and Caelestius, but a general rallying of the Augustinian forces led to a change of view, and by the spring of 418, Zosimus was on Augustine's side. In 419 the Pelagians were banished by the emperor, Honorius, and, in 431, Pelagianism was condemned by the General Council of the church in Ephesus. Thus Augustine's view triumphed officially; but there have never been wanting many who have held essentially the position of Pelagius. It is easy to see, however, that, though Augustine bound the reception of "grace" to membership in the visible church, his doctrine that God chooses whom he will and gives them power to serve him, makes salvation a matter between God and the individual soul, and was, therefore, a doctrine capable of becoming, as at the Reformation, a tower of strength to those who denied that any body of men, of whatever claims to be a church, could come between the soul and its Maker.

A third characteristic of Augustine, of far-reaching influence, was his mysticism, or perhaps it is better to say his spiritual-mindedness. To him God is the end and object of man's love, and even of man's existence. "Thou has formed us for thyself, and our hearts are restless till they find rest in thee," he exclaims in his *Confessions*.[1] But the world he views no less from a spiritual standpoint. The time in which he lived was peculiarly an age of apparent ruin. The Roman Empire was visibly collapsing. Rome itself was captured by the Goths in 410. And

[1] Book I, chap. i.

AUGUSTINE

the remaining heathen were not tardy with their shallow explanation of this apparent downfall of civilization. When Rome worshiped the old gods, they said, it conquered the world. Now Christianity has turned men away from the deities to whom Rome owed her strength, and the barbarians plunder the city itself. To these criticisms, and to the fears of the Christians themselves, Augustine replied in his noble *City of God*, or more truly "Kingdom of God," written between 412 and 426, and presenting his spiritual philosophy of history. Two kingdoms, one that of God, the other that of the world, have existed always side by side. The former owes its life to the grace of God, the latter is necessitated by man's sin. The one is spiritual, the other temporal. While sin exists the temporal kingdom has its use in repressing crime and maintaining peace; but as the spiritual kingdom grows the temporal must diminish. The highest illustration of the kingdom of the world was the empire of heathen Rome, but its passing is no evil. On the contrary, it must decline that the Kingdom of God may more and more come. The grandeur of this spiritual vision made the *City of God* the most beloved of Augustine's works throughout the early Middle Ages. It gave a spiritual interpretation to the woes from which the world suffered. The present might be bad, but better is to come. The golden age—the Kingdom of God—is in the future, not in the fading splendors of a worldly kingdom that could but be temporal. Yet, as Augustine practically identified the Kingdom of God with the visible church, his doctrine greatly aided the growth of the conception that the church should rule the state which the mediaeval papacy was to carry to such heights.

The modern world has departed in many respects from Augustine, but no man since the apostolic age has been more influential as a Christian example or as a Christian thinker than he.

QUESTIONS

1. How did eastern and western Christianity differ in intellectual tendencies?

2. How is our knowledge of Augustine greater than our acquaintance with most of the leaders of the early church?

3. Describe Augustine's early life, his temptations, and his ideals.

4. What was Manichaeanism? Why did Augustine become a Manichaean? How long was he one?

5. Who was Ambrose?

6. Give an account of Augustine's conversion. Its central experience?

7. Outline Augustine's later life.

8. What was the extent of Augustine's influence as a leader of Christian thought? What were his chief controversies?

9. What was Augustine's view of the church? Its defects? Its influence on mediaeval Roman Catholicism?

10. What influence had Augustine's experience on his views of sin and grace?

11. Who was Pelagius and what was his theory of sin and salvation? What importance did he attach to justification by faith alone?

12. What was Augustine's view of the origin of sin? Of

the relation of men to Adam? Of the extent of human sinfulness?

13. Who, according to Augustine, are saved, and how are they saved? What importance had his views in the Reformation age?

14. What influence had Augustine's mysticism? His theory of history as set forth in his *City of God?* Its occasion and influence?

ADDITIONAL READING

F. W. Farrar, *Lives of the Fathers* (New York, 1889), II, 298-459.

Philip Schaff, *History of the Christian Church* (New York, 1884), III, 783-870, 988-1028.

Joseph McCabe, *St. Augustine and His Age* (New York, 1903).

PATRICK

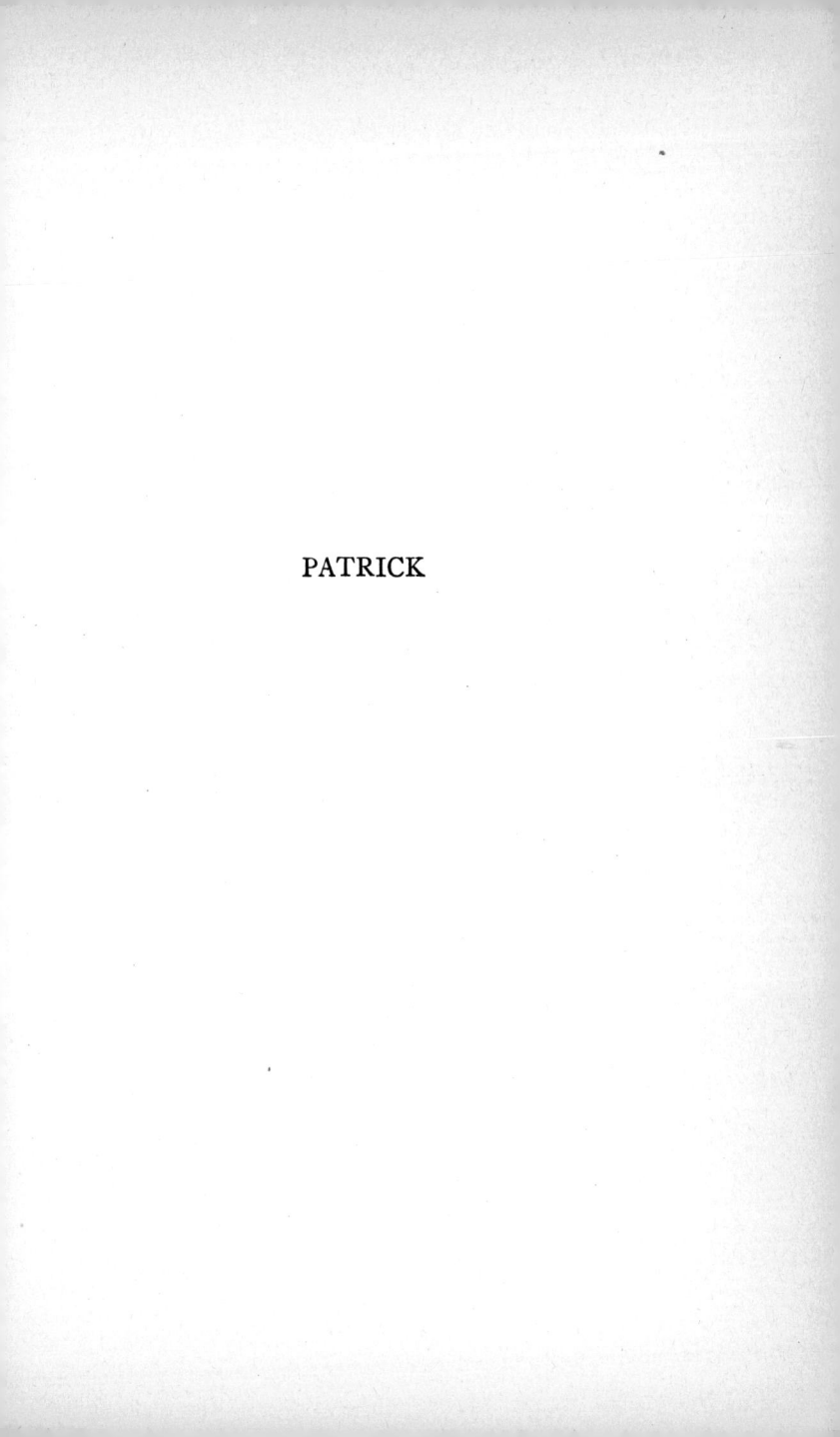

V
PATRICK

The Christian leaders thus far considered labored in the populous cities of the Roman Empire. Rome, Alexandria, Carthage—all centers of government, of education, and of culture—were the scenes of a large part at least of their activities. Patrick's chief work was beyond the bounds of the Roman state, in an age when the institutions of civilization seemed collapsing, among a rude people, and on the remote frontiers of the then known world. The men who have attracted our attention were all of conspicuous scholarship, who moved their own time and after-ages by what they wrote. Patrick was by his own declaration uneducated. But two brief writings of his composition have survived. They are not treatises on deep problems of the Christian faith. He could not have discussed such matters had he wished. He left only a crudely written account of what God had wrought through him (his *Confession*); and an indignant pastoral protest against the capture of men and women of his flock by a British chieftain (the *Letter to Coroticus*). His own life was so obscure that his very existence has been doubted; and competent scholars have most variously estimated the extent and significance of his work.[1] Yet Christianity has been

[1] All earlier literature regarding Patrick has been superseded by the recent studies of Professors Zimmer and Bury. Professor

advanced by men of lowly capacities and attainments, as well as by those of education and high station; and a consideration of Patrick may exhibit the forces by which it has made progress as truly as a study of Athanasius or of Augustine.

In Roman days what are now England, Ireland, and Scotland were inhabited by Kelts, of whom the Irish, the Highlanders of Scotland, and the Welsh are now the representatives. Though divided into two main language groups, the Irish-Scotch and the British, they were similar in original habits of thought and intercommunication was easy. Roman arms, however, subdued only what is now England and southern Scotland, with the result that a considerable degree of Roman culture was introduced into the conquered portions, while the rest largely remained in their primitive state. In the Roman section the church at length obtained a footing; but, as in the northwestern part of the Empire generally, it was feebly represented till after the conversion of Constantine. Bishops of London, York, and Lincoln were

Zimmer (*Realencyklopädie für protestantische Theologie und Kirche*, 3d. ed., X, 204–21, translated into English as *The Celtic Church in Britain and Ireland*, 1902) minimizes his significance, and regards him as identical with Palladius, of which more will be said. Professor Bury (*The Life of St. Patrick and His Place in History*, 1905) has answered Zimmer, in the main successfully, and has shown the real importance of Patrick's work. He attempts, less successfully, to distinguish Patrick from Palladius. The writer would acknowledge his large indebtedness to both of these scholars.

present, however, at the Synod of Arles in 314, and Christianity seems to have grown rapidly in Britain, as in the other western regions of the Empire, during the fourth century. In estimating the intellectual state of British Christianity one recalls that Pelagius was from that land.

With the collapse of the Roman power at the beginning of the fifth century, the civilization of Britain rapidly deteriorated, and the invasions of the Saxons drove the older inhabitants largely to the more mountainous western portion of England, and so extensively reintroduced heathenism that, while Christianity did not absolutely perish, most of the land became missionary territory. But before the Saxon conquest had widely extended—certainly by the end of the first quarter of the fifth century (401-25)—Christianity had begun to reach out from Roman Britain into Scotland and Ireland. This growth was doubtless aided by the ease of communication where speech was so similar, and in Ireland especially by the settlement of Irish in southwestern England. There was therefore a considerable degree of Christianity in Ireland before Patrick began his work, and he cannot be called "the Apostle of Ireland" in the sense that he introduced Christianity into a wholly heathen country. Yet the land was in a very rude stage of civilization, divided into tribes ruled over by petty chieftains, whom it is almost absurd to designate by the name of kings. Some of these "kings" were subject to others, and all were under the overlordship of the "high king" whose seat was at Tara, northwestward of Dublin. Irish Christianity was in an unorganized state, and undoubtedly very much heathenism still existed at the time Patrick began his work.

Like that of Augustine, though in much humbler surroundings, the story of Patrick's awakening to his mission in life is that of a transformation wrought in him by the Spirit of God. Born about 389, in a village called Bannaventa, probably in the region of southwestern England near the river Severn, but not yet identified with even approximate assurance, he was by race a Briton. His father was a man of some local distinction, a municipal councilor (decurion), Calpurnius by name. His grandfather, Potitus, had been a priest. He was therefore of a family long Christian; and the married state of his father and grandfather, though in clerical orders, is not strange; for though clerical celibacy was urged by councils and popes, it was still far from universal. To the boy the British name Sucat, "Ready for Battle," was given, and probably also the Latin name Patrick (Patricius), though this may have been later self-assumed in view of his father's prominence in the local community.[1] Though in far-off Britain, it was with a strong sense of belonging to the great Roman

[1] The latter is Professor Zimmer's conjecture; the former, and more probable, that of Professor Bury.

Empire that Patrick grew up. That Empire had fallen on evil days. The death of the able Theodosius in 395 was followed by the division of the Empire between his feeble sons, Arcadius and Honorius. The Germanic tribes promptly began their devastating invasions which resulted in the capture of Rome itself in 410. In the peril of the central provinces the troops were withdrawn from the Roman frontier. One legion was removed from Britain in 401, and practically all the remaining forces in 407. Thus left well-nigh defenseless, the Romanized portions of the islands were attacked by their less civilized foes on all sides, by Irish, Picts, and Saxons, and became a prey to plunder and soon to conquest.

In one of these invasions, probably in 405, at all events when Patrick was sixteen, he was taken prisoner by Irish raiders, and carried a slave to the western portion of Ireland, into the region now known as Connaught. Here, under the hardest of conditions, as a herder of swine, he lived six years. But here, in captivity, his spiritual nature was awakened, as Augustine's had been amid the far different surroundings of cultivated and luxurious Milan. He now turned to God in constant prayer, going out before dawn, or whenever he could steal away from his work to seek him. Spiritual things now became to him the most important of realities. At last he attempted to escape. With difficulty he made his way to the east coast, probably to Wicklow; and there he found a vessel about to sail, the heathen crew of which he persuaded with difficulty, and as he believed only through divine answer to his prayers, to take him with them. As part of the cargo was Irish hounds, they may have felt the readier to allow his presence as able, from his rough woodland life, to handle these fierce dogs. The ship bore him in three days to what is now France; but he was not easily rid of his new-found and distasteful companions, who kept him with them as they carefully avoided the towns and even the farms of that land, then just desolated by the invasions of the Vandals. It seems probable that they thus journeyed to northern Italy, though Patrick's description of the experience is most perplexing; and that it was in Italy, also, in 411 or 412, that he broke away from the associates whom he had accompanied since sailing from Ireland. At all events it seems certain that for several years he now found a peaceful home in the monastery which Honoratus had just founded on one of the little islands of Lérins, in the Mediterranean, off the extreme southeastern coast of what is now France.

Patrick's course is hard to trace, but it would appear that, not far from 415, he was once more in his old home in England. There he had a remarkable dream, like to that of Paul at Troas.[1] It seemed to him that a messenger stood by him with letters from

[1] Acts 16:9.

Ireland summoning him to labor for Christ where once he had been a slave. Thenceforth he never doubted his divine call to preach the gospel in that land. He would not undertake the work, however, without further preparation and the support of the ecclesiastical authorities; and, therefore, he now went to Auxerre in France, ninety-three miles southeast of Paris, for study and to enlist friends. Here he was ordained a deacon by Bishop Amator. But evidently the realization of his plan was difficult, and it is easy to imagine that his want of education, and what must have seemed to many his visionary nature, led to the obstacles which he found in his way. It was to be fourteen years at least after his arrival in Auxerre before his wish to be sent to Ireland was to be gratified.

The accomplishment of his desires came about in a way that involves one of the most perplexing historical questions connected with Patrick's career. Amator had been succeeded by Germanus as bishop of Auxerre. The Pelagian controversy was at its height. Pelagius himself was a native of Britain, or even possibly of Ireland, and his views had no little following among the Christians of those lands. In 429, at the request of British opponents of Pelagianism, and with the approval of Pope Celestine (422–32) secured by a deacon "Palladius," Germanus went to England and waged spiritual warfare against Pelagian opinions. The Irish Christians could at most have been few, and they were thus far unorganized. The pope's attention was attracted by Palladius to Irish affairs, and, probably in 431, he consecrated the deeply interested Palladius as bishop for Ireland. In 432 Patrick entered on his work in Ireland as a bishop. The question naturally arises whether Palladius and Patrick were not the same person; and whether Patrick did not, therefore, go to Ireland with the approval of the Bishop of Rome. Competent scholars are divided on the problem. To the present writer, the conclusion that the same person is indicated by both names seems much the more probable, though a positive affirmation or denial awaits more evidence than is at present available.[1] If Palladius and Patrick were not one, then it may be concluded that Pope Celestine sent Palladius, and that probably on news of his early death, Patrick, always so eager to labor in Ireland, but thus far

[1] Professor Zimmer regards them as identical, Professor Bury as separate personalities. For the identity may be urged the close connection of dates; the interest of "Palladius" in Irish affairs; the fact that both were ordained bishop for Ireland; that both had relations with Germanus and Auxerre; and not least, that "Palladius" seems to be a Latinized equivalent of Patrick's British name, Sucat = "Ready for Battle." Against it may be presented the tradition represented by Muirchus' *Life of Patrick*, late in the seventh century, that is, two hundred years after Patrick's death, that "Palladius" had a brief mission to Ireland, ending in his early demise, and was followed by Patrick. Then, too, the fact that the seventh-century literature regarding Patrick does not represent him as ordained by the pope, presents a serious argument against the identity claimed.

hindered, was consecrated to the bishopric so recently established and vacated. In that case he was probably ordained by Germanus of Auxerre. At all events Palladius-Patrick, or Patrick, if Palladius and Patrick are not identical, entered on his life-task in Ireland in 432. All had been thus far a long preparation, the difficulties of which had been surmounted by his Christian enthusiasm and his confidence that God had called him to this service.

From 432 to his death on March 17, 461, with the probable exception of a brief journey to Rome about 441–43, Patrick labored in Ireland. The accounts of his work are so overlaid with legend that its amount or its places are difficult to trace; but certain it is that it was of a threefold character. He preached as a missionary to the heathen, and with marked success. He himself recorded that he had baptized thousands. Such a statement involves of course much superficiality in his presentation of Christianity; but there is no reason to doubt that a large proportion of the heathen population of the island were won by him to at least an outward acknowledgment of the gospel. He ordained priests and bishops, and gave to the church of Ireland a definite form. He founded monasteries, for which the Irish of his day seem to have had a peculiar aptitude; and in Ireland the church became monastic in its form for the next two centuries at least to a degree not elsewhere characteristic of it. Indeed, it may be believed that this monastic tendency went much farther than Patrick himself desired. He would have preferred a nearer approximation to conditions as they existed on the continent. He made Latin the language of worship in the Irish church. He was, that is, not so much the representative of the papacy, as of the unity of western Christendom, into conformity with which he would bring the weak Irish Christianity which he found at the beginning of his activities, and which he greatly extended and strengthened.

The scenes of Patrick's labors in Ireland are largely obscured by legend; but his work centered probably in the northeast portion of the island. There he founded the church of Armagh about 444, which was destined to be the leading see of Ireland, and to have an ecclesiastical distinction among its bishoprics like that of Canterbury in England. At Saul, in the present County of Down, he was buried. Besides these efforts to spread Christianity in northeastern Ireland, he worked also in Meath, and in the western districts which compose Connaught. His activities were therefore chiefly in the northern half of the island. That he regarded it all as the field of his charge is evident, and there is reason to think that he preached yet more widely than has been indicated; but these labors are exceedingly obscure.

Enough of the picture of Patrick appears through the mists of time, however, to show not merely that he was a man of rare Christian enthusiasm and indomitable persistence, who, in spite of all limitations through lack of education, did a large missionary work; but that he aimed to serve the general cause of Christianity well in a critical age. The Roman world was falling into ruin. In Britain, invasions of Angles and Saxons were beginning which were to make large portions of England once more heathen. Patrick sought to organize the feeble Christian beginnings of Ireland. He brought them, for a time at least, into closer connection with the Christianity of continental Europe. He helped to extend the conquests of Christianity beyond the farthest reach of Roman arms. He had no thought of fostering a church independent of the papacy, or of the church of the Empire. Rather, he sought for the Christians of far-off Ireland closer fellowship with the rest of western Christendom. That the type of unity which has Rome as its center was to prove full of peril he could not see. That result was still veiled in the future. But that he should wish the Christians of Ireland not only increased in numbers, but organized and brought fully into the great sisterhood of churches of western Christendom, shows the strong impression which the imperial unity that had its center at Rome had made on one of Rome's citizens, though he was born in the farthest confines of the Empire and in the time of its physical decay.

Yet Patrick's desires for organization and unity were but imperfectly realized. The tribal division of Ireland, its passion for monasticism, and its actual separation from the Christianity of the continent, made the type of religion in Ireland for more than a century and a half after his death essentially monastic. Monasteries, rather than bishoprics, were the seats of its life. The island was covered with them; and from the monasteries came missionaries who not merely carried Christianity to western Scotland, like Columba (563), but spread it in northern England, and even reached Italy, Germany, and ultimately far-off Iceland with their labors. It was not till long after Roman missions, begun in 597, had converted a large portion of Anglo-Saxon England, that Ireland fully entered into the Roman obedience. That history of semi-independence was on the whole most creditable; but under the conditions of the early Middle Ages, the larger unity in which Patrick believed, and for which he strove, was well-nigh essential to ultimate progress.

QUESTIONS

1. What is true of Patrick's education and intellectual abilities?

2. What was the nature of the population of the British islands? In how far was it Christian at the beginning of the fifth century?

3. What was the effect of the Anglo-Saxon conquest of England?

4. Was Ireland a wholly heathen land when Patrick began his work?

5. Where and when was Patrick born? His captivity and escape?

6. What was the nature of Patrick's spiritual awakening, and what did it lead him to desire to do?

7. What relation had the Pelagian controversy to Patrick's going to Ireland?

8. Was Patrick ordained and sent by Pope Celestine?

9. What was the nature of Patrick's work in Ireland? Its threefold aim?

10. Where did he labor and where was he buried?

11. What was the value, and what the results of Patrick's work?

ADDITIONAL READING

H. Zimmer (translated by Miss A. Meyer), *The Celtic Church in Britain and Ireland* (London, 1902).

J. B. Bury, *The Life of St. Patrick and His Place in History* (London, 1905).

Philip Schaff, *History of the Christian Church* (New York, 1888), IV, 43–52.

BENEDICT

VI
BENEDICT

There has already been abundant occasion to mention monasticism in these sketches. The institution, as has been seen, was favored by men as widely divided geographically as Athanasius, Augustine, Ambrose, and Patrick. In the fourth and fifth centuries it was rapidly spreading, and down to the time of Luther, who was himself a monk, almost every leader of the church who rendered it conspicuous service was either himself a monk or a warm supporter of monasticism. Such unanimity of approval shows that the institution must have appealed to men for centuries as the highest manifestation of the Christian life. Though Protestantism rightly repudiated it, it is still regarded with favor by large sections of the church.

Monasticism was the normal outcome of ascetic tendencies which have their beginnings even in apostolic times. A life of abstinence and especially of celibacy was very early regarded as of superior sanctity, and was approved by such men as Tertullian, Origen, and Cyprian. Long before the conversion of the Empire many took such vows, though at first without withdrawing from the ordinary life of the cities. The first separate society of ascetics dates from the dawn of the fourth century and was founded by Hierakas of Leontopolis in Egypt. Its members were pledged to abstain from marriage, wine, and meat. But the tendency which it represented went back almost to the beginnings of Christianity. Its fundamental principle, the basis of later monasticism, was the feeling that in withdrawal from the ordinary associations of the world and in the conquest of the passions the highest type of Christian life is to be found. It was favored by the conviction, as old as the time of Hermas (130-40), that the New Testament teaches a lower and a higher morality, its precepts of faith, hope, and charity being binding on all; but its advice being for those who would do more than is required of the ordinary Christian. Chief of such works of supererogation are voluntary poverty and voluntary abstinence from marriage.[1] They constituted the elements, it was thought, of the holier life.

Monasticism itself, which had its roots in this earlier asceticism, originated in Egypt. Its first form, and one long continuing, especially in the East, was that of the hermit life. Anthony, the earliest example of Christian monasticism, was born, about 251, in the village of Koma. Under the impulse of Christ's words to the rich young man,[2] which may be called the golden text of monasticism, he gave away his

[1] Matt. 19:10-22; I Cor. 7:7, 8.

[2] Matt. 19:21.

property when twenty, and soon took up a lonely hermit's life in a tomb. His example was contagious, and he speedily had scores of imitators. Later legend loved to recount his battles with temptations assailing him in visible forms. His long life was protracted to one hundred and five years, and he was the friend and supporter of Athanasius in the great Arian conflict. While the hermit type long continued popular in Egypt, a great improvement was effected there by Pachomius, when, not far from the year 322, he instituted the first Christian monastery. Instead of permitting the monks to live singly or in groups of hermits, each a law to himself, Pachomius established a regulated common life, in which the monks ate, labored, and worshiped, keeping fixed hours, doing manual work, dressed in uniform garb, and were under strict discipline. Pachomius' reform was an immense advance on the hermit life with its liability to idleness and eccentricity. It brought monasticism into system and restraint. It made the monastic life easy for women, for whom the hermit form was well-nigh impossible.

Undoubtedly the strongest appeal made by monasticism to the church of the fourth and fifth centuries was due to the belief, already noticed, that it was the most Christian form of life. Its spread was aided, however, by the general misery of the declining Empire, especially the grinding system of taxing the middle classes of the population, to which, more than to any other single cause, the economic and military collapse of the Empire was due. Politically and socially monasticism was most unfortunate. At the time the Empire was most suffering from lack of men to fill its armies and money for its treasury, it took thousands from family life and productive industry. Religiously considered, its effects were twofold. While the system undoubtedly harmed ordinary Christian life by fostering the feeling that the truest Christian service could not be rendered under the ordinary and natural conditions of human society, it produced, not merely in its early period, but throughout mediaeval history, a noble army of missionaries, preachers, scholars, and consecrated men and women.

Monasticism soon spread far beyond the bounds of Egypt. Syria was its next great conquest; and Asia Minor was won, especially through the influence of Basil, Gregory of Nazianzen, and Gregory of Nyssa, the champions of the Nicene faith of the generation that succeeded Athanasius. To Basil, who died in 379, was due the "Rule" under which the monasticism of the Greek church is organized to the present day.

From the East monasticism was speedily introduced into western Europe, in spite of some opposition, by the efforts of Athanasius, though it was not till between 370 and 380 that the first monastery was there established. Furthered in Rome by Jerome,

BENEDICT

in Milan by Ambrose, in North Africa by Augustine, in France by Martin of Tours, the institution spread with immense rapidity through all western Christendom. Great diversity of organization existed, however; some monasteries following the "Rule" of Pachomius, others that of Basil, and yet others those composed by western leaders. In this want of uniformity was a source of much irregularity, and, as time soon proved, of much corruption. The systematizer and organizer of western monasticism, the man who gave to early monasticism its noblest expression, was to be Benedict.

Benedict was born in Nursia (Norcia), about eighty-five miles northeast of Rome, late in the fifth century. His education in Rome had advanced but little when he adopted the extremest form of asceticism, and dwelt as a hermit in a cave near Subiaco, in the mountains some forty miles eastward of the city. Here he spent three years in the study of the Scriptures and in severe self-mortification, till the monks of a neighboring monastery chose him for their abbot. His strict discipline proved irksome to them, however. He narrowly escaped death by poison at their hands, and gladly betook himself once more to his cave. He could not now be alone, for his fame attracted disciples. He taught children, he established a group of small monasteries. Subiaco proved at length, however, an uncomfortable place of sojourn by reason of the jealous opposition to Benedict of one of its clergy; and, therefore, he left it, now a man of ripened observation and experience. In 529, he laid, at Monte Cassino, eighty-five miles southeast of Rome, the foundations of what was to be the most famous monastery in Europe, the motherhouse of the Benedictine order. For this monastery he wrote his celebrated "Rule." Here he taught, preached, and lived, a pattern of monastic piety till his death, which occurred after the summer of 542.[1]

Benedict was no scholar, but he had the Roman genius for administration, an earnest belief in monasticism as the ideal Christian life, and a profound knowledge of human nature. In the creation of his "Rule" he built on the work of the regulators of monasticism who had gone before him, but with a moderation and good sense that reveal the keenness of his observation and his capacity to meet existing needs. Monasticism, in his judgment, had its grave perils. Many monks lived unworthily of their profession. Some were no better than vagabonds. These evils were due to lack of discipline. Discipline was a fundamental need; yet it must not be made too heavy a yoke for ordinary men. It is this remarkable combination of strict restraint with some real degree of freedom, of lifelong vows with moderation in requirements, that above all distinguished Benedict's "Rule."

[1] The traditional date, March 21, 543, is without adequate historic support. The East-Gothic king, Totila, visited him in the summer of 542. That is the last certain event in his life.

Benedict's conception of the monastic career seems to have been that of a spiritual garrison holding duty for Christ in a hostile world. As such, its discipline was a necessary part of its life. None should enter its service until he had tried the life fully for at least a year's novitiate, during which he should be free to leave. This completed, the would-be monk took the threefold vows which forever cut him off from the world, binding himself to permanent life in the monastery, poverty and chastity, and obedience to its rule and its head. The government of the monastery was vested in an abbot; and nowhere does Benedict's skill more signally appear than in his provisions for its exercise. While each monk was vowed to absolute obedience to the abbot's commands, even if they seemed to him impossible of fulfilment, the abbot was chosen by the free suffrage of all the monks, he could decide weighty matters only after calling for the judgment of the whole body, and smaller concerns affecting the monastery only on hearing the opinion of the elder brethren. Benedict was wise enough to know that a sensible man, even if given absolute authority in theory, would not long resist the wishes of the majority of those whose advice he was obliged to take in all cases of importance. Under the abbot, and appointed by him "with the advice of the brethren," was to be a provost as an assistant in government, and in large monasteries "deans," also, chosen for the same purpose. That the separation of the monks from the world should be as complete as possible, Benedict prescribed that each monastery, wherever feasible, should be equipped to furnish the necessaries of life, since he deemed wandering outside its walls a chief spiritual danger.

Benedict's regulations concerning food and drink exhibited a similar moderation and wisdom. He would have neither luxury nor undue fasting, and he was especially considerate in the care of those who were ill. Since worship was a large part of monastic life, careful requirements were made for its observance in the "Rule." On the supposed authority of Scripture, Benedict required not merely seven services in the twenty-four hours, but made much of that appointed for two in the morning, the "vigil."[1] In contrast to the prescriptions of some other "Rules," however, the services appointed by Benedict, except the "vigil," were notably brief, demanding only about twenty minutes each. They consisted chiefly in the recitation of the Psalms, the whole book being used each week.

Benedict's most fruitful requirements were regarding labor. "Idleness," said he, in the "Rule," "is hostile to the soul, and therefore the brethren should be occupied at fixed times in manual labor, and at definite hours in religious reading." He saw clearly the moral value of work; and he was broad-minded enough in his conception of labor to

[1] Ps. 119 : 62, 164.

include in it that of the mind as well as that of the hands. The proportion naturally varied with the seasons. In the harvest time of summer the manual labor of the fields was the first duty; in the comparative rest of winter, especially in Lent, opportunities, and consequently requirements, for reading were increased. Those who could not read were to have additional manual work assigned to them, that they might have no relaxation of duties by reason of their ignorance. Besides reading, the instruction of boys placed in charge of the monastery was a duty of the monks following the example of Benedict himself.

A Benedictine monastery that was true to the purposes of the founder of the order was, therefore, a little world in itself, in which the monks lived a strenuous but not overburdened life, involving worship, vigorous labor in the shop and fields, and serious reading. It made every Benedictine monastery the possessor of something of a library; and, though Benedict himself says nothing about classical learning, his aim being primarily religious, the Benedictine monasteries soon copied and read the great literary examples of Latin antiquity. Perhaps a considerable influence in this direction of study came from the monastery near Squillace, in extreme southern Italy, founded before Benedict's death by Cassiodorius, in which the cultivation of the classics was one of the duties of the monks. At all events, it is to the monasteries of the order of Benedict that we owe not merely the preservation of the writings of the Latin Church Fathers but the masterpieces of Roman literature.

From Italy the Benedictine "Rule" spread rapidly over western Europe. It is almost impossible to exaggerate the services of these monks in the transition period caused by the ruin of the old Roman civilization and the growth in its place of the new life of the Germanic conquerors. That that new life preserved so much of the best the old had to offer in Christianity and civilization alike was largely due to this Benedictine monasticism. Northern Europe was then much like North America at the coming of the first European settlers. It was in large measure a land of forests and untilled soil. The monasteries did what a modern mission station does among barbarous peoples. They instructed in the principles of Christianity, they relieved distress and sickness to a considerable degree, they taught agriculture to the peoples of northern Europe, they preserved such learning as survived the Germanic invasions, they gave the only schools. Above all, they made it possible, in a rude age when men won and held property and place in the world by the sword, for peace-loving, religious-minded people to find a comparatively quiet and sheltered life. They gave the only opportunity that the early Middle Ages had to offer for study, for protection amid constant warfare, and for rest. They were a great missionary force, and a constant reminder to a rude population that there are other interests than those of the body.

It is easy to see that monasticism had its perils. Some of them have already been pointed out. While the individual monk might vow himself to poverty, the monasteries often grew immensely rich through gifts, especially of land. Their discipline frequently became lax. Their original strenuousness was not easily preserved. The history of the Middle Ages shows constant efforts for their reform; and the foundation of new branches designed to repair the corruption into which the old had fallen. Above all, their conception of the Christian life was essentially unnatural. To enter a monastery was to separate from the world, to abandon the ordinary relationships of social life, to eschew marriage and all that the Christian home signifies. These were the fundamental evils of monasticism and they grew out of an ascetic interpretation of Christianity which is much earlier than the monastic system. But to recognize this now is not to say that these faults were apparent to the men of the declining Roman Empire or of the Middle Ages. For them, generally, the monastic seemed the truest type of the Christian life. Nor should we, in noting the evils of monasticism, in any way underrate the immense services of the system to the spread and development alike of Christianity and of civilization in the most trying period of European history, and, in fact, throughout the Middle Ages to the Reformation. Early European monasticism owed its usefulness in higher degree than to any other of its founders to the organizing ability, good sense, and consecration of Benedict.

QUESTIONS

1. What were the fundamental principles of Christian asceticism? How early did it appear in the church? How widely did it spread?

2. In what country did monasticism originate? Who was the first Christian hermit?

3. What improvement did Pachomius introduce?

4. How did the declining state of the Roman Empire aid the growth of monasticism?

5. What influence had Basil on its spread and organization?

6. Under whose auspices was monasticism introduced into the West?

7. What was the early religious life of Benedict? Where and how did he labor? What great monastery did he establish?

8. What evils did Benedict attempt to correct? What was the importance of his "Rule"? What was his conception of the monastic life?

9. How did one become a monk? How was a monastery governed? How did Benedict combine obedience with some degree of freedom?

10. What can be said of Benedict's prescriptions as to food and worship?

11. What importance did Benedict attach to labor? Why? Was this labor manual only?

12. Some services of monasticism to Europe?

13. The good and evil in monasticism?

ADDITIONAL READING

Philip Schaff, *History of the Christian Church* (New York, 1884), III, 147–233.

Ephraim Emerton, *An Introduction to the Study of the Middle Ages* (Boston, 1888), pp. 135–49.

———, *Mediaeval Europe* (Boston, 1894), pp. 555–81.

F. Guizot, *History of Civilization in France*, Lecture XIV (1830), English translation (New York, 1882).

Adolf Harnack, *Monasticism* (London 1901).

HILDEBRAND

VII
HILDEBRAND

There has been frequent occasion to mention the growth of the power of the Bishop of Rome. That increase had many causes and was by no means uniform. Even before the close of the first century, Clement, writing to the Corinthians in the name of the Roman church, uses a tone of admonition that, though fraternal, implied that Rome ought to be heard. The Gnostic controversy strengthened Rome's position as the great church of the West in which apostles had worked, and therefore as the bearer of the apostolic tradition. Irenaeus and Tertullian, before the latter became a Montanist, thus looked up to it as the head of Christendom. Its position in the capital favored its growth in honor, and no less the large size and conspicuous benevolence of its congregation. In the great Nicene and christological controversies the church of Rome could boast its orthodoxy. The exigencies of the Nicene quarrel led the Council of Sardica, in 343, to give to the Bishop of Rome the right of deciding disputed possession of bishoprics. An edict of the emperor Theodosius, in 380, ordered all to be of the faith given by Peter to the Romans and laid legal foundations for the authority of the pope over all western Christendom.

Pope Innocent I (401-17) claimed judicial power over the whole church, and Leo I (440-61) renewed the pretentions in yet more drastic form, the more effectively because an edict of the western emperor Valentinian III, in 445, recognized the pope as the head of the church, with power to call bishops to judgment, and with authority to declare what should be held by all as law in ecclesiastical questions.

The Germanic invasions, so destructive of the political fabric of the Roman Empire, helped mightily the growth of the papacy. They completed the separation of East and West, thus giving the papacy an independent field for development. They removed imperial control such as still pressed on the patriarch of Constantinople. They made the pope the heir of the honor and reverence which attached, even in its political decay, to the city which had once been the capital of the world. Above all, they presented a splendid missionary opportunity of which the papacy amply availed itself, not merely for the spread of Christianity, but for the extension of its own authority. The missions of the monk Augustine to England, in 596, sent by Gregory I (590-604), and of Boniface to Germany (719-55) added strong churches in those lands to the Roman communion, which were much more directly champions of the papacy than the older ecclesiastical bodies of western Europe.

Nor did the papacy neglect the new monarchies

that rose on the ruins of the Roman state. It early entered into relations with the Franks. With papal approval the crown was transferred from the last of the incapable Merovingians to Pippin the Short (751, 754). In turn, the papacy received from that Frankish king the beginnings of its territorial sovereignty, the "States of the Church," which it was to hold till 1870. Whatever other factors may have entered into the transfer of the Roman imperial dignity, in the judgment of western Europe, from the feeble Constantine VI of Constantinople to Charlemagne, it was Pope Leo III who crowned the new emperor at Rome in 800. It was Nicholas I (858–67) who compelled a royal great-grandson of Charlemagne to take back a discarded wife, who humbled the chief bishops of Germany, France, and Italy, and who asserted the rights of the papacy even in the case of the patriarch of Constantinople. In his claims and deeds the programme of the mediaeval papacy may be said to have been presented. Even Hildebrand went but little farther than Nicholas.

Nothing was more remarkable about the Roman Empire than the long-continued sway which it held over the imaginations of men. Even after its political institutions had crumbled into ruin, it seemed to the Middle Ages that it could not die. The civilized world, however, actually divided, still continued theoretically a unit, having, as Pope Gelasius I had declared to the emperor Anastasius in 494, two heads, the one temporal, represented by the emperor, the other spiritual, by the Bishop of Rome. Hence, when a Germanic leader of imperial size appeared in Charlemagne, the sentiment of western Christendom approved what it regarded as the transfer of the Roman Empire to him; and when his line ran out in inefficiency, it believed that the Empire was continued in the new rulers of Germany. In 962, when Pope John XII crowned Otto I of Germany emperor, the "Holy Roman Empire" began that was to last till 1806; but in the judgment of the time it was no new institution. Otto had simply been given a place in the long line of heads of the temporal world which had continued since Augustus.

In mediaeval theory, therefore, church and state were but two aspects of Christendom; the one representing Christian society organized to secure spiritual blessings, the other the same society united to preserve justice and temporal well-being. Theoretically church and state were in harmonious interplay, each aiming to secure the good of mankind; but as the soul is more important than the body, and man's salvation more desirable than his temporal happiness, the church is the higher in dignity of the two divinely co-ordinated powers.

It is easy to see, however, that such a theory led to constant rivalry in practice. Theoretically harmonious, church and state were actually contestants, the question being should the church rule the state, or the state control the church? This contest was illustrated on countless fields, large and small, throughout the Middle Ages, but nowhere so conspicuously as between the heads of the two orders—the popes and the emperors. Sometimes the one predominated, sometimes the other. Under Charlemagne's masterful rule, the leader of the state was unquestionably the superior; his weak great-grandsons found in Nicholas I, as has been seen, a spiritual ruler of greater force than theirs. But, after Nicholas, the weight of influence for nearly two centuries was unquestionably on the imperial side. The popes, nominally chosen by the clergy and people of Rome, were from the last quarter of the ninth to nearly the middle of the eleventh centuries really the creatures of the unscrupulous nobility of Rome and its vicinity. When these lords had their way their appointees were, with some exceptions, unworthy of their high office. The papacy fell to its lowest depths. The emperors repeatedly interfered and secured the deposition of some of the worst, practically controlling the papal chair itself. Thus Otto I (963 and 966) interfered in papal affairs and compelled the people of Rome to swear to choose no pope without imperial consent. Otto III (in 996 and 999) placed his own friends on the papal throne. Henry III at the Synod of Sutri (1046) secured the deposition of three rival Italian popes, and vindicated for himself the right to nominate to the office. The Empire was thus actually the superior of the papacy. While emperors thus occasionally controlled even the choice of popes, the sovereigns of the period naturally exercised a practical right of nomination and appointment to high ecclesiastical office in their own territories. These appointments were often made for the most unspiritual reasons, personal favoritism, political influence, or money considerations. In the Empire, control of ecclesiastical appointments became vital for the maintenance of the imperial power itself. The great lay fiefs were hereditary. With them the emperor could interfere but little. But if he could control the heads of the monasteries and the bishops, he could, by filling these posts with his friends, offset the lay nobility and raise sufficient taxes and troops. To take from the emperor the control of appointment to the chief ecclesiastical posts of Germany was to strike at the very foundations on which the imperial power of the eleventh century rested.

It was inevitable, however, that many good men looked with disfavor on this systematic filling of ecclesiastical posts for other than religious reasons. They felt that the church should be independent of secular control. They believed that if the papacy could be occupied by men of character and power, strong enough to force the appointment of worthy candidates to church offices, and to take from the emperors their control, the religious situation would be materially bettered. This desire first found organized expression in a reform movement known as that of Cluny. The monastery of Cluny had been founded in eastern France in 910, and, though Benedictine in government, had gradually become the head of a large group of monastic foundations, owing allegiance to its abbot. Of these dependencies, one was that of St. Mary on the Aventine Hill in Rome. From the first, the Cluny movement had a strongly reformatory character, its opposition being directed against "Simony," that is appointment to ecclesiastical office for any other than religious considerations, and "Nicolaitanism," meaning any breach of priestly celibacy, especially by the still widely prevalent marriage of priests.[1] The general tendency of the Cluny reform was, therefore, to emphasize the churchly rather than the secular forces of the time, and at the beginning of the eleventh century, many of its supporters were holding that by the establishment of a strong, independent, authoritative papacy alone could the desired reforms be accomplished. The papacy itself must be freed from dependence either on Roman nobles or on emperors, and made forceful enough to take high clerical appointments out of the hands of secular princes.

Cluny principles were carried to the papacy itself

[1] For the scriptural instances from which these names were derived, see Acts 8:18, 19; and Rev. 2:14, 15.

by Bishop Bruno of Toul, a relative of the emperor Henry III, and practically appointed by him, who became pope as Leo IX (1048-54). Of high character, forceful, learned, and popular, he revived the prestige of the papacy by numerous synods under his supervision in Germany, France, and Italy, and without forfeiting imperial support by too strenuous opposition, fought "Simony" and "Nicolaitanism." Above all, he brought the cardinalate into its modern significance. The pope had long had as his immediate advisors the bishops in the vicinity of Rome who looked up to him as their local archbishop, the priests in charge of the chief churches of the city, and the deacons at the head of the fourteen districts into which Rome was divided for charitable relief. These had been almost universally Romans. Leo IX now appointed to these offices men from anywhere in western Christendom, thus making the cardinalate in a sense representative of the church as a whole—and naturally, he chose sympathizers with the Cluny movement. Under him, Hildebrand came into prominence, though as yet far from shaping the papal policy, and the pupil rather than the teacher of Leo IX.

Hildebrand was born, in humble circumstances, in the region of Italy known as Tuscany; but as he was early committed to the charge of an uncle who was abbot of St. Mary on the Aventine—the monastery of Cluny affiliations in Rome—he always regarded himself as a Roman.[1] There he grew up, filled with Cluny ideas, and we first meet him in intimate relations with the unhappy Gregory VI, whom Henry III sent into exile in Germany in 1046. Hildebrand accompanied that ex-pope, showing thereby his fidelity, and remained in Germany till his patron's speedy death. Then, probably after a brief stay in Cluny itself, he accompanied the newly appointed Leo IX back to Rome. By Leo he was ordained a sub-deacon, and apparently intrusted with much of the secular and financial business of the papal see. Short of figure, and insignificant in appearance, he was soon recognized as of great talents and iron determination; and, though his rôle under Leo IX was subordinate, it was not long after that vigorous pontiff's death before he was recognized as the most forceful man in Rome and the most efficient supporter of the extreme claims of the papacy, as well as an energetic opponent of "Simony" and "Nicolaitanism." Such a man was needed to aid in carrying the papacy through the next stormy years. He and his party would free it first of all from dependence on the emperor or the Roman nobles. It was a most difficult task. Henry III died in 1056, leaving the Empire in confusion. Hildebrand largely aided in securing the recognition of Stephen IX (1057-58); but on his death, the cardinals were driven from Rome

[1] The year of his birth is unknown, but must have been about 1020.

and the Roman nobles once more set up a pope to their liking. A weaker man than Hildebrand would have yielded. But, largely by his skill, the Romans were divided, the consent of the empress-regent was secured, and a reformatory pope, Nicholas II (1058–61) was chosen by the exiled cardinals at Siena.

The circumstances of this choice were now enacted into a new law regulating papal election that essentially rules the choice of popes to this day. Whether the drafting of this constitution was Hildebrand's own work may be doubted, but the policy which it embodied was his. In terms intentionally indefinite, because it was impossible to see how far the new policy could be carried out, it was provided that in papal elections the cardinals should be the "leaders." Only indefinite and wholly secondary rights were allowed the emperor or the Roman people. Furthermore, the cardinals could meet anywhere for an election, and choose the pope from the local Roman congregation only when they saw fit. This great constitution placed the choice of the pope thus in the hands of the cardinals, now mostly of the reform party, and took control at once from the Romans and the emperors. To prepare for the inevitable opposition, Hildebrand entered into political combinations with such Italian forces as he could, notably with the Normans, who were conquering the southern portion of the peninsula. On the death of Nicholas II the struggle came. But, thanks primarily to

Hildebrand's political skill, in spite of the opposition of Romans, Germans, and Lombards, at the end of a most doubtful conflict, Hildebrand's candidate, Alexander II (1061–73), was safely secured in possession of the papacy, which made great strides under his leadership, aided by Hildebrand's abilities, toward an effective control not merely of the whole western church, but of the political situation of the hour. Under Alexander's approval, and with his aid, William the Conqueror gained England (1066), and the rulers of France, Germany, and Denmark, though unwillingly, had to yield much to his demands.

It was but fitting that when Alexander II died in 1073, Hildebrand was chosen his successor, under the name of Gregory VII. His policy had long been determined. To his thinking the church is by divine appointment superior to the state, and the head of the church, the pope, superior to all secular princes. As such, the pope could judge their worthiness to rule, could depose them when unfit, and exercise judgment thus over the political as well as over the religious interests of Christendom. The loftiness of this ideal is undeniable. In Hildebrand's theory, a pope, of high character, and with absolute authority, speaking with divine authority the moral judgment of Christendom, should be the final arbiter of all conduct. From him as God's representative rulers should take commands, and to him princes should be responsible. A visible Kingdom of God ought to be the result. Actually impossible of realization this ideal was, but experience had not yet proved the fact, and Hildebrand undoubtedly believed in full sincerity that his lofty claims were really those of the gospel.

The elements of the contest were at hand. Henry III's successor in Germany was his son, Henry IV, now twenty-three years of age, whose own disposition and mistakes had alienated a considerable portion of his subjects, notably the Saxons, but who was at his best in adversity, and was marked by firmness, courage, and resourcefulness—an opponent in no way to be despised. Alexander II and Henry IV had quarreled over Henry's claim to fill the archbishopric of Milan as he wished, and the dispute was still unsettled. Alexander, just before his death, had threatened some of Henry's counselors with excommunication on charges of "Simony." Nicholas II, as early as 1059, had forbidden all investiture with ecclesiastical office by laymen, and Alexander II had repeated the prohibition. If Henry persisted in filling the bishoprics of the Empire, as he undoubtedly would, a quarrel was inevitable with a pope of Hildebrand's principles.

But, at first, the situation seemed favorable to the pope. Henry's hands were tied by a rebellion of the Saxons. So friendly to Hildebrand did he show himself in this distress, that the pope, in 1074, proposed to Henry a crusade to aid the hard-pressed

Christians of the Orient and to drive back their Mohammedan foes—the first and almost unheeded note of a call that a little more than twenty years later was to rouse Europe to the greatest united effort of the Middle Ages. In 1075, however, Henry defeated the Saxons. His hands were free. His attitude toward Hildebrand's claims at once altered. He nominated a new archbishop for Milan, and sought to draw the Normans from the pope. The open quarrel at once began, and its scenes moved with tragic swiftness.

In December, 1075, Hildebrand threatened Henry with excommunication. In January, following, Henry, and the majority of the German bishops and nobles assembled at Worms, declared Hildebrand no pope, refused obedience, and ordered him, in insulting terms, to leave the papal chair. At the lenten synod in Rome, in 1076, Hildebrand replied by a counterblast of unexampled papal action. He pronounced Henry excommunicated, deposed from sovereignty, and released the German vassals from their oaths of allegiance. Could Hildebrand make this sentence effective, the pope would be in truth, what he claimed, the ruler of kings and the arbiter of the disputes of nations. To a large extent he succeeded for the moment. Henry's support was at once divided. A great part of Germany fell away from him in a measure for religious, but even more for political reasons. Henry tried vainly to raise an army to march to Italy; instead, by the autumn of

1076, his nobles compelled him to lay aside all royal state, and proposed to consider his further continuance in the kingly office at an assembly to be held in Augsburg beginning February 2, 1077, provided that before the end of that month he should be relieved from excommunication. At this convention the pope was invited to be present.

It was now a vital issue with Henry to secure the removal of his excommunication before the fatal assembly should meet. In vain he sought to move Hildebrand by appeals. He now resolved on a course of action which showed him an adroit politician if the success of the moment is considered, but which involved the most spectacular humiliation of the state, as represented in him, before the church, in the person of the pope, that the Middle Ages witnessed. Escaping with difficulty from Speyer, Henry made his way over the Alps just before Christmas, determined to meet Hildebrand as the pope journeyed toward Augsburg. Hildebrand, uncertain of Henry's intentions, sought refuge in the strong castle of Canossa, belonging to his devoted supporter, Matilda, Marchioness of Tuscany. Thither Henry hurried, not as a warrior but as a penitent. The pope at first refused to receive him, as the decision of the future of the German kingship at such an assembly as that proposed at Augsburg, under papal guidance, would have been a mighty triumph for Hildebrand's claims. Henry was determined to forestall that result by such a humiliation of apparent repentance that, in deference to public opinion, the pope must remove the excommunication. On three successive days he appeared barefoot, and in penitential attire, before the castle gate. It was such a manifestation of contrition as was then expected of great offenders, and could hardly be rejected, however its real sincerity might be doubted. So, against his wishes, on January 28, 1077, Hildebrand admitted Henry to communion, though leaving the question of his restoration to the kingdom still open. For Henry this was enough. He was able now to render ineffective the dreaded assembly at Augsburg; though a rival king was chosen in the person of Rudolf of Swabia, by his German opponents. He was once more the head of a large force in his own land. He had saved his throne, and in many respects thwarted the pope, though at the cost of a terrible humiliation of his own dignity, and dishonor to his own conscience, for his "repentance" at Canossa had never been more than a political expedient. For the next three years, 1077–80, Hildebrand held a largely neutral position between the two rival German kings, helping neither effectively, but striving to have their claims, and, therefore, the determination of the rightful sovereignty of the Empire, submitted to his decision. In this he failed, and finding he must take sides openly he favored Rudolf, and once more, in March, 1080, pronounced Henry excommunicated deposed, and his subjects released from allegiance. The same weapons of political warfare can seldom twice be used effectively. This time the papal sentence produced little effect. Public opinion in Germany had turned against Hildebrand; and the death of Rudolf, in October, 1080, placed Henry in a stronger position than he had ever thus far enjoyed. Henry now determined to carry the struggle to Rome itself. After long efforts, he captured an important part of the city in June, 1083. Even now he would recognize Hildebrand's papacy, provided the pope would give up opposition to lay appointments. But Hildebrand had the courage of his convictions, and absolutely refused to compromise his claims. Many, even of his cardinals, now regarded Hildebrand's cause as lost, and fell away from him. In March, 1084, Henry placed a partisan of his own as Clement III, on the papal throne. Hildebrand held only the Roman fortress, the Castle of San Angelo. The coming of the Normans to his aid alone saved him from falling into Henry's power; but their cruel plundering of Rome embittered the Romans themselves against him as the cause of this devastation. When the Normans withdrew he had to go under their protection, leaving Clement III in possession of the papal city. At Salerno the sad remaining months of his life were spent, and there he died, in exile, on May 25, 1085.

Hildebrand's relations to Henry only have been

considered. Did space permit, it would be interesting to trace his dealings with England, France, Spain, and Denmark. Everywhere he pursued the same policy, though nowhere was the conflict so sharp or so picturesque as with Germany. His ideal was a divinely appointed church, having its highest representative in the pope, ruling the affairs of men. With equal zeal he fought, also, against "Simony" and "Nicolaitanism." Apparently he died defeated. Really, the firmness with which he fought brought a large degree of victory to his cause. He lives in history as the ideal of a mediaeval pope. He placed the papacy of the Middle Ages, if not superior to all worldly powers as he wished, at least equal to any of them. His ideas lived after him. In 1122, when Henry IV had been succeeded by Henry V and Calixtus II was on the papal throne, the Concordat of Worms largely settled the dispute with Germany by a compromise on the whole favorable to papal claims. Each bishop or abbot was to receive his investiture with spiritual authority from the church, his temporal possessions from the state. It was by no means all that Hildebrand wished, but it assured the independent share of the church in all ecclesiastical elections, and the impulse toward sovereignty given by him to the papacy was long enduring. In methods he was unscrupulous; in his own personal religious life simple and sincere. That he believed his cause that of God there can be no question. It is equally evident that he had departed widely from the conceptions of the gospel, and that his principles are utterly impossible of application to the modern world.

QUESTIONS

1. What geographical and political circumstances aided the growth of the papacy?

2. What were the claims of Innocent I and Leo I?

3. What effect had the Germanic invasions on the papacy? Its relations to the new monarchies?

4. What was the influence of Nicholas I?

5. Describe the mediaeval theory of the relations of church and state. Was it possible to realize it in practice?

6. What was the "Holy Roman Empire"? Speak of interferences of the German Empire with the papacy.

7. Describe the origin and aims of the Cluny reform movement. What was meant by "Simony" and "Nicolaitanism"?

8. How were Cluny principles advanced by Leo IX? What is the cardinalate? How did Leo IX modify it?

9. Outline Hildebrand's early career. What were his aims?

10. What modification in the method of choosing popes was effected under Nicholas II? Its purpose and permanency?

11. Outline Hildebrand's contest with Henry IV. What did Hildebrand attempt to take from Henry? Why? What principles were involved?

12. What was the scene at Canossa? How did it come to be? What advantages did Henry draw from it? What was its larger significance?

13. How did Hildebrand's struggle with Henry end? When and where did Hildebrand die?

14. Estimate the results of Hildebrand's work.

ADDITIONAL READING

W. R. W. Stephens, *Hildebrand and His Time* (New York, no date) ("Epochs of Church History" Series).

Marvin R. Vincent, *The Age of Hildebrand* (New York, 1896).

James Bryce, *The Holy Roman Empire* (New York, 1904).

Ephraim Emerton, *Mediaeval Europe* (Boston, 1894, pp. 135–269).

Schaff (continued by David S. Schaff), *History of the Christian Church* (New York, 1907), V, Pt. I, 1–80.

GODFREY

VIII
GODFREY

It will be remembered that during the brief season at the beginning of his pontificate in which Hildebrand cherished the thought that Henry IV would yield to his wishes he proposed to that monarch a crusade to aid the eastern Empire and to resist recent Moslem advances (1074).[1] The immediate occasion of his proposal was the conquest of Asia Minor by the Seljuk Turks. Doubtless the zeal of the great pope who first planned a crusade was stimulated in part by the hope that it would bring the Greek church into obedience to Rome; but there is no reason to doubt that he was in this proposal, as in so much else, the interpreter of the spirit of his age, and that conceptions of a vitally religious nature had a large share in the formation of his plan.

All religions have exhibited a strong tendency to the veneration of sacred places. Christianity has been no exception. By the time of the conversion of the Roman Empire the graves and relics of the marytrs were held in high honor; and this reverence rapidly grew. Chief of all sacred places where it was thought prayer would more readily be heard, and whither pilgrimages were meritorious, was the

[1] *Ante*, p. 130.

land where Christ had walked with his disciples, had suffered, lain in the tomb, and risen again. To see the scenes on which he had gazed, to kneel where he was born, to pray where his body had been buried, seemed to be in some sense to draw near to him. Hence Constantine founded great churches in Bethlehem and Jerusalem, and pilgrimages thither became at once frequent. These journeys to the holy places continued throughout the Middle Ages. The capture of Jerusalem by the Mohammedans in 637 placed the sacred sites in Moslem control, but for the most part, the pilgrims, though taxed, were not interrupted. The conquest of Palestine by the Seljuk Turks altered the situation. Their fanatical zeal destroyed churches, oppressed the native Christians, and made pilgrimages exceedingly dangerous.

This momentous change in the situation in Palestine occurred when religious enthusiasm in the West, especially where the Cluny movement was powerful, was producing what can be described as nothing less than a religious revival. That revival was accompanied by an emphasis on the future life, and an outburst of religious mysticism, that was the more intense because of the general misery in which all classes of society found themselves, by reason of famines, constant warfare, and general unrest. To men in a world which offered so little of peace or comfort, the heaven of the gospels appealed as an unspeakable boon; but the age was rough, violent, and gross, and men have perhaps never been more conscious of their unfitness for heaven than then. No better way thither could they conceive than to journey in penitence to pray where Christ had suffered and been glorified. Then, too, the age was one of knightly adventure. In particular, the Normans had recently conquered England and southern Italy, and were fighting with the Moslems in Sicily. They were eager, adventure-loving. The Crusades were to appeal to three great passions: desire to come near to Christ by following in his earthly footsteps; longing for forgiveness of sins by the performance of some great act pleasing to God; and love of adventure promising fighting, booty, territorial aggrandizement, and betterment of prospects in life. Some were moved primarily by one, some by another of these motives; but in many all three were so blended that it seems impossible to say which predominated. We should misjudge the Crusaders if we did not recognize that they felt they were doing something for Christ; we should credit them with far too great disinterestedness if we did not also perceive that they were doing something very human for themselves.

The actual impulse to the First Crusade came from an appeal of the hard-pressed emperor at Constantinople to Urban II. That able pope (1088–99) was by birth a Frenchman, had been a member of the Cluny order, and president of the cardinals under

Hildebrand, whose purposes and ideals he fully shared, though of a far more conciliatory spirit. He had maintained the Hildebrandian cause with great skill, and in March, 1095, in the pursuit of that control, he held a council of Piacenza, in northern Italy. Here the emperor Alexios presented his appeal through his messengers. The pope gave it a favorable hearing; but the matrimonial irregularities of King Philip I of France led him to summon a further council at Clermont, in that land, for November, that the king's misdeeds might there be considered, and to this council Urban determined to present the thought of a crusade, not now, primarily, to help the eastern emperor, but for the rescue of the sacred places from Moslem hands. To Urban II was due the conception of a crusade, in the form which was actually to appeal to Europe; to his great teacher Hildebrand was due the origin of the idea of a crusade in any form. Urban's thought was more purely religious than Hildebrand's had been. It was not the help of the eastern Empire, or the extension of p pal authority, that he had in mind so much as Christian control of the land hallowed by the earthly life of Christ.

As the plan of the Crusade was Urban's, so the impulse which set the armies in motion came from him. To the assembled multitude at Clermont he spoke on November 27, 1095, in words which have not been exactly preserved, but the general purport and effect of which are clear. He pictured the insults offered to the Christians and sacred places of the Holy Land, he called on western Christendom to cleanse the holy sites from such unbelievers, and promised the divine blessing on the undertaking. As he ended, the enthusiasm of the hearers swept all before it. "God wishes it," they shouted, and pledged themselves by hundreds to the accomplishment of the task.

The pope's summons was taken up, throughout the length of France and the Rhineland, by preachers who fanned the enthusiasm for the Crusade, of whom the most famous, and probably the ablest, was Peter, called "the Hermit," or "of Amiens," from the city of northern France in or near which he was born. Slight, gray-bearded, ascetic, eloquent, he fired men's hearts for the work. Later tradition, and probably a desire, also, to claim for monasticism a leading share in the great enterprise, represented Peter as the originator of the Crusade. That he was not.[1] The honor belonged to Urban II, but of his power as a preacher there can be no question. He was, however, but one of many preachers whom the pope's zeal and popular enthusiasm aroused.

Under the impulse thus given thousands of the lower classes, ill prepared, and ill led, started from

[1] The ablest recent defense of a greater share by Peter in the origin of the Crusade than is here assigned him is that of David S. Schaff, in Schaff's *History of the Christian Church*, V, Pt. I, 241-45. To the writer it is not wholly convincing.

France and the Rhineland in the spring of 1096. One such band was under the lead of Peter himself. But their own disorders won the hatred of the peoples through whose lands they passed, especially in Hungary and the Balkan countries. They reached Constantinople with fearful losses, and proved utterly unable to do effective work against the Turks. The real task of the Crusade was to be accomplished under the lead of the feudal nobility of the age. Four main armies were raised: one from the region of the lower Rhine; a second from southern France under Count Raymond of Toulouse; a third from the Normans of southern Italy, having as leaders Bohemond and Tancred; and a fourth under counts Robert of Normandy and Stephen of Blois, from the territories of France which their titles indicated. Of these armies, the first named chiefly concerns us.

The forces from the Rhineland, which may have numbered ten thousand horsemen and thirty thousand foot soldiers, were under the general leadership —it can hardly be called a command in the modern sense—of the noblest knightly character that the First Crusade produced, Godfrey of Bouillon, duke of Lower Lorraine, a region embracing territories now included in northern and eastern Belgium and stretching southward over a portion of what is now northern France and western Germany.[1] Born about 1060, he was the son of an earnestly religious

[1] Bouillon itself is in extreme southeastern Belgium.

mother. His churchly sympathies did not prevent him, however, from taking an active part on the side of Henry IV in the campaign in Italy which resulted in the political downfall of Hildebrand. What led him to the Crusade we do not know; but his land was deeply penetrated by the Cluny spirit, and in the years immediately preceding the expedition it had suffered in unusual degree from famine and consequent misery. To him, as to his brothers and companions Eustace and Baldwin, and to the Crusaders generally, the call was not merely to service but to sacrifice. He sold or mortgaged a large part of his possessions, parting even with the castle of Bouillon, for the expenses of the great undertaking.

In August, 1096, the long march was begun. They journeyed probably up the Rhine and down the Danube nearly to Vienna, then across Hungary to Belgrade, the skill and good faith of Godfrey defending them from many of the hostilities from which the peasant bands of Crusaders had deservedly suffered. From Belgrade, where they entered the territories of the emperor Alexios, they pushed forward by Sofia, Philippopolis, and Adrianople, to Constantinople, reaching there two days before Christmas, after a march of not less than 1,450 miles. Here, in the neighborhood of the city, the winter was spent, waiting for the other crusading armies, and in constant, sometimes warlike, controversy with Alexios, who wished to be free of such troublesome guests.

In these disputes the wisdom and firmness of Godfrey were conspicuously evidenced.

By the spring of 1097 all was ready for the advance. On May 6 the Christian army laid siege to the first city in Turkish territory, the ancient Nicaea, where Constantine had held the first general council in 325.[1] The crusading host had no single commander, but, on June 19, Nicaea surrendered to Alexios, justly hoping to be better treated by him than by the Crusaders, and the first success of the expedition was achieved. Thence the army marched diagonally across Asia Minor toward the ancient province of Cilicia. At Dorylaeum, about 180 miles from Constantinople, what seemed at first a defeat was turned, on July 1, into a great crusading victory that opened free way for the further march of the army. But thenceforward nearly till Iconium was reached, it suffered terrible losses from hunger and thirst under the scorching summer sun. Thence, by a long circle to the northeast through the ancient Cappadocian Caesarea (Kaisariyeh and Marash), they journeyed, till on October 20, 1097, they reached Antioch, where the disciples had first been called Christians,[2] the strongest city of Syria.

Such a place would have been formidable to any army before the use of canon. To the Crusaders, unaccustomed to large cities, it seemed an almost insurmountable obstacle. With its sieges and the

[1] *Ante*, p. 51.   [2] Acts 11:26.

successful repulse of the Turkish army that came to its relief the highest military achievements of the Crusade were associated. By immense effort the Christian forces carried on the siege from October, 1097, to the following June, and even then would not have become masters of the city had it not been for the aid of one of its inhabitants who enabled them to effect a lodgment on its lofty walls. Its capture was none too soon, for the Turkish sultan, Kerboga of Mossul, was on his way with an immense relieving army. Most courageously delayed at Edessa by the pluck of Godfrey's brother, Baldwin, Kerboga did not reach Antioch till two days after its capture (June 5). The Christians now found themselves besieged in the city which had so recently fallen into their hands. With little food, and surrounded by an immense army, many now gave themselves up to despair; but the enthusiasm of others was heightened. Men believed they saw visions in which Christ and the saints promised help. It was thought that the very lance head that pierced the Savior's side as he hung on the cross was found beneath the floor of the Church of St. Peter and would bring sure victory. Thus encouraged, the host marched out, in desperate effort, and on June 28, in a tremendous battle, put Kerboga and his Moslem army completely to flight.

In all this Godfrey bore his full share, but his part was not as distinguished as that of Bohemond or Tancred. Godfrey, however, had in mind more than any of the other leaders the main purpose of the Crusade, and while Bohemond and Raymond quarreled as to whose Antioch should be, and the Christian leaders tried to make conquests in its vicinity, he urged an advance on Jerusalem. It was not till May, 1099, however, that the army started. On June 7 it was in sight of the Holy City. It had seen tremendous fighting and had accomplished a march since the Crusade began of not less than 2,500 miles. As rank after rank beheld Jerusalem the Crusaders fell on their knees in gratitude that the goal of their pilgrimage was so close at hand. But severe contest was needful before the city was theirs. Jerusalem is strong of situation and was bravely defended. On July 15, the Crusaders, Godfrey among the first, effected a lodgment on the wall, and Jerusalem was soon theirs. Mercy was no thought of the victors. The Mohammedan inhabitants were slain; and their bloody work accomplished, the Crusaders marched in penitential thanksgiving to the Church of the Holy Sepulcher. The work was done. The goal was reached, which had cost such suffering and so many lives. It remained now to provide for the government and defense of the Holy Land, and for the majority of the surviving Crusaders to seek the homes that they had left three years before.

On July 22, 1099, the leaders at Jerusalem unanimously chose Godfrey as head of the new state. He took for his title "Protector of the Holy Sepulcher."

There was in him that which commanded general trust. His modesty, his steadfastness, his courage, his simple piety, all commended him, and of all the leaders it was most fitting that he should keep what had been won. One task remained to be done before the main body of the Crusaders could depart. The Moslem ruler of Egypt was sending a large army to avenge the capture of Jerusalem. On August 12, it was wholly defeated near Ascalon, and the last great danger that threatened the new conquests of the Crusaders was overcome. The Christian territories, divided in feudal fashion under princes, counts, and barons, now stretched from Tarsus and Edessa on the north to the southern borders of ancient Philistia on the south—a realm greater than that of David.

Godfrey did not long survive his entrance on his new and responsible office. On July 18, 1100, he died, universally lamented, and was buried in the Church of the Holy Sepulcher in Jerusalem. He was succeeded by his brother, Baldwin I (1100–18), who did not hesitate to take the kingly title. The region so hardly won could not be held save by constant fighting; and a steady stream of knights and humbler folk poured from the West to the Holy Land, most of whom gave their lives in the cause, or perished from the hardships and illnesses incident to the journey. To aid in the defense of the sacred places, a military order, pledged to monastic vows and to fight for the Christian possessions in the

Orient, the Templars, was organized in 1118; and soon after 1130 a brotherhood founded for the care of the ill in Jerusalem, the Hospitallers, or Knights of St. John, was reorganized with a similar aim. In 1198 the Teutonic Knights were established. These orders attracted the gifts of hundreds at home who could not themselves take part in a crusade, but who could thus share in the cause as those now interested in missions may do by the support of missionary societies.

The Holy Land was pressed hard by the Moslems. From 1147 to 1149 a second great crusade under Conrad III of Germany and Louis VII of France sought its relief; but failed miserably in Asia Minor and before Damascus. In October, 1187, the Mohammedan leader, Saladin, took Jerusalem from the Christians who had held it since 1099. A third great crusade, led by Frederick Barbarossa of Germany, Philip II of France, and Richard Cœur de Lion of England, sought to regain it; but wholly failed. The crusading spirit was now largely spent, though subsequent expeditions took place, some of them on a large scale. None had, however, the enthusiam and success of the First Crusade. The zeal for the Holy Land gradually died out, and, in 1291, the Christians lost the last of their hard-won possessions on the mainland of Palestine.

The crusading movement was the highest exemplification of the Hildebrandian idea of the church.

All Christendom, aroused by the pope as its spiritual head, should lay aside its worldly interests and strive for the rescue of the holy places. But the appeal of the movement was to a feeling far deeper than honor for the papacy or obedience to its call. It was the desire to draw near to Christ by following in his earthly footsteps that animated such a man as Godfrey to suffer and to dare. We may hold that the Crusades showed little appreciation of the real spirit of Christianity; but we cannot understand the Christianity of their age without seeing in them a great embodiment of the conception of the religious life then prevalent.

Viewed narrowly in the light of what they directly accomplished, the Crusades were a failure. They cost the lives of thousands. They failed permanently to hold the Holy Land. But their effect on the intellectual life of Europe was worth all they cost. They broke up the isolation which had prevailed since the Germanic invasions. They united western Europe in a common enterprise. They opened men's eyes to the world as they revealed the splendid cities and the civilization of the East. They aroused Italian commerce, and made the revived influence of that land possible. The century and a half which followed their beginning saw an awakening of Europe, religiously, intellectually, and artistically, which, though much less thorough, can only be compared with that which took place in the closing years of the fifteenth and the first half of the sixteenth centuries, when a similar enlargement of men's mental outlook was to be effected by the revival of learning, the discovery of the New World, and the opening of the sea route to India. The beginnings of some features of this awakening, indeed, antedated the Crusades, but all received powerful influence from that great enterprise.

QUESTIONS

1. With whom did the idea of a crusade originate? Why was it not then carried out?

2. What were the causes of the Crusades?

3. From whom, how, and when did the actual call to the First Crusade come? The response?

4. What was the real share of Peter the Hermit? What has been ascribed to him?

5. From what regions did the main armies come?

6. What was the early history of Godfrey of Bouillon?

7. What were the preparations made for the Crusade? Describe its march. Nicaea? Dorylaeum? Antioch?

8. How was the Crusade hindered by internal causes?

9. What share did Godfrey have in the capture of Jerusalem? To what office was he chosen? How long did he serve? His death? His character?

10. What were the military orders? How were they supported?

11. Were there other crusades? What was the ultimate fate of Palestine?

12. What do the Crusades illustrate? Their value?

ADDITIONAL READING

James M. Ludlow, *The Age of the Crusades* (New York, 1896).
Ephraim Emerton, *Mediaeval Europe* (Boston, 1894), pp. 357-97.
G. W. Cox, *The Crusades* ("Epochs of History" Series) (Boston, 1874).
Schaff (continued by David S. Schaff), *History of the Christian Church* (New York, 1907), V, Pt. I, 211-307.

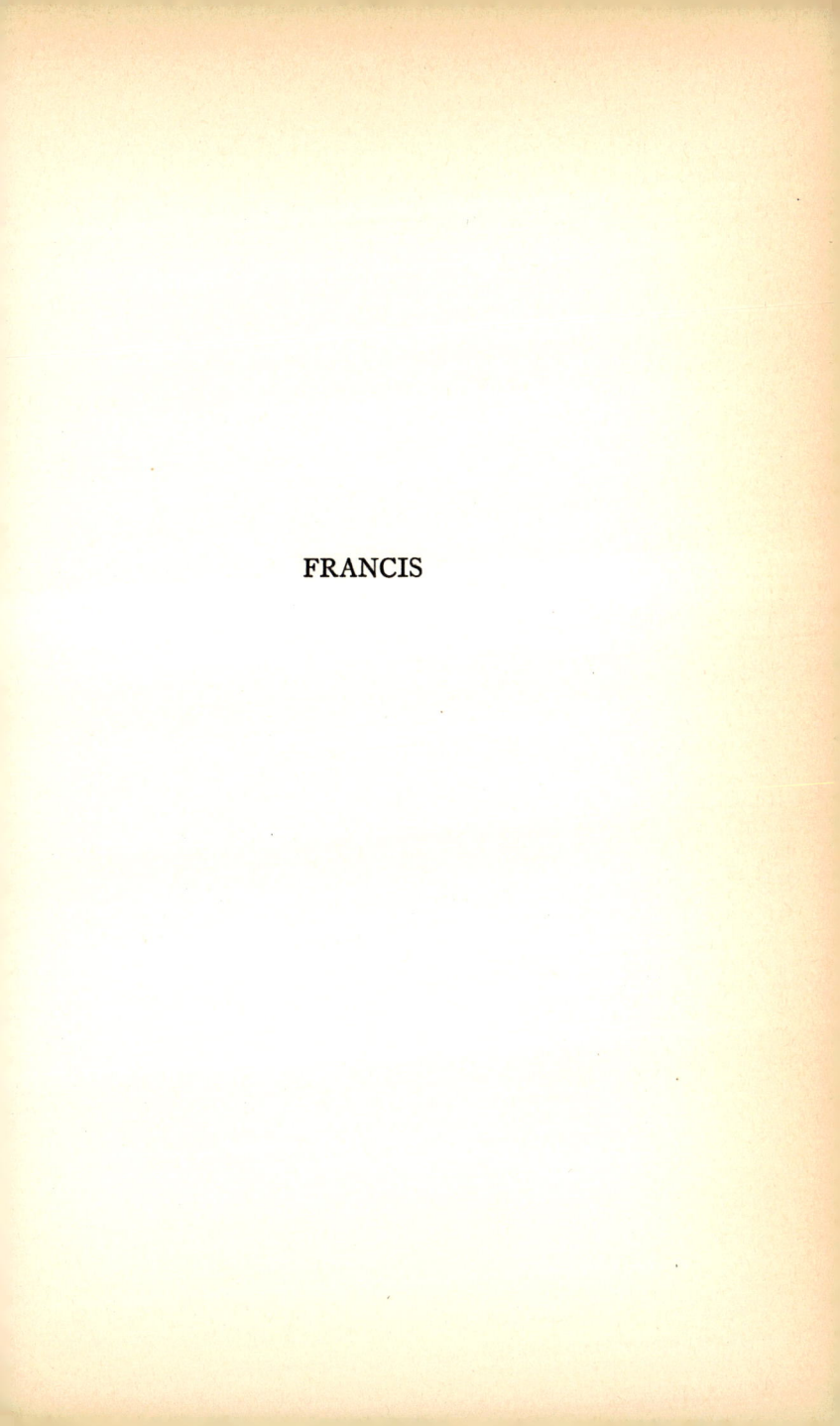

FRANCIS

IX
FRANCIS

In following the experiences of a crusader such as Godfrey one aspect of the religious life of the Middle Ages has been considered. It would be a mistake to suppose that the only type, or to conclude that the churchly ideal of a Hildebrand or an Urban II, was the only form in which religion appeared. Besides, and not infrequently antagonistic to the largely political conceptions of the popes and high clergy, there was widely manifested a relatively simple religious spirit that sought to find its expression in a literal acceptance of what it believed to be Christ's commands and an imitation of his life. The age was crude. Its conception of religion was ascetic; and the only kind of imitation of Christ and the apostles which most men could grasp was an imitation in externals. Christ and his disciples had been poor. "Apostolic poverty" was therefore a mark of the truly consecrated life. He never married. The disciples should so imitate him. He sent forth his disciples two by two, to preach, wearing sandals, without money, and depending on the gifts of their hearers for their support. So his disciples should now go. He told them to use a fixed form of prayer. That should constitute their only public petition. He forbade them to swear. They should take no oaths.

Probably there has never been a time when the Sermon on the Mount and Christ's commands to the apostles,[1] interpreted in the most literal fashion, seemed to so many earnest souls the charter of conduct, however inferior their actual practice might be. Nor was the feeling of Christian men different in that age from what it is now. They and we alike desire to imitate Christ; but we see that real imitation is likeness of spirit. That age grasped such imitation imperfectly. To be like him and the apostles in the circumstances of their lives was what men could most easily conceive.

It was evident that, if "apostolic poverty" is the Christian ideal, the rich prelates and the monks in wealthy cloisters were not living the Christian life. So many thought; and the result was not merely the inauguration of many reform movements in the church itself, but of sects that broke or were driven from its communion, and a widespread revival of ancient Manichaean or Gnostic speculations with their denunciation of all that savored of the material world as evil.

Of these movements that most foreign to the genius of Christianity, though holding itself Christian, was known as that of the Cathari. Though Manichaeanism, such as existed in Augustine's time,[2] probably persisted in western Christendom,

[1] Matt., chaps. 5 to 7; 10:1–13; Luke 9:1–6.
[2] *Ante*, p. 69.

the main impulse toward Catharite views seems to have come into France, Italy, and Germany, nearly a century before the Crusades, from the Orient. Like the ancient Manichaeans, the Cathari held that the universe is the scene of eternal conflict between two powers, the one good, the other evil. Matter is the work of the evil power. The Old Testament is largely his book. The good God, revealed by Christ, is to be served spiritually, by simple worship, without elaborate churches or ritual, and by abstinence as far as possible from defiling contact with the world of matter through marriage, landed possessions, or the eating of flesh. Stimulated by the religious interest awakened in the crusading age, the Cathari grew rapidly, becoming the most powerful party in many sections of southern France, where they were known as "Albigenses" from the city of Albi. In Italy, too, they were strongly represented, controlling the government of Assisi, for instance, for a time when Francis was a young man. To the Roman church they were an immense peril; and after more than half a century of sporadic, and mostly vain, attempts to win them back by missionary effort, they were crushed in France by military force, through the combined efforts of the church and the French monarchy (1209–29). Their political collapse, in 1229, was followed by the more complete establishment of the Inquisition for their uprooting; and, since they had made much use of the Bible in defense of their position, by the prohibition of the reading of translations of the Scriptures.[1]

The Catharite movement was fundamentally hostile to Christianity. Not so the Waldensian. It was simply an earnest attempt to live the Christlike life, and intentionally within the church. Valdez, or Waldo, was a wealthy merchant of Lyons in France. Awakened religiously, he was moved, in 1173, by the legends of the saints, and especially by Christ's directions to the rich young man,[2] to give his property to the poor. He now obtained translations of the gospels and some other books of the Bible, gathered a few disciples about him, and felt himself called with his friends to carry out Christ's injunctions to the apostles,[3] by going throughout the country, without money or shoes, proclaiming Christ's message and dependent on the gifts of those to whom he preached. He had no thought of hostility toward the ecclesiastical authorities. Beginning this mission in 1178, he sought the approval of Pope Alexander III, and of the third Lateran Council at Rome in 1179. Here he was not judged a heretic, but he and his followers were thought ignorant laymen and ordered not to preach without ecclesiastical permission. To Valdez not to preach was to disobey Christ. He persisted; and, in 1184, the Waldenses were excommunicated

[1] For scriptural excuse for this prohibition, see II Peter 3:16.
[2] Mark 10:21.
[3] Matt. 10:5-14; Luke 9:1-6.

by Pope Lucius III. A little more than twenty years later, Pope Innocent III, seeing the mistake of his predecessor, tried to draw the Waldenses as a preaching association into the Roman church; but it was too late. They grew and spread, being represented not merely in eastern France but in northern Italy, and ultimately in Germany. As they developed they came more and more to feel that no teaching but that of Christ was binding, and to reject all in the Roman church for which they could not find clear scriptural warrant. Yet they were slow in forming a church for themselves. They consisted of an inner circle, the society proper, bound by monastic vows, and worshiping by simpler services, and an outer body of "friends" who still remained in the Roman communion, but from whom the society was recruited and by whom it was supported. Pressed by persecution, the Waldenses were driven into the high valleys of the Alps west of Turin, where they maintained their independence. They became fully Protestant at the Reformation, still exist in vigor, and now that religious freedom has been established in Italy, carry on Christian work in its chief cities.

All these movements, notably that of the Waldenses, were not merely ascetic, but semi-monastic in form. But their monasticism differed from the older types in two important particulars. Earlier monasticism emphasized separation from the world. Its aim was to seek personal salvation. Though it had engaged in much missionary work when established, it was essentially aristocratic, even if its recruits were from all classes of society. The new movements, especially that of the Waldenses, had for their aim work for others. They affiliated with the common people. They were fundamentally democratic. They introduced a new purpose into monastic life. What Valdez attempted, and that for which he was most unwisely driven from the Roman church, was taken up into the service of that church by a Spaniard, Dominick (1170–1221), the founder of the "Order of the Preachers," or Dominicans, and especially by Francis of Assisi, the man who in the judgment of his age lived nearest of all men like Christ, and who was therefore the most typical mediaeval saint. Francis, or as he was baptized, John, Bernardone, was born in 1182, in Assisi, a little Umbrian city, about eighty-five miles north of Rome. His father, Peter, was a wealthy cloth merchant. From boyhood, Francis showed himself a leader, but at first with no intimation of interest in religion, for it was as a leader of the young men of the city, associated in a kind of club for riotous amusement, that he first won distinction. Of learning he had comparatively little. Assisi was distracted by quarrels between the aristocrats and common people, and the former, being worsted in 1202, called in the aid of the citizens of Perugia, only thirteen miles distant, but, such was the distracted condition of Italian politics, a bitter rival of Francis' native town. In the battle that followed Francis fought on the popular side, and, the Assisan forces being beaten, he was taken a prisoner of war to Perugia, where he remained a year. Even now he was distinguished for his cheerfulness and courage. His return from this imprisonment was followed by a severe illness. Recovered, he was more earnest in purpose than he had thus far been, but not yet determined to devote himself to the Christian life, for he now decided to seek a soldier's career in southern Italy. He started on this quest, but only to abandon it when a few miles from Assisi and to return to his home. His conversion was beginning, however. With Francis it was no sudden change, but a gradual process. His sympathy went out to the poor. He gave largely of his means to their relief; but even more largely of his interest and personal help. He cared for the sick, even for the lepers whom most shunned. At Rome, on a pilgrimage, he borrowed a beggar's clothes, and supplicated his food that he might understand the lot of the unfortunate. He meditated and prayed much in solitude. He believed that he heard a divine call to "restore the fallen church of God." Taking the vision literally, he sold his horse and some pieces of cloth, and offered the sum thus obtained to rebuild the chapel of St. Damian. Francis' father had long been disgusted by what he deemed his son's unbusiness-like ways and had used even force to win him back. This act seemed to him the climax. In the quarrel that followed, Francis was summoned before the bishop, and now formally renounced to his father not merely the money, but his clothing, declaring that henceforth he had no father but the Father in heaven. Men derided him as insane, but he persisted with unabated courage.

For about two years after this event Francis labored with his own hands and by begging aid for the restoration not only of St. Damian but of the Portiuncula and other chapels near Assisi. In 1209, however, a larger vision of his work came to him. He heard read from the gospels that command of Christ to the apostles to preach the good news of the Kingdom which had once made such an impression on Valdez. At once he began to put it into practice. His message was to living men in the name of Christ. Soon he gathered a few associates, kindled by his enthusiasm. In a few months they grew to eleven in number. In their "apostolic poverty" they should go, clad only in a long robe of undyed wool bound at the waist by a bit of rope. Two by two the new preachers went, with singing and much expression of happiness, not merely as those who were serving Christ, but who found all God's creatures their friends. This appreciation of nature as God's work, and therefore to be loved and desired, was one of the most remarkable of Francis' characteristics, fanciful as was often the form in which it expressed itself. In "brother sun" and "brother fire" he saw, no less than in his fellow-men, God's servants and therefore his brethren. Among men, Francis felt that his work was primarily for the neediest and lowliest. His own association was of "humble" brethren, a term that of itself implied affiliation with the lower rather than the higher social classes. It was to the people little in the world's regard, the poor, the sick, the lowly, that he was to go in "apostolic poverty," with the message of repentance.

For this little brotherhood Francis prepared in 1209 a simple "Rule," not now existent; but containing little more than Christ's injunction to take up the cross, his advice to the rich young man, and his directions to the apostles; and, also, brief regulations regarding fasting, humble carriage toward all men in imitation of Christ's humiliation, and speaking and living as good Catholics, for Francis was anxious to serve the church and to recognize the authority of its officers. With this "Rule" he and his companions went to Pope Innocent III. It was almost exactly the same proposal with which Valdez had vainly approached Pope Alexander III in 1179; but times had changed. Innocent III saw the mistake which his predecessor had made; he had just been engaged in trying to persuade some of the Waldenses to return to the Roman church. Under such circumstances it is not surprising that Francis' fate was very unlike that of Valdez, and that Innocent III, most wisely, gave his approval to the work. It was still a wholly simple association of those who would live and preach as Jesus taught; but it was now approved by the pope (1210) and by papal injunction had in Francis a responsible head with whom the ecclesiastical authorities could deal. The first step toward the Franciscan order had been taken.

In little huts grouped round the church known as Portiuncula near Assisi the brethren had their first headquarters. Here at each Pentecost they gathered to relate their experiences and strengthen themselves for their work. From this meeting the annual "general chapter" was soon to grow. But Portiuncula was simply their center. Thence they went forth to preach, to aid the poor, nurse the sick, and care for the neglected. They were to help the peasants in the fields, to work in return for food and lodging; but to take no money, and to beg only in illness or incapacity. It was a working, helpful association, not a mendicant order that Francis planned.

Francis' followers rapidly multiplied, and were not confined to his own sex. Impressed by a fiery sermon on the duty of forsaking all to follow Christ, a girl of eighteen, of noble lineage, Clara Scifi, dedicated herself to a similar work; and her vows were received by Francis himself in the Portiuncula church on March 18, 1212. With her the nuns of the Franciscan order, or Clarissines, had their beginning. Francis himself preached widely through

Italy, and soon his disciples were carrying his work not merely throughout the peninsula, but to Spain, France, Hungary, and Germany. Such a man could not be possessed of a burning desire to bring disciples to his Master without his heart going forth in love to those who rejected the lordship of Christ. Francis would lead in foreign missions. The crusading expedition of 1219 to Egypt gave him his opportunity. With eleven companions he accompanied the army, and even preached before the sultan, by whom his courage and sincerity were respected. The converts from Mohammedanism that he desired were not made—he had too little preparation for the work—but his own consecration of spirit was abundantly revealed. From Egypt he visited the holy places in Palestine, and it was only after an absence of more than a year (June, 1219, to July, 1220) that he again saw Italy.

During this absence serious changes took place in the association, part of which were inevitable. It was growing rapidly. Its very popularity was a peril to its original ideals. The simple enthusiasm for the life of "apostolic poverty," and strict obedience to Christ, the motive spring of which was love, was hard to maintain as numbers increased. The need of organization, rules, and careful supervision grew in proportion to the enlargement of the body. It is always thus. The enthusiasm of the few can be carried to the many only in greatly weakened form, and with the many, organization must attempt to make good the defect. Then, too, the ecclesiastical authorities, notably Cardinal Ugolino, the later Pope Gregory IX, who soon became by appointment of Pope Honorius III the "protector" of the association, saw the possibilities of the movement as an aid to the papacy and the advancement of the interests of the Roman church, where its authority had been undermined by Cathari, Waldenses, and other "heretics." A society of three thousand members, as that of Francis had grown to be, was very different from a little company of eleven like-minded enthusiasts.

Its development into a full monastic order went rapidly forward. A bull of Pope Honorius III, of September, 1220, regulated entrance, required perpetual observance of vows, and placed the monks under the strict command of their superiors. A new "Rule," in which Francis had some share, but on which others labored, was issued in 1221; only to be replaced by another, prepared chiefly by Cardinal Ugolino, two years later. This revised rule made begging a fundamental characteristic of the order. In it the eager reference to Christ's commands, which marked the earlier "Rule," became a series of relatively minute and legalistic regulations, characteristic of the spirit of monasticism in general. It was more ecclesiastical, less free and fresh-spirited. Among the brethren themselves, moreover, two tendencies appeared, the one to preserve, and if anything to increase, the ascetic inclinations rather than the loving spirit of the founder; the other toward a laxer interpretation of his conception of Christlike poverty, and an emphasis on organization, mechanical discipline, and the development of a great monastic body. Francis himself was no organizer. He was a preacher, a lover of his fellow-men, and an enthusiastic disciple of his Master. Elias of Cortona, his friend and associate, possessed the administrative talents which he lacked, without his enthusiastic spiritual insight, and with decided inclination to the more worldly of the two tendencies within the order of which mention has been made. The reins had fallen by 1220 from Francis' hands, and from 1223 Elias was the controlling spirit. The tendencies were at work which were to lead to long-persisting quarrels between the stricter and looser elements in the order.

Francis' last years were, therefore, filled with grief and apprehension. He saw the ideal of his association changing. He feared the spread of worldliness in the order. He dreaded the growth of devotion to learning, lest the service of the poor and lowly should be supplanted by it. He spoke forth his anxiety in bitterness of spirit. Broken in health from the time of his return from his mission to the East, he withdrew more and more from the activities of life. He sang his praises to God, he prayed, he fasted, he was much alone in ecstatic meditation. In one of these long vigils, in 1224, there appeared on his body the marks of the Savior's wounds, constituting in his own thought an honor similar to that which he believed the apostle Paul to have received.[1] The fact of these "stigmata" is assured; the question of how they came to be is more difficult. The best solution seems to lie in that but partially understood influence of the mind, dwelling intensely on a desired experience, on a body enfeebled by extreme asceticism. As his end grew near, Francis had himself carried to the vicinity of his beloved church of Portiuncula, and in it he died in full humility and triumphant peace on October 3, 1226. He was of his age and race in many of the circumstances of his career; but he belongs to all the Christian centuries in spirit, for he tried in utmost love and humility to live the very life of Christian discipleship as he believed Christ taught his first followers to live it.

Much as the order which he founded departed from his ideal, it was a great power for good in the Roman church for more than a century after his death, and remains in usefulness to this day. It spread with marvelous rapidity throughout Europe, welcomed by the common people, to whom its friars came as preachers and as helpers. It did much for

[1] Gal. 6:17, where the reference is probably not to the wounds Christ received on the cross, but to disfigurements resulting from stoning at Lystra, Acts 14:19.

the unchurched and neglected in the cities. It presented a democratic conception of monasticism, in contrast to the essential aristocracy of the older orders. To a large degree it was true to the principle that in work for others rather than for oneself lies the highest value of the Christian life. For the Roman church and the papacy the Franciscan order was of utmost usefulness. It and the Dominican body largely won back the popular support which had seemed to be slipping away from the church. They presented a type of piety that appealed to the best men of the age. They took up into the service of the church that which had most attracted men in the Cathari and Waldenses, and by so doing overcame the opposition which had given to those "heretical" movements their chief support. They profoundly deepened and quickened the popular religious life.

QUESTIONS

1. How did men of the twelfth century conceive of imitating Christ? What did they mean by "apostolic poverty"?

2. What was the result of this valuation of "apostolic poverty" on men's attitude toward the rich prelates and the wealthy monasteries? Was the period one of many sects?

3. Who were the Cathari? Their beliefs? How were they suppressed?

4. Who was Valdez, when did he live, how was he converted, and what did he attempt? How was he treated by the Roman church? Who were and are the Waldenses?

5. What new methods and spirit did these protesters repre-

sent, and by whom were these principles taken up into the service of the Roman church?

6. Outline the early life of Francis. His birthplace, parentage, youth, captivity?

7. Describe the nature of Francis' conversion. What spirit animated him? What text impressed him?

8. How did Francis conceive of the Christian life? What were the original purposes of his brotherhood? Its earliest "Rule"?

9. Give some account of Clara Scifi, and of the founding of the Clarissines.

10. How did Francis attempt to engage in foreign missions?

11. How were the original ideals of Francis' association transformed? Was this change unavoidable? The "Rules" of 1221 and 1223? Francis' feeling toward these changes?

12. Francis' last years? Their occupations? The "stigmata"? His death? His character?

13. The influence of the Franciscan order?

ADDITIONAL READING

Paul Sabatier, *Life of St. Francis of Assisi* (English translation) (New York, 1894).

J. W. Knox-Little, *Saint Francis of Assisi, His Times, Life, and Work* (London, 1897).

Schaff (continued by David S. Schaff), *History of the Christian Church* (New York, 1907), V, Pt. I, 379-533.

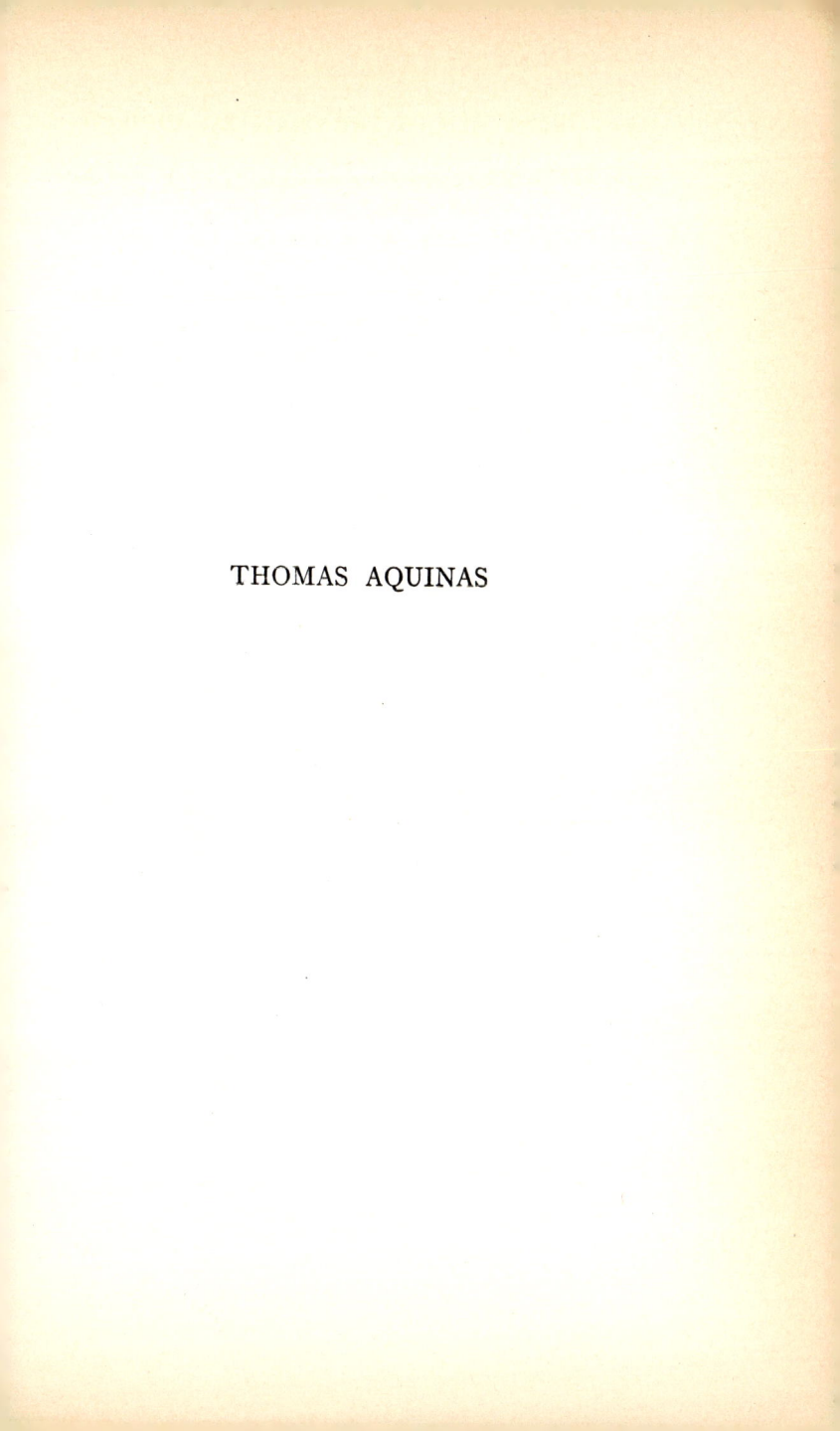

THOMAS AQUINAS

X
THOMAS AQUINAS

The consideration already given to Godfrey and to Francis has shown something of two very unlike aspects of the religious life of the crusading period. With Aquinas we turn to a third feature of the age, its theological learning. The intellectual efforts of the Middle Ages have often been unduly belittled, and the title given to them—that of "Scholasticism" —interpreted so as to imply an undeserved contempt. The aim of the schoolmen was not, indeed, a free inquiry as to the truth or falsity of the Christian religion, as if that were a matter open to debate. The chief doctrines of the faith were regarded as fixed; and the object of discussion was to show their reasonableness and to explain their philosophic implications. But, under this apparent rigidity, an immense amount of freedom of discussion was actually enjoyed, objections of the most weighty character were stated and answered, and the whole field of systematic theology was carefully investigated. It was a noble attempt to explain and interpret the great doctrines of the Christian faith.

The intellectual stagnation consequent upon the collapse of the ancient Roman world through the Germanic invasions was nowhere more evident or more slowly overcome than in the domain of theological speculation. While many doctrines were modified in the early Middle Ages by what may be called the general spirit of the time, conscious discussion of theology, as far as it existed, was essentially a reproduction of the positions of the great teachers of the declining Roman Empire. But with the gradual increase of enlightenment, this branch of intellectual activity was stimulated also, and in the period of the First Crusade there appeared in Anselm (1033–1109), the Italian-born Archbishop of Canterbury, a theologian who gave a new and influential interpretation to the doctrine of the atonement, who presented an impressive demonstration of the existence of God, and deserved to be called "the father of the schoolmen."

In Abelard (1079–1142), who taught in Paris, scholasticism was represented by a great critic, whose free handling of the current theology shocked many of his contemporaries, but undoubtedly stimulated inquiry by its defense of the rights of intellectual investigation as against dependence on traditional authority. This tendency found a vigorous opponent in Bernhard of Clairvaux (1090–1153), the greatest preacher of his age, and one of the noblest characters of church history, whose own deep mystical piety was nourished and developed by that of Augustine, but who had a much clearer conception of justification by faith alone than the great African theologian, so that Luther was to be profoundly influenced by him. It is easy to see, however, that the desire to know truth scientifically, and to feel it religiously—the intellectual and the mystical tendencies—are not necessarily mutually exclusive. They were united in Bernhard's friend Hugo of St. Victor (1097?-1141), and even more in Peter Lombard (?-1160?), both of whom taught in Paris. The latter, a disciple both of Abelard and Hugo, combined the new and the old methods in his *Four Books of Sentences* so skilfully that his work held its place as the main textbook of theological instruction till the Reformation. A collection of authoritative extracts ("sentences") from the Bible and the Fathers was gathered, in the older fashion, but interpreted and explained by the new philosophic discussion. Thanks to the work of these men, the "new theology," as it was called, won its way, in spite of opposition; and by the middle of the twelfth century the scholastic, systematic treatment of Christian truth, as contrasted with the traditional acceptance of ancient statements, was fully developed. A great period of theological discussion was well begun.

Some of these teachers had been connected with monastic or cathedral schools, others had been independent; but in many of the cities of Europe scholars were gathering about them and others like them. Various studies were preferred in different cities. Thus Paris and soon Oxford were centers of theology, Bologna of law, and Salerno of medicine. Shortly before 1200 a great change, however, began. In the Middle Ages each trade in a town was incorporated, and had its own laws and government. The whole body of teachers and scholars in a particular community were now similarly associated, and thus the "University" came into being. Of these probably the earliest except Bologna and Salerno, and certainly the most famous and influential, was the University of Paris, the most celebrated seat of theology in the later Middle Ages. In this institution, which became the model of many similar foundations, studies were begun under the faculty of arts, and continued under one of the three higher faculties of theology, law, or medicine. The universal use of Latin made it possible for teachers and students from all nations to share in the work, and soon the attendance was counted, in the larger institutions, by thousands.

Contemporary with this change in instruction through the development of universities, learning, and especially the discussion of theology, were given a great impetus by the revived knowledge of the Greek philosopher, Aristotle. Studied among the Mohammedans and Jews of Spain, Aristotle's writings began to be influential by the beginning of the thirteenth century among Christian scholars, at first through Arabian and Jewish commentaries, and then by direct translation. Though the influence of Aristotle was looked upon with suspicion as too rationalistic by orthodox churchmen, who represented the traditional neo-Platonism of Augustine, his philosophic standpoint so approved itself that, by the middle of the thirteenth century, it was dominant in theologic investigation. The result was the golden age of scholasticism, illustrated in the work of a series of brilliant and profound thinkers, of whom the most conspicuous were Alexander of Hales (?-1245), an English-born teacher of Paris; Albertus Magnus (1193–1280), a German, who labored principally in Cologne; Thomas Aquinas, an Italian of whom more will be said; Bonaventura (1221–74), likewise an Italian, who worked much in Paris; and Duns Scotus (1265?–1308), of English or possibly Scottish origin, who taught in Oxford and Paris. All the scholars just named were members of the Franciscan or Dominican orders, then representing the warmest type of religious life. All were men of character. All regarded the Bible as the final authority. While they differed much among themselves, all pursued essentially similar methods of investigation and presentation. Of them all, Aquinas was the first in clearness of presentation, and in the completeness with which he made the Aristotelian philosophy subservient to the development of a great theological explanation of Christian truth. His aim was to show the reasonableness, naturalness, and verity of the Christian system, as then understood, when explained in the light of the science of the age; and in its accomplishment he showed himself not merely the greatest theologian of the Middle Ages, but the classic exponent of Roman Catholic doctrine to the present day.

Thomas was born in the castle of Rocca Sicca, near Aquino, from which place his father, Landulf, took the title of count, in 1225 or, less probably, 1227. Though thus Italian in origin, he was related to some of the most eminent families of Europe. His father was a connection of the great German imperial house of Hohenstaufen, his mother traced her ancestry to the Norman Tancred who distinguished himself as a leader of the forces of southern Italy in the First Crusade. The family was in every way one of distinction, and prominent in the political conflicts between the popes and emperors. Monte Cassino, the mother monastery of the Benedictine order,[1] is only eight miles from Aquino, and thither Thomas was sent in childhood for education. Thence he went, while still in boyhood, to Naples; and there fell under the influence of the Dominicans, then in the height of their early fame. Their zeal, their scholarship, and their self-denial all attracted him, and the eighteen-year-old boy determined to become a monk of the order. His family, who hoped for him a brilliant secular career, bitterly opposed this. He was imprisoned, worldly inducements, even tempta-

[1] *Ante*, p. 108.

tions, were employed to turn his purpose; but he persisted, and, in 1244, he was admitted a Dominican. His superior in the order perceived his scholastic promise, and soon sent him (1245) to Cologne to have the benefit of instruction by Albertus Magnus.[1] Here his large frame and silent manner made him rather the butt of the lighter-minded of his fellow-students, and he was nicknamed "the dumb ox;" but his teachers saw what was in him, and he now went with Albertus Magnus for further study to Paris. By 1248 he was teaching with great success as second in the school at Cologne, and four years later established himself in Paris, where his lectures were thronged, though the university refused to give him full standing among its teachers of theology till 1257, because of a jealous fear lest the mendicant orders should thus obtain a footing in its faculty.

Such conspicuity in learning was accompanied, however, by great modesty. Splendid ecclesiastical posts were offered him, but Aquinas refused them all. He never forgot that he was a member of a preaching order, and his sermons were marked by great simplicity, directness, and effectiveness. His judgment was so sound and disinterested, even in worldly matters, that his advice was sought by nobles and princes. In all his work he sought divine guidance by prayer, and his piety was as unaffected as it was sincere. Summoned to Italy by Urban IV

[1] *Ante*, p. 181.

in 1261, he taught in Rome, Pisa, Bologna, and again in Paris, till in 1272 he became professor in the University of Naples. Gregory X invited him to the Council of Lyons, but the journey thither was never completed. He died on March 7, 1274, at the age probably of forty-nine, in the monastery of Fossa Nuova, only a few miles from the place of his birth. He was a noble example of the Christian scholar, humble, prayerful, teachable, yet profoundly learned, and universally recognized as of transcendent abilities as a teacher and an interpreter of Christian theology.

Throughout these brief years of study, teaching, preaching, and travel, which most men would have found exhaustingly filled by these labors, Thomas was constantly busy with his pen; and the fecundity displayed is amazing, his works filling no less than twenty-eight good-sized volumes.[1] Nor is the quality of his discussions less remarkable. He is the profoundest of the mediaeval scholars, and at the same time one of the most lucid in expression. In ethics Thomas is ranked by good judges as second only to Augustine in his contribution to the development of a scientific treatment of Christian morals. In government, even in so remote a subject as trade, his views command great historic interest. But speculative theology was to him the crown of all studies, and his ripest work is therefore the *Summa*

[1] E. g., in the Venice edition of 1787. The new Roman edition, begun by Leo XIII, will have twenty-five volumes.

theologica, his general view of the whole body of Christian belief.

In its form the *Summa* is exceedingly mechanical, some 518 questions being treated in 2,652 articles, the discussion of each following the same order. The proposition presented is clearly defined and defended by authority and argument, the objections equally fairly stated and carefully answered. This form, whatever its defects, had the merits of thoroughness and full consideration of opposing views. In his citation of authorities it is interesting to observe that Thomas regarded nothing but the Bible, and that literally understood, as conclusive. All the more striking, therefore, as showing how fully he was under the influence of the spirit of his age, it is that he is able to defend not only the whole of the traditional creed, but all important parts of contemporary churchly practice and of papal claim.

Our space will permit but a hasty glance at the contents of this great outline of theology. The chief end of all investigation of religious truth, Thomas held, is to give knowledge of God, and of man's origin and destiny. Much can be known by the use of reason —natural theology—but full knowledge must have a higher source. It comes only by revelation from God himself. This revelation reason alone cannot reach. It cannot prove or disprove it. But revelation contains nothing contrary to reason, and reason can show the weakness of the objections brought against its doctrines.

This revelation, so necessary for man, is contained in the Bible. We accept it because the divine Spirit moves our hearts to credence as we read it, because of the miracles by which the message was accompanied, because of the fulfilment of prophecy which it witnesses, and because of what it has done in the world. Yet its acceptance is not forced on our reason, even by these arguments, as are the demonstrations of mathematics. We believe because we trust the character of the divine Revealer whose Word the Bible is, and such belief is meritorious, for it is pleasing to God thus to be trusted.

Aquinas next takes up the discussion of God's existence and nature, the Trinity, and divine Providence, holding that the latter extends to all persons and events, and manifests itself, among various ways, in the predestination of some to eternal life, and the relegation of others to everlasting death.

The second part of the *Summa* treats of the nature of man. He was made for the vision and enjoyment of God; in these blessings his highest good is to be found. But this vision and enjoyment cannot be obtained without the possession of the three Christian virtues of faith, hope, and love. The power to exercise these virtues is not man's by nature. His natural endowment extended to the attainment of the four natural virtues, prudence, justice, courage, and self-control; but though these bring honor and a certain degree of happiness, so that he who practices them is far worthier than he who does not, the natural virtues are inadequate to secure the vision of God. To enable him to practice the Christian virtues man, as originally created, was endowed with a "superadded gift," a divine bestowment of power that was in addition to his natural capacities. This gift Adam had, and lost for himself and all his descendants by his sin, thus leaving them incapable of the higher virtues. This sinful condition, this lack of original righteousness, is original sin, and has become the condition by his disobedience of all who are descended from Adam.

The restoration of the lost gift, and with it the power to attain the Christian virtues, and ultimately to reach the blessed vision of God, is the work of Christ. God could, indeed, have restored men without that sacrifice, but it did not seem fitting or wise for him so to do. Christ, by his life and death of humble obedience, merited grace for us; he made satisfaction for our sins by taking their punishment upon himself; he wrought reconciliation between us and God. As a result of Christ's work, those who are the recipients of its benefits are justified—an instantaneous experience made possible by God's wholly unmerited grace, involving faith on man's part, and bringing with it forgiveness of sins. But, as with

Augustine,[1] the most important element in the work of salvation thus begun is not the instantaneous remission of sins, but the constant infusion after justification of "co-operating grace," whereby the Christian virtues—above all, love—are stimulated in the soul. By the aid to this co-operating grace, a Christian man is enabled to do works to which God is pleased to attach merit, and to reward with eternal life. Aquinas thus finds large room for a doctrine of "works," though holding that salvation is dependent on Christ and made possible only by the free grace of God.

In one very important division of doctrine the schoolmen, and notably Thomas, greatly improved the work of Augustine in logical completeness—that of the sacraments. Augustine had taught that men are saved by God's grace, and yet only in the church.[2] The exact connection of the two thoughts he had failed always to make clear. They were now brought into logical association by the doctrine that the grace won by Christ for men comes to them exclusively through the channel of divinely appointed sacraments placed in the keeping of the church. In Thomas' view, as in that of the schoolmen generally, this church is the visible, hierarchically organized Roman body, of which the pope is the head. Indeed, so convinced a defender of the papacy was he that he affirmed that

[1] *Ante*, pp. 77, 79.
[2] *Ante*, pp. 75, 76, 80.

submission to the pope is needful for salvation. To the priesthood an all-important position was assigned as the divinely appointed agents in the dispensation of the sacraments; and in the administration, reception, and due use of the sacraments the most vital part of the religious life of the church was placed.

According to Thomas, following Peter Lombard, the sacraments are seven in number, though not all are received by all Christians. To the normal adult disciple five would be administered, Baptism, by which he is ingrafted into the body of Christ, and original sin is forgiven; Confirmation, by which vows made in one's behalf in infant baptism are made one's own, and the graces of the Holy Spirit augmented; the Lord's Supper, by which the disciple receives the body and blood of Christ; Penance, by which his lapses are healed; and Extreme Unction, by which he is spiritually strengthened for the ordeal of death. Of these, Baptism and the Supper are the pre-eminent. Two further sacraments may come to some Christians: Marriage, and Ordination. By the latter a spiritual power is imparted, notably to be the agent through whom the miracle of Christ's presence in the Lord's Supper is wrought. No layman possesses this gift. The ordained priest, and he alone, it is, upon whose words of consecration God miraculously changes the bread and wine of the sacrament into the body and blood of Christ.

Regarding two of these sacraments something more

should be said. The Lord's Supper was to Thomas, as it had long been to the church in general, the highest act of worship. In it Christ is really present, comes into fellowship with the believer, and is offered to the Father. It is not merely a communion in which the disciple partakes of Christ; it is a sacrifice, continuing that of Christ on the cross, and inclining God to be gracious to those in whose behalf it is offered. In it the bread and wine are changed into the actual body and blood of Christ—a doctrine known as "transubstantiation," to which Thomas gave the classic presentation.

Penance is the sacrament by which the lapses of the believer since baptism are healed. According to Thomas, it consists of three elements, contrition or sincere sorrow for the sin; confession to the priest as the spiritual physician who can apply the appropriate remedy and pronounce absolution; and satisfaction, by which the evil effects of the sin can be made good. Yet this doctrine of Penance was further modified by the practice of indulgences which had come into prominence in connection with the Crusades, and which Thomas, though with great caution, defends. In his exposition, the work of Christ has more than made satisfaction for human sin. The saints, also, have done meritorious deeds through God's co-operating grace. Hence a treasury of merit is laid up for the church in the sight of God, and its officers can transfer something from it, on proper conditions, to those who have not sufficient merit of their own.

At their deaths the wicked pass into hell. Those who, by faithful use of the means of grace, are fit for heaven go thither immediately; but the mass of mankind, who while Christian in desire, and participants in the sacraments, have followed Christ but imperfectly, will have further purification in purgatory before attaining heavenly blessedness. The church, as the body of Christ, whether on earth, in purgatory, or in heaven, is one; and on this unity of the church is grounded the doctrines of prayers to the saints and for the dead. As members of the one body the blessed in heaven are interested in the struggling souls on earth, and those in purgatory are not beyond the help of our intercession. The goal of all Christian hope is heaven, and its chief joy will consist in the vision, the comprehension, and the enjoyment of God. Then shall we know as we are known.

Such in barest outline is the great theological system to which Thomas gave expression. Very little was original with him; but he gave to it its classic form. Here and there his definitions were altered by those who came after him. It was attacked in many subsidiary points by Duns Scotus and his successors. It profoundly influenced all the later Middle Ages. It is, for instance, the theological basis of Dante's *Divine Comedy*. By declaration of the late pope, Leo XIII, as recently as 1879, Thomas' expositions of theology and philosophy have been affirmed to be of the highest value as a guide to Christian theology. He is, therefore, a living force in a large portion of Christendom to the present day.

QUESTIONS

1. What was the aim and significance of scholasticism?
2. Who were Anselm? Abelard? Bernhard? Peter Lombard? Their efforts?
3. How did the universities come into existence?
4. What was the influence of the revival of Aristotle?
5. Who were some of the great schoolmen of the thirteenth century? To what monastic orders did they belong? What inference can be drawn, in general, as to their piety? Why?
6. Sketch the early life of Thomas Aquinas. His parentage? Of what order was he a member?
7. What was Aquinas' career as a teacher? His death? His character?
8. What was Aquinas' productivity as a writer? His *Summa?* Its method?
9. What, according to Aquinas, is the object of theology? What are the sources of theology? Why is revelation necessary? Why do we believe the Bible? Why is that belief meritorious?
10. Wherein does Aquinas find the highest good? What virtues are necessary for its attainment? Are they man's by nature? What did Adam lose?
11. How is Adam's loss restored to man? What is the effect of justification? What the work of co-operating grace?
12. What is the importance of Aquinas' treatment of the sacraments? How many are there?

13. What is the value of the sacraments? The Lord's Supper? Penance? Indulgences?

14. What is his doctrine of purgatory? Of prayers to the saints and for the dead? Wherein is the blessedness of heaven?

15. What is the present significance of Aquinas?

ADDITIONAL READING

W. J. Townsend, *The Great Schoolmen of the Middle Ages* (London, 1881), pp. 199-241.

Schaff (continued by David S. Schaff), *History of the Christian Church* (New York, 1907), V, Pt. I, 659-77.

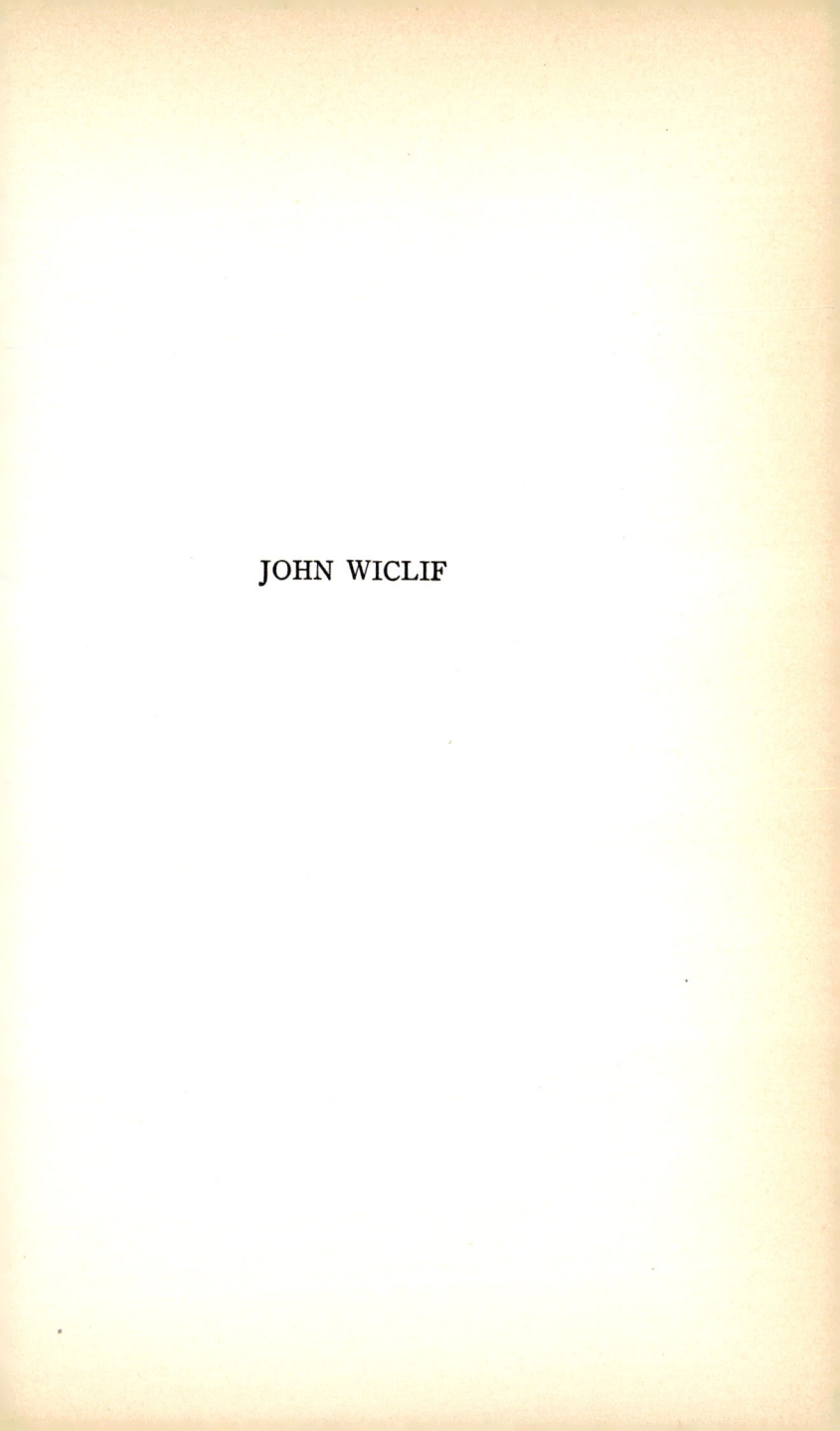

JOHN WICLIF

XI
JOHN WICLIF

The fourteenth century was an epoch of great changes. Mediaeval feudalism, with its strongly divisive spirit, was giving way to a new national feeling. A real sense of common unity of interest was beginning to be felt by the peoples of France, of England, and in a less degree of Germany. A new power was therefore rising, that of national life. It speedily entered into conflict with the papacy, and with momentous results. Though Boniface VIII asserted the extremest papal claims, and even declared in essential agreement with the teachings of Aquinas, in a bull of 1302,[1] not only that the papacy ruled all secular princes, but that obedience to the pope is needful for salvation, he encountered the most determined opposition of the French king, Philip IV, and of the French people. So strong did the newly awakened French monarchy show itself, that from 1305 to 1377 the papacy itself left its ancient seat at Rome, and the popes lived for the most part in Avignon. All were Frenchmen, and were largely subservient to French political interests. One or two were men of low moral standards and almost purely secular ambitions. This transfer of

[1] The bull *Unam sanctam ecclesiam*.

residence and submission to French influence lost the papacy much of its prestige in the rest of Europe, while the popes of this period carried their system of taxation to a height heretofore unexampled. The papacy never was more burdensome, but it had lost the leadership and high spiritual purpose which alone could make its burdens endurable. Men were beginning to criticize it from many points of view.

The Franciscans and Dominicans had lost much of the zeal which had made them so useful in the years following their foundation, while the popes were supporting the looser element in them in laxer interpretation of the "rules." The character of the clergy was too often unworthy. Theology, which in the teachings of Aquinas had seemed a science solidly buttressed by philosophy, was now largely held to be philosophically improbable, to be accepted only because taught by the church. Religion was not declining; but the mediaeval institutions of religion were more and more showing themselves inadequate. Earnest men, like Dante[1] and William of Occam, were opposing the claims of the papacy to control the state; and one bold voice, that of Marsilius of Padua, in 1324,[2] questioned the whole papal system; but they were yet relatively few, and the mediaeval scheme of doctrine, with its great hierarch-

[1] In his *De monarchia*.

[2] In his *Defensor pacis*, written when a professor in the University of Paris.

JOHN WICLIF

ical structure, though inwardly weakened, stood apparently as strongly as ever.

Yet in one region of Europe, before the fourteenth century came to a close, the most effective, if not the most logical, critic of the papacy that had yet appeared was to arise and to lead in a movement for reform of no little importance. This reformer was John Wiclif. England, thanks to its insular position and the direct relations of its kings since the time of William the Conqueror to the great land-holders, had possessed an unusual sense of solidarity of interest. The national feeling had there developed to a degree only comparable to that of France. Under Edward III, in 1339, England began the long war with France, incidents of which were to be the English victories of Crécy (1346) and Poitiers (1356). It was at the time that the papacy had its seat at Avignon, and was largely under French influences. Naturally the payment of taxes to such popes, and the appointment by them of their French protégés to English ecclesiastical posts, were looked upon by a large party in England as aids to England's enemies. Statutes known as those of "Provisors" and "Praemunire" were passed by Parliament, in 1351 and 1353, intended to limit papal appointments and appeals to the papal courts; and, in 1366, Parliament refused to pay to the pope the taxes granted by King John in 1213. It was this feeling of resistance to what seemed foreign aggression that Wiclif was to share, and it was to be the beginning from which he was to advance to far more radical criticisms of the papacy.

John Wiclif was born probably in the village of Hipswell in the county of northern England known as Yorkshire, at some unknown date which has been conjectured to have been about 1324. Of his early life almost nothing is known, save that he went as a young student to Oxford, and gained great distinction there as a scholar and a teacher. When he emerges into the light of history it is as a man of high philosophical attainments, who departed from current theological conceptions in the direction of a renewed Augustinianism, such as Thomas of Bradwardine (1290–1349) had made influential at Oxford. We shall see this in his emphasis on predestination, and his strong sense that religion is a relation of God to the individual human soul.

It was not merely in Oxford that Wiclif had won distinction. In 1366 or 1367, as one of the chaplains of Edward III, he put forth a vigorous defense of the action of Parliament, already mentioned, in refusing further payment of taxes to the pope. From this publication Wiclif's open opposition to papal encroachments may be dated. He soon followed it with others. By 1374 he had become a doctor of divinity. In April of that year he was nominated by the king to the pastorate of Lutterworth, and, in July, he was sent as a royal commissioner to treat with the representatives of Pope Gregory XI, regarding the vexed question of ecclesiastical appointments in England. He was evidently in high favor at court.

Thus far Wiclif had gone but little, if at all, farther in his criticisms than many of the Franciscans had done. His motives were opposition to the wealth and corruption of the church, and patriotic resistance to papal encroachments. His argument was curiously mediaeval. All authority is a "lordship," a fief, held by its possessor from God, who is overlord of all. As a temporal fief, if misused, is forfeited, so spiritual lordships are vacated if not rightly employed, or if the holder is unfit. If an ecclesiastic is of bad character, in "mortal sin," or if he uses his office to accumulate riches or gain temporal power, things inconsistent with the purpose for which the ministry was established by Christ, his "lordship" is forfeited, and may be taken from him by the civil authorities. The enforcement of ecclesiastical claims by spiritual penalties, which in mediaeval practice would have followed such attempts to seize the possessions of the clergy, is not to be feared, since even the pope's excommunication is ineffective unless he against whom it is directed is really deserving of condemnation in the sight of God. Only the "law of Christ" as laid down in the New Testament is of final authority as a criterion of rightful action. In its last analysis the church consists only of the "predestinate;" but as they are not easily distinguished, the practical test is apparent conformity to the "law of Christ."

These views commended Wiclif to the favor of the most powerful, but one of the least popular, of the English nobles, John of Gaunt, duke of Lancaster, fourth son of Edward III. John was without a spark of religious sympathy with Wiclif, but he headed a hungry party who thought to profit by despoiling the English church, and believed that in Wiclif he had one whom he could use as a tool for that purpose. John's support was to be a safeguard to Wiclif, but the latter was too profoundly religious to enter into real sympathy with that greedy noble's hopes, and probably too guileless wholly to fathom his plans. Thanks to this support, an attempt to bring Wiclif to trial before the Convocation of the Province of Canterbury, gathered in St. Paul's in London in February, 1377, utterly failed, the proceedings being frustrated by an angry personal encounter in the church between John of Gaunt and the Bishop of London. Gregory XI now issued five bulls condemning Wiclif's opinions in the matters of the withdrawal of property from its unworthy possessors and excommunication, and comparing him with Marsilius of Padua. But court favor still served the reformer. Though Edward III died in June, 1377, and John of Gaunt went into temporary political eclipse, the mother of the young king, Richard II, proved Wiclif's friend, and through her aid an attempt of the Archbishop of Canterbury and the Bishop of London to discipline him was frustrated in 1378. For the next three years Wiclif was not molested.

It was during these three years of comparative peace, apparently, that he achieved two of his greatest services. Convinced of the need of popular preaching, as Valdez and Francis had been before, and as John Wesley was to be in a later age, he now began sending out "poor priests," that is, unendowed preachers, not necessarily clergymen, who should proclaim the gospel in churches, in marketplaces, in the fields, wherever they could gather an audience. The condition of the lower classes of England was such as to secure them a ready hearing. That frightful pestilence known as the "black death"[1] had ravaged England in 1348–49, 1361, and 1369, and, especially in the first attack, had been terribly destructive. Probably half the population, possibly more, had perished. The whole labor situation was unsettled for years by the consequent scarcity of workmen, and the attempts of Parliament to regulate work and wages by legislation. The lower classes of the population were in a state of profound discontent; and they listened eagerly to

[1] The same disease as that known as the "bubonic plague," and fatal at the present, 1908, in India. The unsanitary conditions of the Middle Ages made it destructive throughout Europe.

Wiclif's "poor priests," whose denunciation of the wealth and arrogance of the high clergy, and assertion that the "law of Christ" demanded "humility, love, and poverty"—to quote Wiclif's own phrase—found ready response.

To aid these preachers, and to give to the people generally the Word of God which Wiclif was convinced was the only final authority for the Christian, he now undertook with his friends the translation of the Scriptures from the Latin Vulgate into English. It was a time of much interest in the developing language. Sermons were being widely preached in it. Its use had recently been established in law-court practice. Wiclif was therefore following the spirit of the age in putting the Bible into the English tongue. Of the greatness of his service there can be no question. The gospels and Psalms had been translated or paraphrased repeatedly from early Anglo-Saxon times; but these versions had at best a very limited circulation. The new work, especially the New Testament which was from Wiclif's own pen, was idiomatic, forceful, readable. He gave the whole Bible to his nation; and, in so doing, not merely contributed to its religious development, but exercised a formative influence upon all subsequent English versions of the Scriptures, and upon the general growth of the English language.

While engaged in this work during his three years of comparative peace, events were occurring which caused Wiclif to advance to far more radical criticisms of the papacy than he had hitherto uttered. The death of Gregory XI in 1378 found the cardinals, a majority of whom were Frenchmen, at Rome. The pressure of the Roman populace and other influences compelled the choice of an Italian pope, Urban VI; but that election the same cardinals repudiated a few months later and selected another head for the church in the person of Clement VII, who returned to Avignon. All Europe was distressed at the spectacle of two rivals in office, each with about an equal following. The French pope ultimately had the allegiance of France, Spain, Naples, and Scotland; the Roman, of England, Germany, and most of Italy. The scandalous schism thus begun was to last till healed, after infinite labor, by the Council of Constance in 1417. The sight of two popes mutually anathematizing each other, and proclaiming crusades, the one against the other, turned Wiclif now fully against the papacy. Could men so un-Christlike in action be living rightly according to "the law of Christ;" and if not so living, had they not forfeited their "lordship"? He could but answer that such popes were "vicars of Anti-christ." But he now went farther. He criticized not the papacy only, but the whole priestly order which drew its income from revenues and endowments, the monks with their landed possessions, and even the mendicant friars, whom he had formerly favored, whose vow of poverty was so often really ignored. Applying the test of conformity to Scripture, Wiclif now rejected indulgences, a treasury of good works, private confession, the worship of saints, pilgrimages, and purgatory, and asserted the spiritual equality of all priests.

Wiclif's greatest breach with popular religious conceptions was occasioned by his denial, in the spring of 1381, of the doctrine of transubstantiation. It aroused antagonism as almost nothing else could have done. No belief was more widespread at the period, and none seemed more sacred to multitudes than the faith that when the priest pronounces the words of consecration the elements are transformed in their substance into the very body and blood of Christ.[1] Roman Catholic devotion still clings with peculiar affection to this doctrine which seems to bring Christ into vital contact with present life. To Wiclif, however, it appeared unscriptural and irrational. His own view was essentially that of a spiritual presence of Christ in the sacrament which Augustine had taught. But something more than its supposed unscripturalness or irrationality may have led Wiclif to the dangerous task of attacking transubstantiation. He was at war with what he deemed an un-Christlike body of clergy who were unjustly lording over God's heritage. Their highest power, the power no layman was believed to possess, was

[1] See *ante*, p. 190.

that on their consecrating act, the miracle of transubstantiation is wrought. Deny that miracle, and the chief distinction between clergy and laity, the main spiritual buttress of clerical claims, is swept away.[1]

This attack by Wiclif cost him many friends. The University of Oxford condemned his opinions, though, such was the esteem in which he was there held, without mentioning his name. Even untheological John of Gaunt urged him to silence. Within a few weeks, however, a great disaster overtook the Wiclifian cause—a disaster for which Wiclif was only in remote degree responsible. The years-long discontent of the lower classes has already been mentioned.[2] In June, 1381, it flared up in a terrible insurrection directed against what the peasants deemed the forces of oppression. Deeds and mortgages were burned, lawyers killed, the inns of court at the Temple in London and John of Gaunt's palace were destroyed, the Archbishop of Canterbury and some of the king's leading agents in the collection of taxes were murdered. King Richard II, himself, was in great peril. Fierce as it was, the storm soon passed; but the nobles were ruthless in their acts of repression and the feeling was widespread that Wiclif's attacks on the clergy, and especially the preaching of his "poor priests," were responsible for the disorder. Some

[1] The suggestion is that of R. L. Poole, *Wycliffe and Movements for Reform*, p. 104.

[2] *Ante*, p. 203.

influence may have come from Wiclif's preachers, though he himself had no direct share in the revolt; but the movement as a whole was due to the working of long-standing economic grievances.

The discredit into which the peasant revolt brought Wiclif's cause for the time being emboldened his enemies, and in May, 1382, his doctrines were condemned by a synod held in London. His popularity remained too great, however, for successful personal attack. He wrote much in vigorous English tracts and in Latin. He pushed forward the cause he had at heart to his utmost. It was while in his own church at Lutterworth on December 28, 1384, that he suffered the paralytic stroke from which he died three days later.

Wiclif's chief characteristic was moral earnestness. He was a patriot anxious to save England from foreign tyranny; but even more he was a Christian intent on advancing the Kingdom of God. He broke with the current religious system on many points. He rejected the papacy, at least of such popes as were then in power, denounced the wealth of the clergy, criticized the monks, rejected transubstantiation, urged preaching, proclaimed the unique authority of the Scriptures, gave England the Bible in its own tongue. He evidently regarded vital religion as an inward and personal experience. His view of it was far deeper than that of most men of his age. These are great services; but they hardly entitle him to be called, as he has often been styled, "the morning-star of the Reformation." His conceptions of religion, however profound, were the familiar mediaeval Roman Catholic thoughts of ascetic "apostolic poverty," and of the gospel as a "new law." He had no new theory of the way of salvation, or of Christ's relations to men, to offer. Hence he was no Luther. Rather he was one of the most radical and deserving of the mediaeval reformers—a man who belonged to the Middle Ages, not to the new day.

This failure to give to his age that which was vitally new probably accounts for the surprising fruitlessness of his movement in England. At his death he had a large following, and on the whole royal tolerance made easy the path of his party till the downfall of Richard II in 1399. No church was founded, however. On the accession of John of Gaunt's son, Henry IV, first of the House of Lancaster, the royal policy was changed to one of persecution. The political significance of the "Lollards," as Wiclif's followers were called, ended with the execution of their leader, Sir John Oldcastle, in 1417, and their religious importance did not long survive. The one lasting influence of the movement in England was the impulse which it undoubtedly gave to the reading of the Bible; and the number of manuscripts of Wiclif's translation which have survived, in spite of attempts to destroy them, is remarkable.

In one remote region of Europe, however, Wiclif's work was to have a powerful influence. The Bohemian reformer, John Huss, did little more doctrinally than reproduce Wiclif's opinions, often in Wiclif's very words. More conservative intellectually, Huss did not share Wiclif's rejection of transubstantiation. Unlike Wiclif, he urged the right of the laity to partake of the wine as well as of the bread in communion. In conduct Huss was much more a man of action than Wiclif. A teacher in the University of Prague from 1398 onward, he became, in 1402, the preacher of the Bethlehem church in that city. During the reign of Richard II of England, whose queen was a Bohemian princess, many Bohemian students had been attracted to Oxford and had returned with Wiclif's writings. Of these Huss made a thorough study. They appealed to his Bohemian patriotism by reason of their rejection of foreign authority, and soon to his religious spirit by their bold criticism of the evils of the age. To him, as to Wiclif, Christ is the sole head of the church,[1] only the "predestinate" are its members, and all ministers are essentially equal in spiritual powers. In sermons of great popular influence Huss denounced the corruption of the Bohemian clergy, and advocated Wiclifian positions. The Bohemian element

[1] Too much must not be made of this as a "Protestant" declaration. Even so good a churchman as Pierre d'Ailli, who was a leader in Huss's condemnation at Constance, taught the headship of Christ in the most explicit terms.

JOHN WICLIF

in the University and city of Prague largely sympathized with him, and through his influence a decree was obtained from King Wenzel, by which the Bohemians, though a decided minority, were given a controlling influence in the University. The result was that Huss became the chief power in that seat of learning, while the disgruntled Germans and other foreigners regarded it as unorthodox and established, in 1409, the University of Leipzig.

These events led to a breach between Huss and his archbishop, and in 1410 he was excommunicated for Wiclifianism. The contest was now fully on, and Huss enjoyed large popular support as well as the somewhat fickle favor of King Wenzel. The situation attracted European attention, and the emperor Sigismund now summoned Huss to appear before the great general Council of Constance, which had been called, primarily, through the work of the leading theologians of the University of Paris, to heal the schism and effect reforms in the church. Thither he went, protected, as he certainly supposed, by a safe conduct from the emperor. He was, however, promptly imprisoned, and a pitiful contest ensued. On May 4, 1415, the council condemned Wiclif's views, and ordered his body cast out of consecrated ground. It urged Huss to yield his opinions to its authority. The leaders of the church sincerely felt not only that a council was wiser than any individual in the church, but that only by the recognition of the duty of all Christians to submit their private convictions to its authority could they rid the church of its rival popes and end the scandal of the schism. To allow Huss to assert his judgment against that of the council would be to lose all that the council had won for church unity. They were perfectly honest in this position. But Huss was equally sincere. He would play no tricks with his conscience. He would not deny what he believed to be the truth even when the council declared him in error. It was a contest of opposing principles, and the future was with Huss, for the principle for which he stood was essentially the right of private judgment which Protestantism was to assert. Firm in his opinions, he was condemned by the council as a heretic, and on July 6, 1415, was burned at Constance, meeting his death with heroic firmness and Christian courage.

In Bohemia Huss was regarded as a national hero. A large part of its population openly supported his cause, and, in 1419, the terrible civil wars began. The Hussites gradually divided into conservative and radical parties, and the latter was nearly extinguished in battle, in 1434; but its remnants survived. Out of some of them, and of others influenced by Waldensian views, which had long found a following in Bohemia, the *Unitas Fratrum* came into being soon after the middle of the fifteenth century. This communion was much modified by the influence of the Lutheran reformation; but it is the spiritual ancestor of the

JOHN WICLIF

modern Moravians. Thus Wiclif's influence long survived, in modified form, in a land which he never saw and which was far from that in which he did his work.

QUESTIONS

1. What influence had the rise of the national spirit on the fortunes of the papacy?

2. How came the papacy to transfer its seat to Avignon and how long did it remain there?

3. Who were some of the opponents of extreme papal claims?

4. What evidences of opposition to the papacy are to be found in England under Edward III?

5. Sketch Wiclif's early life. When and how did he come to oppose the papacy?

6. What was his theory of "lordship"? When did a clergyman forfeit his office?

7. Sketch Wiclif's relations to John of Gaunt. Why?

8. What condition of the lower orders favored Wiclif's work?

9. Speak of his "poor priests" and of his translation of the Bible. Its importance?

10. What effect had the papal schism on Wiclif? To what new positions did he advance after 1378?

11. What were the reasons for Wiclif's rejection of transubstantiation? What was its effect?

12. What consequences for Wiclif's work had the great peasant rising of 1381?

13. Wiclif's last days? His character? Was he "the morning star of the Reformation"?

14. Was Wiclif's work permanent in England? Where was it fruitful?

15. Outline the career of John Huss. How did he resemble and how did he differ from Wiclif?

16. When, how, and for what did Huss die? The results of his work?

ADDITIONAL READING

G. V. Lechler, *John Wiclif and His English Precursors* (London, 1878, 1881, 1884).

Johann Loserth, *Wiclif and Huss* (London, 1885).

Rudolf Buddensieg, *Wiclif, Patriot and Reformer* (London, 1884).

R. L. Poole, *Wycliffe and Movements for Reform* (London, 1889).

Lewis Sergeant, *John Wyclif* (New York, 1893).

J. F. Hurst, *History of the Christian Church* (Cincinnati, 1897), II, 12-42.

MARTIN LUTHER

XII
MARTIN LUTHER

The period from Wiclif to Luther was one of great modification of mediaeval conditions of civil life and habits of thought. The tendency toward national unity, already noted, had increased, and to England and France, Spain was now added as the most forceful sister in the family of nations. In Germany no such unity existed; but even there strong principalities, like Saxony, Hesse, Brandenburg, and Bavaria, were building within the Empire. The discovery of a New World, and of the sea route to India, had immensely widened men's geographical knowledge and spread wide a vague feeling that they stood on the threshold of a new age. The revival of learning had given to the educated world a new point of view, in which interest in the thought of Greece and Rome displaced the influence of scholastic theology. It was essentially a "return to the sources;" and was leading to a re-examination of that which the Middle Ages had accepted as authoritative—a re-examination that was slowly beginning to be applied even in the realm of religious thought. In political administration the layman was wresting his old-time preeminence from the ecclesiastic. A new individualism was taking the place of the strong corporate feeling of the Middle Ages. The world was in ferment to a degree that had not before been manifested since the downfall of the Roman Empire.

In the religious realm the situation was at once discouraging and hopeful. The institutions of religion had become increasingly corrupt and inefficient. The slowly growing sense of the need of reform in the administration not merely of the papacy but of the church in general had found expression, stimulated by the scandal of the papal schism, in the great Councils of Pisa (1409); of Constance (1414-18), when the schism was ended and Huss condemned;[1] and of Basel (1431-49). These had attempted to change the papacy from an absolute to a constitutional spiritual monarchy, controlled by councils as a king is by a parliament. The effort had been an ignominious failure. The church could not be reformed without revolution. In the period following the collapse of the conciliar movement the popes became more and more engrossed in Italian secular politics. Their spiritual interests were largely neglected. But the taxation imposed by the papacy had been rising for a century and a half. The introduction of new means of money raising had been frequent, and the exactions of the Roman court, to which a revenue flowed far greater than that of any contemporary king, were the scandal of Europe. Indeed, so notorious were they, and so widely were

[1] *Ante*, pp. 211, 212.

they the object of hatred, that many scholars are inclined to see in them the principal root of the Reformation. This view, however, fails to do justice to the religious nature of the movement, though it accounts for a large part of Luther's early support. Corruption at the head led of course to much similar inefficiency in the lower officers of the great hierarchical edifice.

On the other hand, there were many signs of a deepening popular religious life. In Spain, under Ferdinand, Isabella, and Cardinal Ximenes, a very thoroughgoing movement for the improvement of the morals and education of the clergy, without any favor toward doctrinal changes, however, was in progress from 1479 onward. Similar, though less extensive, efforts were made a little later in England. In Germany, the Bible was being widely read by laymen, no less than fourteen editions in the language of the people being printed between 1466 and 1520, while the gospels and epistles in German were issued twenty-five times before 1518. Preaching was being encouraged. The religious orders were undergoing a reformation, in which none shared more conspicuously than that of the Augustinians of which Luther was to be a member. There is much evidence of the existence of a simple, heartfelt religious life among the people, and several German governments were even taking steps to improve the clergy and do away with some of the worst abuses. Indeed, the last years of the fifteenth and the opening of the sixteenth centuries were witnessing what can be called nothing less than a revival of religion in Germany. Its dominant notes seem to have a sense of sin and fear of divine judgment, and it led, as men's temperaments inclined, to increased devotion to relics, pilgrimages, and indulgences, which were never more popular, or to more heartfelt and inward evidences of piety. Luther's work was not an awakening out of spiritual deadness. It was made possible by an immense antecedent quickening of popular religious feeling. To note this is, however, to detract in no way from his world-transforming significance.

Martin Luther was born in Eisleben, in central Germany, on November 10, 1483. His parents were peasants. His father was a miner. Both were strict, hard-working, God-fearing people; and of energy and ambition, anxious that their son should have an education and be better placed in the world than they. In 1497, therefore, the boy was sent to school in Magdeburg, and from 1498 to 1501 in Eisenach, where he was befriended by Frau Ursula Cotta. In the year last mentioned he entered the University of Erfurt, from which he graduated as "Master of Arts" in 1505, after a student career of high credit from the standpoints of sociability, scholarship, and character. His father intended him for a lawyer. In spite of his cheerful companionableness, however, the sense of his personal unworthiness in the sight of

God weighed heavily upon him. The question, "How may I gain a gracious God?" which may be called the ground note of the contemporary German religious revival, burdened him. In spite of his father's opposition, he determined to seek spiritual peace in the monastic life, and on July 17, 1505, entered the Augustinian monastery in Erfurt.

Yet the wished-for rest of soul did not come. He studied, he prayed, he practiced monastic austerities, he was looked upon by his associates as a pattern of monastic piety, but he felt that he was wrong in the sight of God. He viewed Christ as a stern judge. But gradually his conversation with some of the earnest men of the order, notably Johann von Staupitz, and his reading of Bernhard, Augustine, and especially of the Pauline epistles, brought him to a new point of view. By 1507 or 1508, he had come to feel that these external efforts after righteousness in the sight of God were valueless; and that justification is a divine gift received through "faith" alone. The soul throws itself in trustful confidence on God's promises, and enters thereby into a new relationship through Christ—a relationship immediate, personal, and full of good-will on God's part. Religion, in his new-found experience, was not an obedient conformity to a great corporate system of life and worship, but a new and personal relation to God, which took as one's own all that Christ offered, and from which the Christian virtues should naturally flow. God gives everything. Man trustfully receives. This conception was not absolutely new. It had been apprehended, none too clearly to be sure, by many of the most spiritual-minded men of the Middle Ages. But they had not drawn its full consequences. They had combined it, as Augustine did, with inconsistent ecclesiastical theories. As Luther now apprehended it, it was a complete breach with current official interpretations of the gospel. It was essentially a revival of the largely forgotten Pauline conception of the way of salvation. It was to be the mainspring of all Luther's later work. Salvation was to him henceforth not something painfully to be won; it was a present, certain experience, based on an undoubting acceptance of the promises of the gospel. In a word, it was a new life of union with God through Christ. He who has this new life must be "saved."[1]

This fresh, Pauline, religious conception of the way of salvation placed Luther far in advance, not merely of mediaeval reformers like Wiclif and Huss, but of the great men of the ancient church. But Luther was naturally a conservative, and it was long after his apprehension of justification by faith alone before he realized its full consequences or broke with the mediaeval hierarchical system. In 1507 he was made a priest; 1508 saw his transfer to Wittenberg,

[1] In this and other paragraphs of this sketch I have taken some sentences from my *The Reformation*.

MARTIN LUTHER

thenceforth to be his home, and the beginning of an influential professorship in the little, recently founded and weak university there situated. He rose to prominence in the Augustinian order, was sent to Rome on its business in 1511, and became superintendent of a group of its monasteries in 1515. Meanwhile, he attained the degree of Doctor of Theology in 1512, his expositions of the Bible in the classroom soon began to attract attention, and his own thinking, under the influence of Augustine and of the German mystics, by 1516 had broken with the Aristotelian explanations of theology which had been characteristic of scholasticism. He was winning great popular approval as a preacher.

Convinced as he was that salvation is based on a new personal relation with God, Luther could not but view with disapproval the coming of Johann Tetzel, in 1517, as a seller of papal indulgences, the proceeds of which were to rebuild St. Peter's in Rome. It was the offer of a stone to those who needed bread. Accordingly, in strict academic custom, he posted on the door of the castle church in Wittenberg, which served the university as a bulletin board, ninety-five "Theses" proposing a discussion of the value of indulgences. The event occurred on October 31, 1517, the eve of "All Saints," when the church was to be crowded with pilgrims. In themselves, the theses were very moderate; but they held that penitence is not an act done once for all, but a lifelong state of the soul; that the real treasury of the church is not one of good works, but the gospel of God's grace; and that every Christian who feels true compunction for his sins has full remission of punishment and guilt. In the existing state of heated opposition to the financial exactions of the Roman court the theses attracted immediate attention throughout Germany. Their effect was far greater than Luther could have anticipated. He had spoken in opposition to the system, and was at once a marked man. Its effect on the sale of indulgences was immediate. Of course Tetzel replied at once, but more powerful defenders of indulgences appeared, chief of whom was the brilliant Johann Maier of Eck, and a Roman Dominican, "Master of the Sacred Palace," Prierias, who affirmed the infallibility of the pope, in whom he declared the church to be virtually embodied, and declared that whatever the Roman church does is right. Luther had wished no quarrel with the papacy; but he now, in 1518, took up the battle with Prierias, asserting the infallibility of the Word of God, and denying that the pope is virtually the church. The struggle was assuming vastly larger dimensions. It was changing from a question of the misuse of indulgences to that of the power of the papacy, and of the hierarchical system of which the papacy was the crown.

A summons to Rome for trial reached Luther in August, 1518, and he would undoubtedly have had to go to his death, had he not been protected by the favor of Elector Friedrich of Saxony, his sovereign, who, though in slight sympathy with Luther's religious position, was proud of his reputation and work in the University of Wittenberg. Friedrich was of political importance for Pope Leo X. The matter was compromised. Luther appeared before the pope's representative, Cardinal Cajetan, at Augsburg in October, 1518; but was ordered to submit. Instead, he issued an appeal to a general council, though without real hope that the appeal would be heard, and in expectation of speedy death. His courage never shone out more conspicuously. But politics still counseled the pope to compromise, and Luther finally agreed, in January, 1519, to submit the questions to a German bishop, and pending the decision to remain silent, provided his opponents would refrain from controversy. This was impossible, and on July 4, 1519, Luther found himself face to face with Eck in a momentous discussion at Leipzig. In his studies preparatory to this debate Luther had made a great advance in the clear apprehension of the consequences of his earlier positions. He had come to the conclusion that the supremacy of the papacy was not merely unnecessary, but was based on many false pretenses and of comparatively recent origin. He had also made up his mind that the seat of ecclesiastical power is the church, not its officers, and that the church is the whole number of

Christian believers, not the hierarchy. With these convictions Luther entered the discussion. Eck was a most skilful debater, and soon showed that many of Luther's positions were those of Huss, who had been condemned by the Council of Constance. It was a moment of decision for Luther. He had doubted the authority of the papacy, but to deny the infallibility of a general council was to break with all mediaeval orthodoxy. It was to break with the whole hierarchical system. It left the sole ultimate authority the Scriptures; and that the Scriptures interpreted by private judgment, since it was in reliance on his own judgment that Luther decided that a general council had erred. Yet he did not shrink from the step. His breach with the mediaeval system was now complete.

Luther's bold stand won him the hearty support of all in Germany who looked in any way with disfavor on the papacy. By many he was regarded as a national hero; and he now began to look upon his own work as a national struggle for freedom from the papacy and all that the papal system represented. Eck hastened to Rome to secure Luther's condemnation as a heretic. In anticipation of its coming and effect Luther now issued two powerful revolutionary treatises of the highest importance. In August, 1520, he put forth in German his appeal *To the Christian Nobles of the German Nation*. He called upon the rulers to redress the grievances from which Germany had long suffered and to take the renovation of the church into their own hands. The spiritual claims of a special priesthood to stand between the layman and God are worthless. God is approachable by all without priestly intervention—a doctrine which swept away the superstitious fear of priestly power which gave its chief strength to the hierarchy of the Middle Ages. "All Christians are truly of the spiritual estate, and there is no difference among them save of office alone." The pope has no monopoly in the interpretation of Scripture or of the summoning of general councils. All honest occupations have on them the divine blessing, and the religious life may be lived in them as truly as in monasticism. A German national church should be guided by a primate of Germany; ministers should be chosen by the communities they serve; priestly celibacy should no longer be required; monasticism should be restricted, and the proper care of the poor be secured.

Two months later, Luther issued an appeal to the learned in Latin—his *Babylonish Captivity*. That bondage he finds in the mediaeval conception of the sacraments. Their number has been exaggerated, their efficacy made magical. Baptism and the Supper—which is no sacrifice offered by the priest to God—are witnesses to and attestations of the divine promise of forgiveness. Hence their value is received by faith only. They evidence to us the truth of God's promises.

Yet such was Luther's inward calmness of spirit, that even in these stormy weeks he could write a third great tract, published in November, 1520—his *Christian Liberty*. It is an untroubled exposition of his faith, as illustrated in the great paradox of Christian experience: "A Christian man is the most free lord of all and subject to none; a Christian man is the most dutiful servant of all and subject to everyone." He is free because justified by faith and united with Christ; he is a servant through love, because he must bring his body into subjection to his regenerated spirit and aid his fellow-men. "A Christian man does not live in himself, but in Christ and in his neighbor, or else is no Christian; in Christ by faith, in his neighbor by love."

The papal bull ordering Luther to make his peace within sixty days or suffer the penalties of a heretic was now in Germany, and Luther answered it by a dramatic act. On December 10, at Wittenberg, with the consenting presence of his colleagues, fellow-townsmen, and students, he burned it, with copies of the papal decretals and canon law. Such an act evidently put a section of Saxony into rebellion against the existing ecclesiastical constitution of Germany, and could not fail to come to the cognizance of the Reichstag. Accordingly, after long discussion, a command and safe-conduct from the Emperor, Charles V, ordered him to appear before it in Worms to declare in what measure he still maintained the positions advanced in his books. On April 17 and 18, 1521, he appeared before that august parliament. It is well-nigh impossible for one of this age to conceive the courage which such a task demanded. Could he, a peasant's son, maintain his independence in the face of the spiritual and temporal rulers of his nation? Was he sure enough of himself to affirm that his own conscientious conviction of the truth of God was more to be relied on than the declarations of the great representative gatherings of Christendom which men generally believed to have been spoken by the power of the Holy Ghost? He was unshaken in his cause. Before the assembly he refused to recant, and declared that he could not do so unless refuted by scriptural testimonies or clear arguments. It was the most heroic moment of his courageous life.

On May 26 Charles V signed the Edict of Worms declaring Luther an outlaw to be seized for punishment; but fortunately, Friedrich still favored him, and for his protection had Luther seized as he journeyed homeward and hidden in the castle known as the Wartburg, near Eisenach. In this safe retreat he lived for eleven months, a period distinguished for his translations of the New Testament into German. As has already been pointed out[1] this was far from the first German translation; but it was fresh, idiomatic, and readable. Its

[1] *Ante*, p. 219.

effect on the popular religious life was almost immeasurable.

Thus far Luther had been steadily growing as a national leader supported by most various classes of Germany. To these years belong his best work, his new, deeply religious appreciation of the way of salvation; his free trust in the universal priesthood of believers, his fresh and suggestive examination and valuation of Scripture in proportion as it taught clearly or imperfectly the doctrine of justification by faith. But from his return from the Wartburg to Wittenberg, in March, 1522, without any alteration in his doctrine of salvation, his position changed gradually, by force of circumstances, to that of a party leader. The vision of a universally purified church, or even of a united Germany, slowly faded, because it proved impossible of realization, and to some extent because of his own conservative fears. That return was compelled by disorders in Wittenberg, which he mastered, but which led to the separation of his more radical followers. Worse by far was the divisive effect of the great peasant revolt of 1524 and 1525. In it he took the side of the nobility who crushed it in blood. Probably in no other way could he have kept their important favor for his cause, and he was thoroughly honest in his attitude. But the results were most unfortunate. Much of Germany charged the revolt to his teaching, and swung back toward the older church; and he himself came to distrust the common man and to feel that all effective reform must be the work of the princes. The same years also witnessed his dispute with Erasmus, and the separation of many of the scholars from his movement. In 1529 came his doctrinal rupture with Zwingli and the leaders of the Swiss reformation at the Marburg Colloquy.

Of the steps by which the Lutheran movement became the Lutheran churches our space will not allow us to speak at length. The year 1526 saw the beginnings of the organization of territorial churches by the rulers of evangelical sympathies. Three years later the protest of these leaders against reactionary Roman Catholic policies in the Reichstag of Speyer fixed the name "Protestant" permanently on the party. In 1530, they presented their creed to the Emperor and Reichstag at Augsburg—the Augsburg Confession. Then followed a quarter of a century of political, and at times military, contest, a period marked by the rapid territorial expansion of the Protestant movement, till by the Peace of Augsburg, in 1555, the Lutherans were recognized as religious bodies having equal rights with the Roman Catholics of the Empire.

In the spiritual battles of this contest Luther bore his full part, assisted by his friend the noble-minded Philip Melanchthon, till his death at Eisleben, the place of his birth, on February 18, 1546. The work far outgrew the power of any one man to direct it;

but as long as he lived he was the foremost figure in his native land, and no son of Germany has been so honored in memory as he.

Luther's work brought Protestantism into being. It had many aspects; but a few of its more significant religious results may be enumerated. Foremost of all it placed in men's minds the conception of the Christian life as a new personal relationship between the soul and God through Christ. Not membership in a great corporation and obedience to its laws, not even nourishment by its sacraments— though Luther greatly valued the sacraments as witnesses to God's promises—are the important things. The one essential is a new and vital relationship to God. Hence saintly intercession or priestly intermediaries are all needless. God gives his gifts and himself directly to the willing soul. A second great result was the fruit of the principles just described. Luther taught the universal priesthood of Christians. The clergy are a ministry who serve by preaching, by guidance, by leadership in the sacraments; they are not a priesthood divinely empowered with authority no layman possesses. In case of need any Christian can be chosen by his fellows their minister. This view swept away the claims of the whole mediaeval hierarchy, either as dispensers of divine grace or as exclusive interpreters of the Word of God. A third feature of his work, of equal significance, was Luther's insistence that the ordinary natural relations of family and society afford the highest opportunities for Christian living. Not in celibacy, or monastic separation from the world, but in its duties and normal relations, is Christian service to be sought. To this vastly important doctrine Luther gave the sanction of his own example by his marriage, on June 13, 1525, to an ex-nun, Catherine von Bora; and in his family life some of the most attractive traits of his character appeared. Less important, probably, but of much significance, were Luther's insistence that worship should be in language understood by the people, his exaltation of the exposition of the Word of God as its central feature, and his vindication for laymen of a share in the government of the church. When every allowance possible has been made for the tendencies of the age which he embodied, and which might conceivably have found other leaders, he still remains one of the few men of whom it may be said that the history of the church has been profoundly modified for all subsequent time to the present by his life and work. Protestantism is his monument and his permanent debtor.

QUESTIONS

1. What tendencies were at work in popular thought on the eve of the Reformation?

2. What criticisms of papal abuses were rife?

3. Were there evidences of reformatory zeal and deepening religious feeling?

4. Speak of Luther's parentage, birth, and rank in life. What were the circumstances of his education? Why did he enter a monastery?

234 GREAT MEN OF THE CHRISTIAN CHURCH

5. How did Luther seek spiritual peace? What did he mean by "justification by faith alone"? Value to him of this experience?

6. Did Luther immediately become a reformer? What was his history from 1507 to 1517? Where was he a professor?

7. How and why did he protest against the abuse of indulgences? The effect of this protest? How did the scope of the controversy enlarge through Prierias' attack?

8. What was the importance for Luther's development of his discussion with Eck at Leipzig? To what clearer views did it bring him?

9. What were his great controversial tracts of 1520? What was their argument?

10. What was his tract on *Christian Liberty?*

11. How did Luther treat the pope's bull of condemnation? Consequences of the action? His appearance before the Reichstag of Worms? Its significance?

12. What action was taken by the emperor against Luther? How did he escape its consequences? How did he employ his sojourn in the Wartburg?

13. What change of position was forced on Luther by the development of the Reformation after his return from the Wartburg? His death?

14. What were the main results of Luther's work? His significance in Christian history?

ADDITIONAL READING

Philip Schaff, *History of the Christian Church* (New York, 1888), VI, 94-744.

Henry E. Jacobs, *Martin Luther* (New York, 1898).

Williston Walker, *The Reformation* (New York, 1900), pp. 71-146, 181-224.

Thomas M. Lindsay, *A History of the Reformation* (New York, 1906), Vol. I.

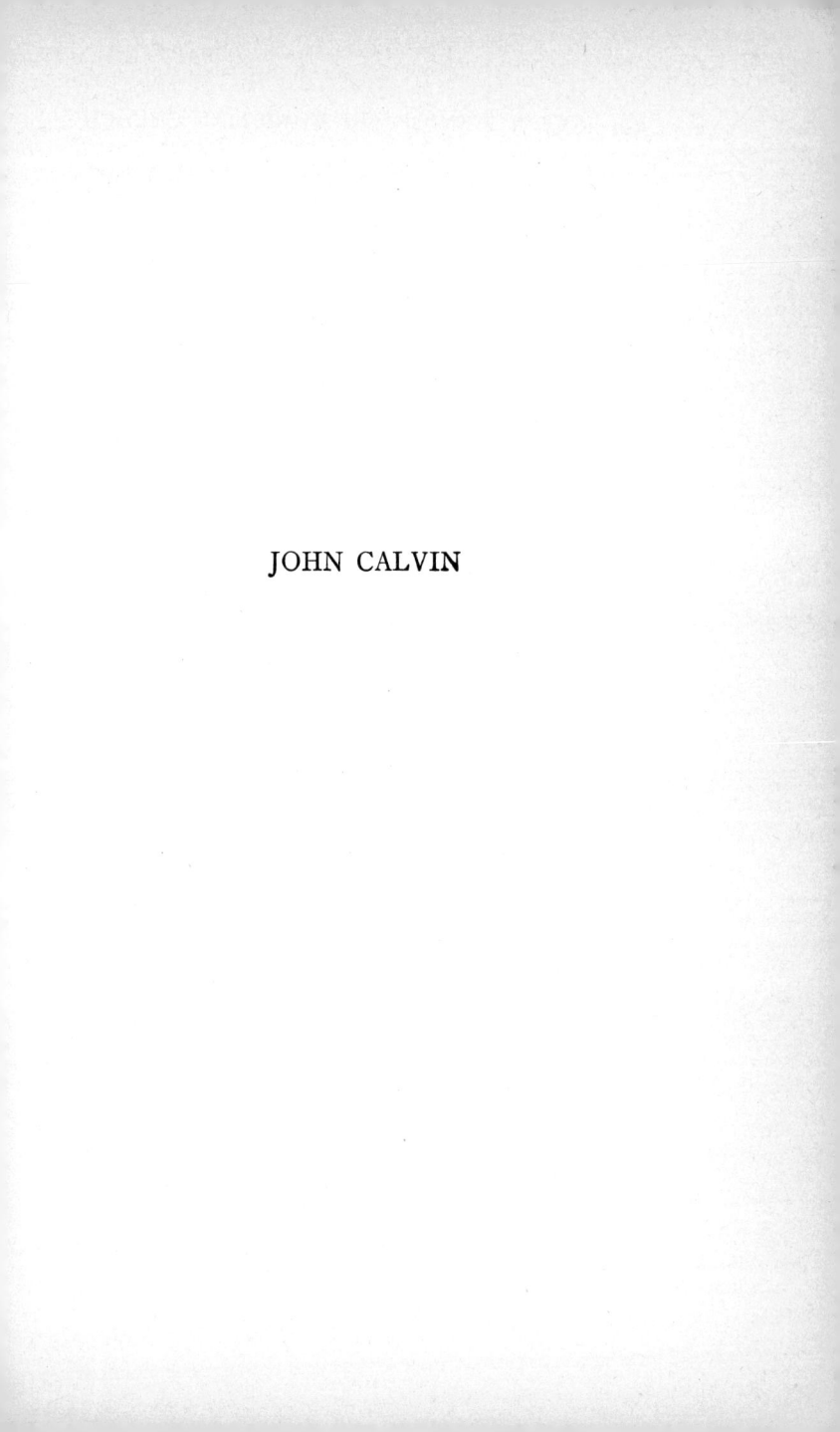

JOHN CALVIN

XIII
JOHN CALVIN

Contemporary with much of Luther's work, though later in its initiation, an independent and more radical reformatory movement ran its course in Switzerland. Its leader was Ulrich Zwingli. Born in Wildhaus, on January 1, 1484, a few weeks later than Luther, Zwingli obtained an excellent education in the "new learning," and was in hearty sympathy with the humanistic feeling that men should go back of the interpretations of the Middle Ages to the grand sources of Christian truth, the Scriptures. It was this impulse, rather than a profound religious experience such as Luther enjoyed, that made him a reformer. His first pastorate in Glarus, from 1506 to 1516, was followed by more than two years in Einsiedeln. In December, 1518, he was called to Zürich, and there his real reformatory work began. By 1522 he had rejected the Lenten fast as without scriptural support. The same year he married. In 1523 he defended in public debate the sole authority of Scripture, and the immediate headship of Christ over the church. With the support of the Zürich magistrates the pictures, crucifixes, and images were removed from the churches in 1524, and in 1525 the communion was substituted for the mass.

Church services were reduced to a Puritan simplicity. Luther, conservative by nature, held that all was allowable in worship which the Word of God did not expressly condemn, thus retaining many of the older usages and adornments. The radical Zwingli felt that nothing should be retained for which express warrant could not be found in the Bible. Hence Swiss worship was from the first of an unadorned and severely intellectual character. This heritage was to pass to the reformed churches of France, Holland, and Scotland, and to the Puritans of England and America.

Zwingli's comparative radicalism appeared also in his doctrine of the Lord's Supper. His rejection of any form of the physical presence of Christ led to a bitter controversy with Luther, and the permanent separation of the Swiss and German reform movements at the Marburg Colloquy in October, 1529.

The reform movement spread rapidly in German-speaking Switzerland. The great canton of Bern was won for it in 1528, and that of Basel in 1529. Appenzell, St. Gall, and Schaffhausen joined the movement. The Zwinglian type of reformation found support also outside of Switzerland in the important German city of Strassburg, where Martin Bucer (1491–1551), surpassed in influence throughout Germany only by Luther and Melanchthon, was disposed to sympathize with Zwingli rather than with Luther. Controversy between the Protestant and

JOHN CALVIN

Catholic cantons in Switzerland led, however, on October 11, 1531, to a battle at Cappel between Zürich and its Roman neighbors in which Zwingli lost his life. His work was not lost, for it came under the wise and patient leadership at Zürich of Heinrich Bullinger (1504-75); and the Swiss movement as a whole was soon to be remodeled and given a world-wide significance by the reformer of French Switzerland, John Calvin.

The beginnings of the reform movement in France, from which land Calvin was to come, were, like those of Switzerland, closely connected with the revival of learning. A group of scholars, of whom Jacques Le Fèvre (?-1536) was the leader in Paris and its vicinity, were actively following the humanistic path of study of the Scriptures and of opposition to superstitions and abuses. These men were seeking a warmer religious life, without thought of breaking with the Roman church, before the fame of Luther's struggle had spread abroad. Their work affected many in high position, though it seems not to have touched the common people, and, indeed, the population of France as a whole had little of that hostility toward the papacy, that was widespread among the masses in Germany. It was in this humanistic, semi-reformatory atmosphere that Calvin's religious life was to have its first awakening.

John Calvin was born in Noyon, a little city about fifty-eight miles north of Paris, on July 10, 1509.

He therefore belonged to the second generation of the Reformers. His father was a self-made man, who had risen to influence in the legal and administrative service of the bishop and chapter of Noyon, a man eagerly ambitious for his sons and anxious to give them all the advantages in his power. Among the boy's friends were the sons of the noble family of Hangest, and this acquaintance doubtless gave to him a familiarity with the ways of polite society such as few of the Reformers enjoyed. After receiving such education as Noyon permitted, Calvin was sent, in 1523, when fourteen, to the University of Paris, where he pursued the undergraduate course till its completion, probably in 1528, and not merely became master of a brilliant Latin style, but gained much skill in logical argument. The expenses of these student days were paid by ecclesiastical appointments in and near Noyon, though Calvin never received ordination either as a Catholic or a Protestant.

Calvin's father had originally intended him for a clerical career, but had now quarreled over business matters with the chapter of the Noyon Cathedral whose agent he was. At his father's insistence he now turned to the study of law, in the universities of Orléans and Bourges. Here he also engaged in the pursuit of the Latin classics and began his acquaintance with Greek. The long hours of labor to which he forced himself gave him a brilliant reputation as a student, but permanently undermined his health, leaving him subject thenceforth to severe attacks of nervous dyspepsia. Throughout his student days, however, he made many warm friendships and was evidently much beloved by such of his companions as shared his intimacy.

The death of his father in 1531, when his course as a lawyer was practically completed, left Calvin free to carry out his own wishes. He therefore took up residence once more in Paris as a student of the classics, with the purpose of pursuing the scholar's career. The fruit of these studies was his first book, his *Commentary on Seneca's Treatise on Clemency*, published in 1532. It is a marvel of classical learning, the more remarkable that its author was not yet twenty-three. It reveals a high sense of moral values, but it shows, equally, that religious considerations had not yet the first place in his regard. He was still primarily interested in questions of scholarship. The year following the printing of this book was spent by Calvin in further study of law in Orléans, but in the autumn of 1533 he was once more in Paris, and in hearty sympathy with his friend Nicolas Cop, whose strongly Protestant address, delivered as rector of the university on November 1, put that institution in turmoil. It has been alleged that Calvin wrote the address. Of this there is no sufficient proof; but that it voiced sentiments with which he was in essential agreement there can be no doubt, and contemporary letters show that religion was now uppermost in his thoughts. A great change had come to him since he wrote his *Seneca*—a change which he himself called his "conversion." Unfortunately the circumstances and the date of this spiritual transformation are exceedingly obscure. It probably took place late in 1532 or early in 1533; and it is evident that it involved not merely spiritual enlightenment, and a recognition of the supreme authority of the Scriptures, but a conscious submission of his will to that of God. In obedience to God's will he must give up the career of scholarly quiet that was opening so brilliantly, and court poverty and danger. This central experience made the divine sovereignty always prominent in Calvin's religious thought. As Luther's consciousness of relief from the sense of guilt placed justification by faith alone in the forefront of his convictions, so Calvin's obedience to God's guidance, as he conceived it, made the divine rulership a cornerstone of his later theology.

The commotion caused by Cop's address compelled Calvin to fly from Paris, and he now spent some months in wandering and concealment. In May, 1534, he was in Noyon, where he resigned his ecclesiastical benefices from which he had thus far drawn revenue, and was briefly imprisoned in connection with a tumult in one of the churches. Part of this time of retirement was spent at Angoulême as the guest of his friend, Louis du Tillet; and in his hospitable home Calvin seems to have carried on the studies which were, a little later, to result in the *Institutes*. The outbreak of severe persecution in the autumn of 1534, however, compelled Calvin and du Tillet to seek refuge in the Protestant city of Basel in northern Switzerland.

The most significant incident of Calvin's residence in Basel was the publication, in March, 1536, of the first edition of his *Institutes*—a work which he had substantially completed in the preceding August, when he was little more than twenty-six years of age. It is the clearest, most logical, and most readable exposition of Protestant doctrine that the Reformation age produced, and it gave its youthful author at once a European fame. Calvin labored on its elaboration nearly all his active life. It may be said to have attained doctrinal completeness in the second edition (1539), and perfection of presentation in its final and much enlarged form issued twenty years later; but its interpretation of Christian truth was always essentially the same. To this masterful treatise Calvin prefaced a remarkable letter to Francis I of France, defending the Protestants of that land from the criticisms of their enemies, and vindicating their rights to a respectful hearing. No man had yet spoken so effectively in their behalf, and with this letter Calvin took a position of assured leadership in the party whose cause he pleaded.

A brief visit to Ferrara in Italy followed the publication of the *Institutes*. Calvin then returned to Paris to secure his brother and sister and settle his business affairs, preliminary to intended removal to Protestant Strassburg. War compelled a detour by Geneva. He reached there late in July, 1536, intending to spend a single night; but was met by the entreaties and admonitions of his friend, Guillaume Farel, to remain and engage with him in the establishment of the Reformation in the city. To Calvin it seemed a call of God, and he now began his Genevan work.

No city could have seemed less promising than Geneva to one who, like Calvin, believed that the prime duty of minister and magistrate alike was the cultivation of strict, conscientious, Christian character. Pressed upon by the Duke of Savoy, with whom its bishop was in sympathy, its liberty-loving citizens had rejected Savoyard influence and driven out the bishop. Farel had labored there since 1532. The mass had been suspended in 1535, and in May, 1536, two months before Calvin's coming, the citizens by formal vote had placed themselves on the Protestant side. Yet their Protestantism was chiefly political hostility to the bishop, not doctrinal conviction. The town was notoriously pleasure-loving, and its religious institutions were all in confusion. It was a most difficult task to which Calvin was thus suddenly invited by Farel.

Calvin began his work with vigor. He would have each inhabitant assent to a Protestant creed, the young instructed in a catechism, all watched over as to moral conduct, the church free to act to the point of excommunication, and the government then to deal with incorrigible offenders. It was the most strenuous programme of moral discipline that Protestantism had yet presented, and it, of course, aroused opposition. The point of attack was the partial freedom from governmental control which Calvin, unlike the German and Swiss reformers before him, demanded for the church. On this issue Calvin and Farel were defeated, and were banished from the city in April, 1538. His work seemed a failure.

The next three years were spent by Calvin in Strassburg and were in many ways the happiest of his life. He was pastor of the church of French refugees and was free to carry out his disciplinary measures; he was a successful teacher of theology; he was honored by the city, and was made its representative in important religious conferences in Germany. Here he married, in August, 1540, the wife who was to be his helpful companion till her death in March, 1549. His Strassburg career did much for him. It enlarged his experience and ripened his thought in every way.

Meanwhile a revolution had occurred in Geneva, his friends were once more in power, and his return was eagerly sought. In September, 1541, with great reluctance, he once more took up the Geneva burden, practically on his own terms. The ecclesiastical constitution of the city now established was not indeed quite what he desired, but it put into effective operation his leading ideas. Its most important feature was the *Consistory*, made up of the ministers of the city and of twelve laymen, to whom the moral oversight of Geneva was referred. It could proceed in discipline as far as excommunication. If that failed to effect amendment, the power of the civil government was called in. Naturally, in practice, this ecclesiastical supervision aroused great opposition, not only from those to whom any discipline was irksome, but from more worthy representatives of old Genevan families to whom Calvin and his associates seemed foreign intruders who had imposed their yoke on the city. His stay was a constant contest, and Calvin was many times on the brink of banishment. But he fought his way courageously, and the influx of exiles for their faith, chiefly from France, whom Calvin attracted to Geneva, constantly increased his following. At the very crisis of the struggle, in 1553, the brilliant but erratic Michel Servetus, the critic of the doctrine of the Trinity, came to the city, and his condemnation became a trial of strength between Calvin and his enemies. Though Calvin wished for Servetus an easier death than that at the stake, which was inflicted on October 27, 1553, he had long determined

JOHN CALVIN

to crush that ill-balanced thinker; and the incident is one which shows Calvin in his least attractive light. A riot in 1555, however, gave Calvin's friends in Geneva the upper hand; and his position was made permanently secure by the admission of a large number of the refugees to citizenship. Thenceforward, to his death, he had no serious opposition in Geneva.

Calvin now crowned his Genevan edifice by the "Academy" in 1559. This famous school, which was for a century the most distinguished seat of education under the control of the Reformed churches, became at once a training institution for the Protestant ministry of France, and its influence was profoundly felt in the Netherlands, England, Scotland, and Germany. For Calvin, Geneva was never an end in itself. He would make it a city of refuge for persecuted Protestants, an example of a strictly disciplined Christian community, and a center for ministerial training whence men should go forth to advance the Reformation cause. In all this he succeeded. And, besides this constant labor in Geneva, Calvin exercised a real, though unofficial, superintendence over all non-German and non-Anglican Protestantism. Before his death, great reform movements bearing his impress had begun, and in some instances had far advanced, in France, the Netherlands, Scotland, Poland, Hungary, and even in the Rhine Valley section of Germany. They reproduced his theology and his conceptions of the well-disciplined Christian life. He trained many of their leaders, and maintained an enormous and far-reaching correspondence. To Calvin was due the essential spiritual likeness that came to exist among the scattered family of non-Lutheran Protestantism; and the territorial growth of Calvinism had but begun at his death. His system was destined powerfully to mold English thought through the Puritans, and American religious development through the Pilgrim and Puritan, the Scotch-Irish, the Dutch, the Huguenot, and the German-Reformed elements in our national life.

With all this multiplicity of tasks Calvin's pen was always busy. His commentaries, which cover the greater part of the Bible, are the best that the Reformation age produced. His *Institutes* were constantly improved. His minor treatises discussed the most important questions of the day. He was unremitting in attention to preaching and to theological lectures. This activity was the more remarkable because his health was always precarious, and in the latter years of his life he was constantly an invalid. He died, worn out by his burdens and disabilities, when not yet fifty-five years of age, in Geneva, on May 27, 1564.

Calvin's theology was essentially Augustinian, without the ecclesiasticism with which the great African thinker combined his doctrine of grace. God is all powerful in creation and providence. In him is the sole source of all good, wherever manifested. The object of all worthy laws, as well as of right individual action, is conformity to the will of God. Man's chief duty and enjoyment is to know him and what he requires and offers. This knowledge is adequately imparted only by the Scriptures, which approve themselves as the very Word of God by the inward testimony of the Holy Spirit in the heart of the believing reader. No other authority than this Word is of value.

Man was created upright, but by Adam's fall has become wholly bad. He is of himself utterly incapable of any good act, and his salvation is totally the work of God. Its basis is what Christ has wrought for men, but to be available that must become man's personal possession. Christ must become ours. We must enter into vital union with him. This union is conditioned on faith; but this faith is itself the gift of God, and comes by "the secret efficacy of the Spirit." Grace therefore flows not through the sacraments alone, but by the divine Spirit who works when and where and how he will. As with Luther, the sacraments are seals attesting God's promises.

The consequence of faith is the Christian life. To Calvin, far more than to Luther, this life is one of strenuous endeavor. Though no longer judged by the law of God, the Christian sees in it the pattern to which his life should conform. "We are justified not without, and yet not by works." No man can be really a Christian without aspiring to holiness of life. This insistence is one of the prime features of Calvinism. It made character a main test of all true religious life.

Since all grace is from God, and man deserves nothing of himself, the salvation or loss of any individual must depend on the divine purpose. Calvin advanced beyond Augustine in holding that no one in whom God had really begun a work of grace could fail to be saved. From this doctrine of election therefore he drew great encouragement.

In his theory of the church, Calvin held that, in the last analysis, it is the invisible company of the elect; but as known to us it is the body of those who profess the Christian faith. It is properly governed only by officers of divine appointment—the pastors, teachers, elders, and deacons of the New Testament, who are called to their duties inwardly by God, and outwardly by the consent of those they serve. Calvin thus recognized a true share of the people in the choice of their church officers.

Calvinism has proved of great service to civil liberty, rather as a consequence of Calvin's principles than of a deliberate purpose on his part. His doctrine that when God's commands are clear no contrary human enactment deserves any obedience, tended to develop independent judgment as to the righteousness of any statute of man's making; while

JOHN CALVIN

his principle that church officers receive their places with the consent of those they serve, led men to regard them as responsible to their congregations—a feeling easily carried to civil governorships and other places of political rule. The debt of America to his work, religiously and politically, is well-nigh immeasurable.

QUESTIONS

1. Give some account of the life and work of Zwingli. How did he resemble and how did he differ from Luther?

2. What influences favored the beginning of the reform movement in France?

3. Describe Calvin's parentage, early life, and education.

4. In what studies did Calvin gain distinction?

5. What was the nature of Calvin's conversion? What experience in it affected his theology?

6. How did Calvin come to leave France?

7. When were the *Institutes* published, and what were their significance?

8. What was the condition of Geneva and how came Calvin to settle there? Why was it a hard field?

9. What did Calvin attempt in his first stay in Geneva? How did it end?

10. What was the value to Calvin of his residence in Strassburg?

11. How came Calvin to return to Geneva? The *Consistory*? The sources of opposition? His success in the struggle?

12. What did Calvin aim to make of Geneva? How far did he succeed?

13. What were the results of Calvin's work outside of Geneva?

14. Calvin's varied activities? His death?
15. Speak of some features of Calvin's theology.
16. What was his service to civil liberty? Why?

ADDITIONAL READING

Philip Schaff, *History of the Christian Church* (New York, 1892), VII, 1-844.

John F. Hurst, *History of the Christian Church* (Cincinnati, 1897), II, 223-304.

Williston Walker, *John Calvin* (New York, 1906).

JOHN KNOX

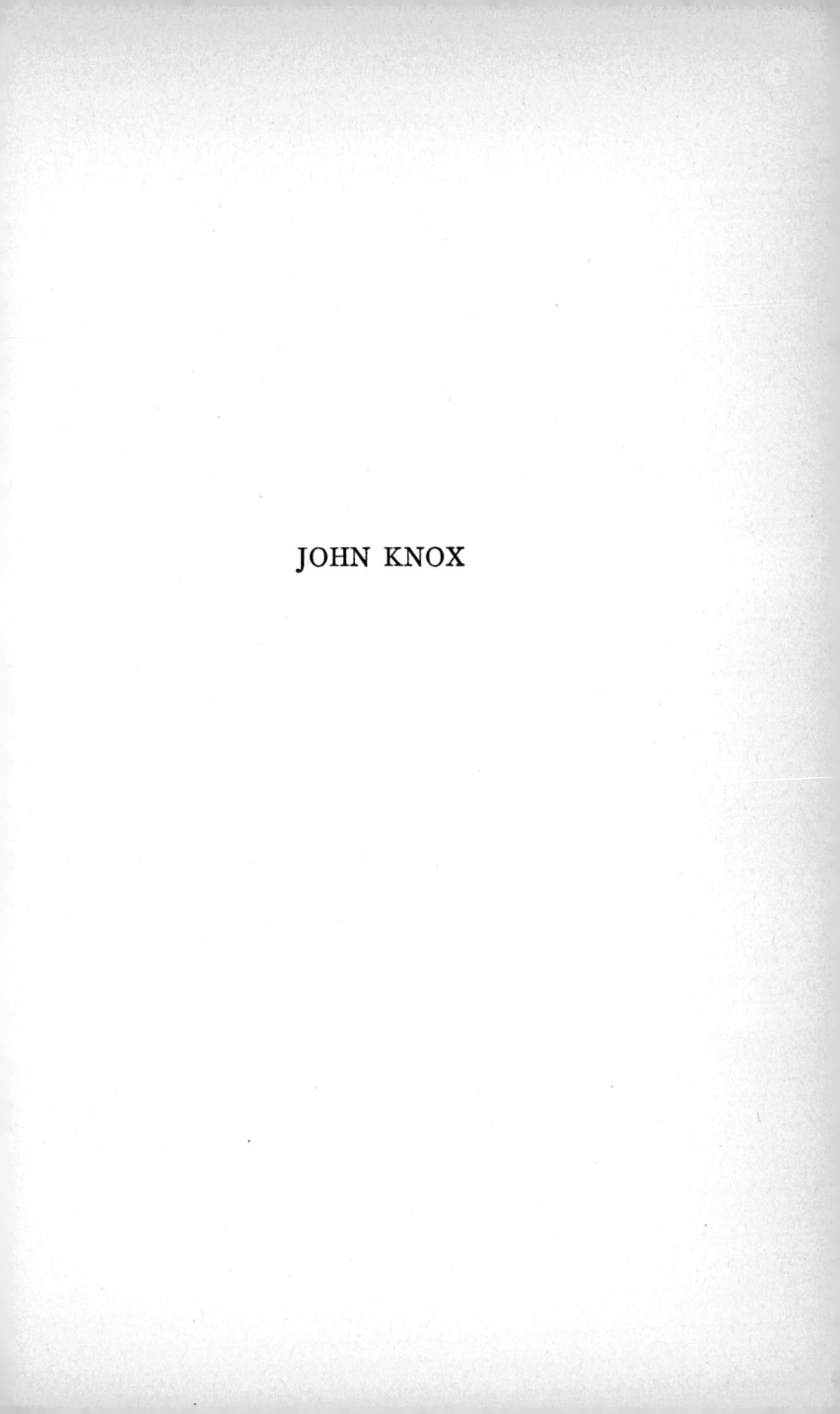

XIV
JOHN KNOX

Calvin's most eminent spiritual disciple was undoubtedly John Knox, if the permanency and widely extended character of his work are the criteria of estimate. He had little of the originality of Luther, Zwingli, or Calvin; but though principally indebted for his theology and his form of church organization to the Genevan reformer, Knox possessed so impressive an individuality and such personal force, and fought so peculiar and successful a battle, that he had high independent significance among the leaders of the Reformation age. His is not only the greatest figure in Scottish history, but the history of the Reformation in Scotland is largely the story of Knox's life.

Scotland before the Reformation was an undeveloped land.[1] Its business and its culture were alike backward, it was torn by internal controversies in which the nobles and the great churchmen bore full share. Its monarchy was weak. Its church, though wealthy enough to possess half the land of the kingdom, was notoriously corrupt. In its political relations, Scotland was harassed by well-grounded fears of English aggression, which inclined the little

[1] In this sketch the writer has made considerable use of what he has already said in his volume *The Reformation*.

kingdom to look for aid to France. The Reformation movement was far advanced on the Continent before it was felt in Scotland. The first Scottish Protestant martyr, Patrick Hamilton, was burned under Archbishop James Beaton at St. Andrews in 1528, and this policy of repression was even more severely carried out under James Beaton's nephew and successor, Cardinal David Beaton; but Protestantism grew very slowly till it found a leader in Knox.

John Knox was born probably in the Giffordgate district of Haddington, thirteen miles east of Edinburgh, on some unknown day probably of the year 1513.[1] His father, William Knox, was in humble circumstances, but the boy had the advantage of a good school in Haddington, and entered a university, probably that of St. Andrews, where he came under the influence of the leading scholastic theologian of Scotland, John Major (1469-1550). While thoroughly Roman in doctrine, Major criticized the papal administration, wished to limit the number of monks, and held that civil authority is derived from the people, who can depose and even execute unjust rulers. In the opinion last described he was

[1] The traditional year of Knox's birth is 1505; but the evidence for 1513 seems stronger. Besides the claim of Giffordgate as the scene of his birth, that event has been assigned to Gifford and to Morham, each village about four miles from Haddington. The subject is well discussed by Professor Henry Cowan, *John Knox* (New York, 1905), pp. 22-29, 45-48.

to have an energetic disciple in Knox. By 1540 Knox had been ordained to the priesthood. He also acted as notary, and served as a tutor, by 1544 having under his care several young sons of Lothian families of position.

It was apparently in 1543 that Knox's spiritual awakening, or at least his conversion to Protestantism, took place under the preaching of a former monk, Thomas William of Athelstaneford, the particular passage of Scripture that first impressed him being the seventeenth chapter of John's Gospel. A few months later he came under the influence of George Wishart (1513–46), a powerful Protestant preacher for whom he conceived a great affection. Knox narrowly escaped sharing Wishart's arrest, and was profoundly moved by that vigorous missionary's death by fire at St. Andrew's on March 1, 1546. Wishart had represented not merely Protestantism but English interests. His opponents had sided with France and the papacy. As a result of this partly religious, partly political, contention, Cardinal Beaton was murdered by some of Wishart's supporters, on May 29, 1546. Knox had no part in the deed; but, once done, he fully approved of it; and when, some time after, the conspirators and their friends took possession of the Castle of St. Andrews for safety, he joined them, in April, 1547. Here he was chosen minister of the little company, and entered on his office with a fiery sermon against the papacy and all its works. Here, first of any in Scotland, he publicly administered the Lord's Supper in Protestant fashion. English help did not come to the beleaguered garrison; but the French party procured aid from France. The castle was captured; and from September, 1547, to February or March, 1549, Knox suffered the fate of a galley-slave, chained to the rowing-bench of a French war-vessel. Even under these circumstances, and the added distress of severe illness, his courage did not desert him; and he confidently trusted, and made others believe, that he would yet preach in his native land.

Knox's release through an exchange of prisoners was followed by a pastorate under the auspices of the Protestant government which ruled England in the name of Edward VI, at Berwick on the Tweed. His success there was great, and resulted in his promotion to Newcastle, his appointment as one of the English royal chaplains, and finally the offer of the bishopric of Rochester. That important dignity he refused, not so much by reason of any opposition to the episcopal office, as from dislike of the revenues and state of the English prelates, and his own patriotic determination to renew his work in Scotland as soon as opportunity might offer. Though in his judgment, as in that of the Reformers generally, all ministers were spiritually equal, he objected no more than Calvin or Melanchthon to the retention of purely

JOHN KNOX

administrative supervision by a "bishop" over the ministers of a district.

The death of Edward VI in 1553 was followed in England by the Roman reaction under Queen Mary. Knox saw that further work in England was impossible for the present, and after waiting quite as long as safety permitted, he, like many of his fellow-Protestants, fled to the Continent early in 1554. He made his way promptly to Geneva, where he was heartily welcomed by Calvin, with whom he was already in spiritual sympathy. His stay at this time in Geneva was short, however. In September, 1554, a call came to him to become the pastor of the English exiles in the German city of Frankfort. Thither he went at Calvin's insistence; but his pastorate proved one of his most stormy experiences. The refugees there gathered had all fled from England in fear for their lives; but even a common misery could not prevent the outbreaking among them of what was soon to be the great Puritan controversy of Queen Elizabeth's reign. Some wished to use the Prayer-Book as it had been established in England in the reign of the late Edward VI; others, of whom Knox was one, thought that it preserved too many vestiges of Romanism and favored a simpler service. Knox found his position untenable, and in March, 1555, was back in the friendly shelter of Geneva.

Meanwhile the situation in Scotland had improved from Knox's point of view. Mary of Guise, the

French mother of the youthful Mary "Queen of Scots," though a devoted Catholic, had coquetted with nobles of Protestant leanings to obtain the regency in 1554. The return of England under Mary to the Roman obedience favored the growth of Protestantism in Scotland by reason of the disposition then characteristic of the hard-pressed little country to follow a policy opposite to that which England pursued. Under such circumstances Knox judged the time opportune, and, in September, 1555, was once more in Scotland. Here he preached widely and with effect; but his success was even greater in organizing a definitely Protestant party. He persuaded the leading Protestant sympathizers to cease attending mass. He entered into relations with three youthful nobles who were to be leaders in the Protestant cause—Lord Erskine, afterward Earl of Mar, Lord James Stuart, afterward Earl of Moray, both to be regents of Scotland, and Lord Lorne, afterward Earl of Argyle. He defied the bishops. But Knox evidently judged the time not fully ripe for successful overthrow of the old church. The Genevan English-speaking congregation urged him to return, and in September, 1556, he was back in the Swiss city.

Here in Geneva Knox made his headquarters till January, 1559. He was pastor of the English congregation. He was on affectionate terms with Calvin, whom he intensely admired. He spoke

JOHN KNOX

French fluently, and his Genevan stay was interrupted with courageous missionary work in Dieppe in France and by visits to other French cities in aid of the Evangelical cause. At Geneva he published, in 1558, what proved later a source of great annoyance to himself, his *First Blast of the Trumpet against the Monstrous Regiment of Women*. Moved by the opposition of Mary Tudor in England, of Catherine de' Medici in France, and of the regent, Mary of Guise, in Scotland, to the Protestant cause, Knox argued that no woman could rightfully exercise sovereignty. He did not foresee that England would soon have a Protestant queen—and Queen Elizabeth never forgave him.

While Knox was thus busied, the Protestant cause was gaining in Scotland. On December 3, 1557, its leaders drafted at Edinburgh the first Scottish "Covenant," agreeing "to maintain, set forward, and establish the most blessed Word of God and His congregation," from which they soon obtained the nickname of the "Lords of the Congregation." The political situation soon strongly favored their cause. Fear of overbearing French influence was increased when the long betrothal of Mary, "Queen of Scots," ended in her marriage in April, 1558, to the heir to the French throne who, in July of the next year, was to become Francis II of France. In November, 1558, Elizabeth became Queen of England. By the Roman party she was held to be illegitimate, as the daughter of Anne Boleyn, whose marriage to Henry VIII that party had never recognized. If she had no right to the English throne, then Mary "Queen of Scots" was queen of England. Mary asserted her claim. Elizabeth in self-defense could do no less than countenance the Protestant party in Scotland, and many not Protestants trembled at the thought of the union of France, England, and Scotland under the joint sovereignty of Francis and Mary. So it was that Knox, from his post of observation in Geneva, deemed the time for battle to have come at last, and on May 2, 1559, arrived in Edinburgh. Intense, religious, argumentative, democratic, fearless, intolerant, forceful, Knox was just the man for leadership in the crisis he had so laboriously prepared. It was not a religious struggle only. To a large degree it was a great national conflict against foreign dominance in which he fought.

At Perth Knox heard that the regent, Mary of Guise, had declared him an outlaw. He replied with a vehement denunciation of the mass. The mob rose. The images in the churches were destroyed and the monasteries were sacked. Both sides raised what troops they could. Scotland was in civil war. Similar scenes of violent abolition took place at St. Andrew's and elsewhere, and the nobles hastened to put themselves in possession of the church lands. The regent was drawing her support from France, and Knox now negotiated success-

JOHN KNOX

fully for pecuniary assistance for his cause from England. On his advice, the "Lords of the Congregation," in October, 1559, suspended Mary of Guise from the regency so far as they could, and the battle was practically decided for the Protestant cause, when, in January, 1560, an English fleet, sent by Elizabeth, came to its assistance, and was soon followed by an English army. The two rival forces struggled ineffectively for a time, but, in June, 1560, the regent died, and within a month the French and English forces were withdrawn by treaty. In the absence of the queen, Mary, in France, it was agreed that the government of Scotland should be in the hands of a council of Scotchmen. It was a great victory for self-government in Scotland, against French interference, as well as for the right of the land to determine its religious affairs, and the chief agent in the result had been Knox himself.

In August the Scottish Parliament met, under radical Protestant control. In form it was not strictly legal, for it lacked the consent of the queen, but it was fairly representative of the nation. Its action was drastic. Romanism was abolished. Death was threatened for a third conviction of celebrating the mass. A Confession of Faith, drafted by Knox and five ministerial associates, and Calvinistic in doctrine, was adopted. The ancient Roman edifice was utterly overthrown.

This radical action made necessary the complete

reorganization of the Scottish church. Knox and his ministerial associates had been laboring on a constitution before the meeting of Parliament, and it was now completed after the adjournment of that body. It is known as the *First Book of Discipline*.[1] The essential features of the system of church government therein outlined were derived from Calvin, and are of the type known as Presbyterian. In each local congregation was a minister, elders, and deacons, all chosen by the people they served, the minister permanently with the approval of other ministers of the region, and the elders and deacons by the congregation for terms of one year. To the deacons the care of the temporalities and the relief of the poor was intrusted. The elders with the minister, the "session" of Presbyterian usage, were the disciplinary council. Neighboring ministers and elders met weekly for Bible-study—an assembly, that after Knox's death became the "Presbytery." The ministers and elders of a district met as a superior court in the "Synod;" and chosen ministers and lay representatives convened as a supreme ecclesiastical court for all Scotland once a year in the "General Assembly," the first session of which gathered in December, 1560. In two features Knox departed from the Genevan system. He would have "superintendents" in administrative supervision over the

[1] That prepared largely by Andrew Melville, and approved by the General Assembly in 1578, is the "Second."

ministers of given districts; and owing to the scarcity of suitable ministers, he provided for "readers" till the want could be supplied. In public worship Knox introduced substantially the Genevan service, in the form in which it had been used in his congregation in that city. This made the sermon central, and provided opportunity both for free and written prayers. Could Knox have done as he wished, the income of the old church would have been used for schools, church expenses, and charity; but he could do nothing with the greedy nobles who seized it for themselves. Owing to their opposition the "Book" was not established by law, but it became the pattern essentially in accordance with which the Scottish church was organized.

Knox's battle seemed about won before the close of 1560. He himself was chosen minister in Edinburgh. But a hard struggle was before him to maintain what had been secured. Mary "Queen of Scots" became a widow in December, 1560, and returned to Scotland in the August following, determined to bring back the country to Rome, and to secure for herself the succession to the English throne. Her charm and shrewdness, and the sympathy felt for her bereavement, won her many friends. In Knox and in the spirit which he had fostered she met her chief obstacles. The struggle was waged on his part with weapons of invective that seemed coarse and often brutal, but the contest was none the less one for popular sovereignty and the right of the majority to determine its form of religion. "What are you in this commonwealth?" asked Mary of Knox in 1563. "A subject born within the same," he replied, "and though neither earl, lord, nor baron, God has made me a profitable member." He criticized her Romanizing policy unsparingly, declaring when she set up Roman worship in her own chapel that "one mass was more fearful to him than ten thousand armed enemies," and boldly affirmed to her face that subjects may rightfully depose a ruler who opposes the Word of God.

Knox, however, could hardly have succeeded as he did in the struggle had it not been for Mary's misdeeds and misfortunes. She angered public sentiment, in 1563, by proposing a marriage with Don Carlos, son of Philip II of Spain. She quarreled with Darnley, whom she married in 1565. She made prominent among her advisers an Italian favorite, David Rizzio, who was murdered in March, 1566, by a conspiracy of disaffected nobles, in which the jealous Darnley himself was involved. On February 10, 1567, Darnley was himself murdered—with what connivance on Mary's part has been ever since one of the battlegrounds of historic discussion. On May 15, following, she married the Earl of Bothwell, who had had a share in Darnley's death. Public opinion was outraged. On June 15 Mary was taken captive by her nobles and soon forced to abdicate in

JOHN KNOX

favor of her infant son, James VI, and a regency to be administered by the Protestant Earl of Moray. In the discussions following Mary's capture, Knox seems to have contributed the decisive influence in favor of forcing her abdication. The Parliament which followed, in December, 1567, gave full legal establishment to the enactments of 1560, and the Scottish church.

Knox hoped that his work was done; but the condition of the land remained a cause of anxiety to him as long as he lived. Mary escaped from imprisonment in 1568, and found many supporters. Her defeat was followed by her flight to England and her imprisonment by Elizabeth, where she remained a scheming captive, menacing the Protestantism of both lands, till her execution as a conspirator against the English queen in 1587.

In October, 1570, Knox suffered a paralytic stroke. He regained partial strength and labored with something of his old fire till shortly before his death. On November 24, 1572, he met his end, in calm assurance, and in full enjoyment of spiritual comfort. To some extent he was a disappointed man in his last days. He saw many of his cherished plans for the church and education frustrated, as he believed, by the greed and unspirituality of the nobles. But when he died at Edinburgh it was in the fulness of an accomplished work of vast dimensions; and no more fitting characterization was ever spoken of him than the often-quoted words of Regent Morton at his burial: "Here lieth a man who in his life never feared the face of man."

QUESTIONS

1. What was the condition of Scotland before the Reformation? Why was Scotland closely bound politically to France?

2. Who was the first Scotchman to die for Protestantism? Was Protestantism late in getting a foothold in Scotland?

3. What were Knox's parentage, birthplace, and education? What influence had John Major on him?

4. Under what influences was Knox converted to Protestantism? What were his relations to Wishart?

5. How came Knox to be in the Castle of St. Andrews? His ministry there? How signalized? His experience as a prisoner?

6. What was Knox's work in England? How was it regarded?

7. What was the value to Knox of his stay in Geneva? The Frankfort episode?

8. How did he organize the Reformation movement in Scotland in 1555–56?

9. What office did Knox fill in his second stay in Geneva? His *First Blast?*

10. What political conditions facilitated his work in Scotland in 1559? Character of the reform movement?

11. The work of the Parliament of 1560? How did Knox organize the church?

12. What were Knox's relations to Mary "Queen of Scots"? How was she injured by her own misdeeds and mistakes?

13. Knox's death? His character and work?

ADDITIONAL READING

Thomas McCrie, *The Life of John Knox* (Edinburgh, 1812, and many later editions).

Peter H. Brown, *John Knox, a Biography* (London, 1895).

Henry Cowan, *John Knox* (New York, 1905).

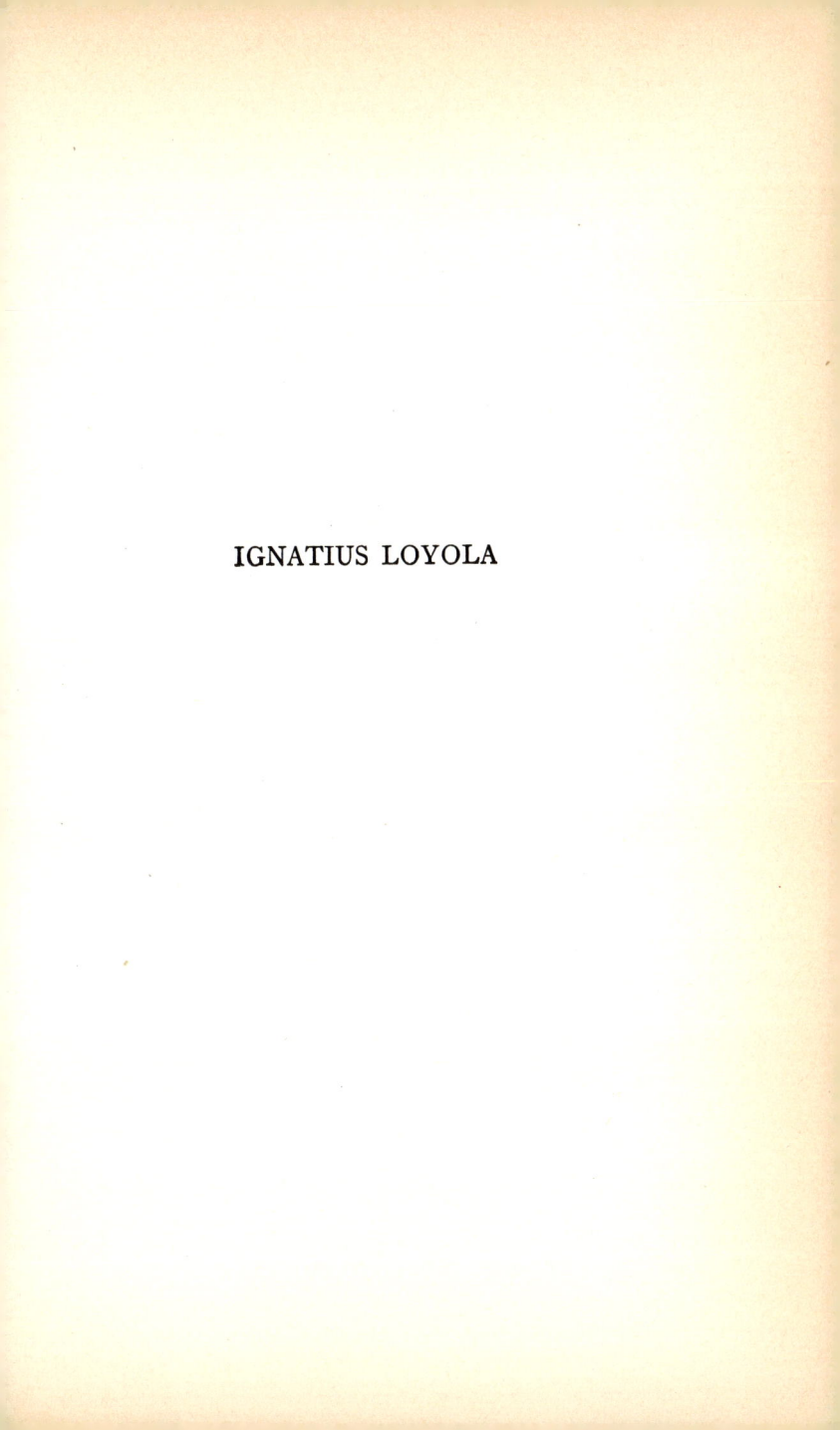

IGNATIUS LOYOLA

XV
IGNATIUS LOYOLA

The Reformation age witnessed not merely the birth of Protestantism; it beheld a great revival of the spiritual life in the Roman Catholic church itself—a movement to which the name "Counter-Reformation" has often, but not wholly adequately, been given. To a large extent this awakening was induced by the great Protestant revolt. But it is not wholly traceable to that upheaval. Its beginnings had been manifested before the time of Luther; and, like the Protestant revival, it owed much to the quickening spirit of the Renaissance. Unlike Protestantism, this awakening had no quarrel with mediaeval doctrine. It was content with a better-educated and more faithful clergy, the abolition of the grosser abuses, and a warmer spiritual life.

In no country in Europe[1] was this Roman revival so conspicuously in evidence as in Spain. That land was rising to a political significance heretofore unsuspected, that made it the marvel of the closing years of the fifteenth century. The marriage of Ferdinand of Aragon and Isabella of Castile, in 1469, ultimately resulted in placing the larger part of the Spanish peninsula under their effective rule. Their

[1] In this sketch the writer has borrowed some sentences from his *The Reformation*.

conquest of Granada, in 1492, ended Moorish sovereignty in that land; and the same year witnessed the discovery, under Spanish auspices, of the New World, from which a wealth soon flowed to the Spanish treasury such as no mediaeval king had enjoyed. Spain, by the beginning of the sixteenth century, had suddenly become well-nigh the most powerful land of Europe; and this political growth had been accompanied by a great effort for the intellectual and moral improvement of the Spanish church in which the deeply religious queen, Isabella, and her trusted religious adviser, Ximenes, had been leaders. The Spanish church had awakened, before 1500, to new zeal. Fanatically tenacious of mediaeval doctrine, it tolerated no change in its theology, but it was the most thoroughly aroused section of Latin Christendom. Of this Spanish awakening the most characteristic and influential product was to be Ignatius Loyola, the founder of the Company of Jesus, or, as its members are generally nicknamed, the Jesuits.

Iñigo Lopez de Recalde was born of the noble Spanish family of Loyola, at its castle in the northern province of Guipuzcoa, in 1491. As a boy, he was trained in the court of Ferdinand and Isabella, and soon developed marked talents as a soldier. Of unshakable courage and a born leader of men, he, though the youngest officer present, decided the slender garrison to defend Pamplona against the overwhelming French army, in 1521. In the storming of the city by its besiegers he showed heroic firmness in defense, but he fell severely wounded by a ball which shattered his leg. Then followed long weeks of invalidism. The young soldier would not readily abandon his career, and the ill-knit bones were repeatedly broken and reset in the vain hope of a more perfect recovery. He had at last to recognize that the soldier's pathway was closed to him forever.

To the man of thirty this was a distressing outcome; but a new vision had come to him in his invalidism. He had read eagerly such books as he could find—a Life of Christ and sketches of the saints. He would imitate them in a new and holier warfare as his great fellow-countryman, Saint Dominick, had done. He would be a knight of the Spirit, waging warfare with the powers of evil. He would serve a nobler lady than any earthly princess—the Virgin herself.

As soon as returning strength permitted, Loyola put his new resolutions into practice. He offered his armor at the shrine of the Virgin in Montserrat, and soon began a life of self-mortification in the Dominican monastery in Manresa. Here he fought the battles for the mastery of his own spirit which ever after colored his religious life. He fasted and prayed. He painfully recalled his sins, till, feeling that their remembrance was a hindrance to his spiritual progress, he resolved to thrust even their recollection behind him and to recount them no more, not even in prayer. He believed that the mysteries of the Trinity, of the Incarnation, and of the creation of the world were revealed to him in vision; but he rejected equally clear spiritual suggestions as of satanic origin; and he made the test of the divine or devilish impulses of his soul their comfort and help, or their disquieting effects. Here he conceived his *Spiritual Exercises*, based indeed in part on earlier treatises by Cisnero of Manresa and the Netherlandish mystics, Zerbolt of Zütphen and Mauburnus of Zwolle, but profoundly original in their treatment. This marvelous work is a drillbook of spiritual self-mastery. Under the guidance of a religious master-at-arms, the disciple is to exercise himself for four weeks in attempts to gain, by strenuous effort of will, a vivid consciousness of man's sinfulness, and of the life and saving work of Christ. The world as a battleground between his Lord and the powers of evil is to be made real to his imagination; and the great facts of salvation are to become part of his mental imagery. Never was there a more remarkable or a more successful attempt to awaken, control, and direct mental pictures. In the order which Ignatius was later to establish each member had to pass through the discipline thus prescribed; and its effects on most minds must have been an unforgettable quickening of the spiritual imagination by which what is usually fantasy was directed into definite pictures of great Christian verities. Loyola would use the visions of the spirit to the full; yet control and direct them absolutely.

This period of spiritual conflict in Manresa was followed by a determined effort to engage in missionary activity. Loyola made his way, in 1523, to Jerusalem. But the Franciscans in authority among the Latin Christians there looked with disfavor on his enterprise; and, finding it impossible to accomplish his purpose, he returned to Spain. The main result of this courageous, but fruitless, enterprise was to convince Loyola that for effective work he must obtain an education. He now began with the very rudiments of Latin in a boys' class in Barcelona. Thence he went for further study at Alcala and to Salamanca. It was hard work; but his perseverance was inexhaustible. Loyola was showing himself, as always, a leader; and he soon gathered a little following, which he drilled in his *Exercises*. This work excited, however, the suspicions of the ecclesiastical authorities, and he narrowly escaped condemnation as an *alumbrado*, or a heretical claimant of special divine illumination. Forbidden to speak on religious themes for four years by the investigators of his orthodoxy, since they deemed him still too ignorant, he left Spain for Paris in 1528, and there took up his studies in the Collège Montaigu, probably just as John Calvin left that seat of learning. In circumstances of great poverty he pursued his work in the university. The years of his stay in Paris were a period of public excitement and involved much of the beginnings of the Reformation in France; but he shared in no conspicuous event. With the utmost persistence, on the contrary, Loyola strove to gain personal influence over his fellow-students, and to train them by his *Exercises*. A group from most various social ranks soon looked to him as its leader. A simple Savoyard, Pierre Lefèvre, a brilliant nobleman of Navarre, Francisco de Xavier, a Spaniard of great learning and organizing talent, Diego Lainez, Alonso Salmeron, likewise a fellow-countryman of Loyola, who was to be a preacher of power, Simon Rodriguez, a Portuguese, and still another Spaniard, Nicolo Bobadilla, with two or three others constituted the little companionship.

With the friends just named Loyola entered into vows in the church of St. Mary on Montmartre, then just outside of Paris, on August 15, 1534. The student associates pledged themselves to engage in missionary labors and the care of the ill in Jerusalem, or, should that prove impossible, wherever the pope should direct. It was at first a student organization for missionary effort, and, as such, the movement was soon carried from the university of Paris to those of Louvain and Cologne.

Ill-health compelled Loyola to return to Spain in 1535, but in 1537 the associates gathered in Venice to carry out their purpose of going to Jerusalem. War rendering that impossible, they began preaching in the cities of Italy. Loyola now determined their name. Italy had seen many military companies in the service of worldly princes; his should be the *Societas Jesu*, the military company of Jesus, for a nobler warfare, but like them bound together by soldierly obedience. The approval of the pope was won with difficulty, but in September, 1540, Paul III sanctioned the association, and, the next year, Loyola was chosen its first "general."

In Loyola's view few were fitted for membership in the society, and all who entered it must undergo long mental and spiritual discipline. As in an army, each must cheerfully and promptly make his superior's will his own, yielding absolute obedience unless the command involved sin. Each should be assigned to the task for which his talents and education best fitted him. That the members should be free for any suitable task, they were burdened with no prescribed dress or lengthy religious duties, such as marked most orders of monks. No religious agency was ever more ingeniously devised. It gave room for the exercise of the most varied and highly trained talents. It appealed to two of the strongest motives that men can feel—labor for others and for self-development in the service of God; but it conditioned their answer to this appeal on a self-surrender and an obedience that, while leaving room for a high degree of individuality, abdicates the highest exercises of the individual judgment and will.

Under Loyola's generalship, which lasted till his death in Rome on July 31, 1556, the society that he founded developed a most manifold activity, and its growth and efficiency but increased under his immediate successors, his early disciple, Diego Lainez (1557-65), and Francisco Borgia (1565-72). It has borne ever since its foundation the impress of his masterful mind. To use Loyola's favorite Pauline quotation, he would have it made "all things to all men." From Italy its preachers were soon reaching out to all the countries of Europe. By Loyola's death it counted more than a thousand members, settled in a hundred places. Under Xavier, appointed to the task by Loyola himself, a great missionary campaign was begun in India in 1542, that before Xavier's death, ten years later, had carried the gospel by his means, all too superficially it is true, to Malacca and Japan. He was but the forerunner of a great company of Jesuit missionaries, who were to labor in India, China, and Japan, and in North and South America. Their story, if not always one of wisdom or of effective method, is one in many instances of intrepid heroism, that shines on the pages of missionary consecration; and in its work for missions the most winsome aspect of the Society of Jesus is to be found.

It was, however, as an opponent of Protestantism

and as a molding force in the revival of Roman Catholicism on the European continent that the society did its most effective, if not its most praiseworthy work. It early devoted itself to the control of higher education, a means of influence the importance of which was clearly perceived by Loyola. Much in the same way as that born leader availed himself of the individualism of his age, and yet made it subservient to a single purpose in his society at large, the Jesuits in their schools took into service the admired humanistic culture of the Renaissance, and yet held it in absolute obedience to the church. Their schools and their instructors who gained a foothold in older seats of learning were greatly admired for more than a century after the founding of the society, and their teaching, the fame of which often attracted pupils whose Protestantism was lukewarm, proved a potent means of extending their influence and renewing the sway of the church which they served.

Though no part of the original intention of the society, its political activity soon became one of its most formidable weapons. That activity was the natural outgrowth of its constitution and principles. The body was international in membership, and bound by strict obedience to generals like Loyola, Lainez, and Borgia, of surpassing political gifts. To them the members reported the minutest affairs of the lands in which they were stationed. The society could not but become a political force. No wonder that the Jesuits proved the chief agents in restoring many of the princes of Germany to the Roman obedience, that they were the terror of such sovereigns as Elizabeth of England or William the Silent of the Netherlands, or that the governments even of the most Catholic lands came ultimately to look upon their activity with fear and hostility.

In their teaching and practice the Jesuits not merely emphasized obedience to the papacy, but those features of Romanism which are most at variance with Protestantism. Devotion to the Virgin was cultivated. Frequent participation in the Lord's Supper was enjoined. The confessional was exalted and its use impressed on the people, and special papal privileges gave the members of the society larger powers of absolution than those ordinarily possessed by simple priests. But this emphasis on the confessional became the doorway to what has seemed to many of the Roman church, as well as to Protestants, a lax conception of moral values. The views of sin characteristic of the society were superficial. An elaborate and unstrenuous system of casuistry was developed. Results were exalted at the expense of the moral worth of the means by which they were achieved; and that only came to be considered fully sin, in the theological sense, which is done with a clear recognition of its evil character, and a conscious consent of the will.

The general tone of Jesuit morality was unstrenuous, not merely when compared with that of Protestantism, but when examined in the light of the stricter teachings of the Roman church itself.

With its faults and virtues, the society founded by Loyola has been since the Reformation the most powerful force in the Roman church. It has had its missionaries, its martyrs, its men of saintly lives and high consecration in abundance. It has also had many a political intriguant and schemer. It did more than any other agency to limit the advance of Protestantism; but it has intensified and developed those tendencies in the Roman church against which Protestantism protested. Its power is still unexhausted, and the work of Loyola must be regarded as one of the most abiding legacies which the sixteenth century has bequeathed to the modern world.

QUESTIONS

1. Was the "Counter-Reformation" wholly a reaction from Protestantism? With what kind of a Reformation was it content?

2. What was the relation of Spain to the Roman awakening? Why?

3. What was the early life of Loyola? How did he turn to Christian things?

4. Describe the chief characteristics of Loyola's religious experience.

5. What were the *Spiritual Exercises?* What did they aim to accomplish?

6. Give some account of Loyola's student life.

7. Who were some of Loyola's early companions and how did he win them?

8. When and with what purpose was the Society of Jesus founded? Its peculiarities? The meaning of the name?

9. When did Loyola die? Who succeeded him in the generalship of the society?

10. What can be said of the missionary work of the society? Who was its most famous missionary? Where did he labor?

11. What was the relation of the society to education?

12. What may be said of its political tendencies?

13. What aspects of Roman Catholicism did the society emphasize? Why have its moral tendencies been criticized?

14. What may be said of the extent of the influence of the society?

ADDITIONAL READING

T. M. Lindsay, *A History of the Reformation* (New York, 1906, 1907), II, 526–63.

Stewart Rose, *Ignatius Loyola and the Early Jesuits* (London, 1891).

GEORGE FOX

XVI
GEORGE FOX

The English Reformation was in many respects unlike that on the Continent. Under Henry VIII political interests were far more potent than religious considerations. The country as a whole was not anxious for doctrinal revolution and was not profoundly moved spiritually. It looked upon the papal authority as foreign, and willingly saw it rejected by the masterful sovereign. It acquiesced in his confiscation of monastic property. It accepted the relatively slight changes that he made in worship; but, like the king, the people had little criticism of the broad fundamentals of mediaeval belief. At the close of Henry VIII's reign, in 1547, three parties existed—a large body, of whom the king himself was fairly representative, insistent that England should be for Englishmen, in church as well as in state, but not sympathizing with a Reformation like that of Luther; and two small factions, one holding to the ancient connection with Rome, and the other Protestant as Germany and Switzerland understood Protestantism.

After the death of Henry VIII the small parties successively controlled England. Under the nominal rule of Edward VI, to 1553, the Protestants were in power, and to their supremacy were due the English Prayer-Book and the Protestant Articles of Faith. Under Mary, to 1558, the Roman faction was uppermost; and persecutions, mild, indeed, compared with those on the Continent, but sufficient to give her the name "Bloody" in memory, marked her reign. At her accession, in 1558, Elizabeth was confronted by a most difficult problem. She would rule the English church, independently of the pope, as her father had done. To this end, and to maintain her foreign politics and even her own claim to the throne, she must rule as a Protestant. But she could not afford to alienate those of her subjects to whom any extreme Protestantism was distasteful. Hence her own policy was one of compromise—a course which her own lack of deep religious convictions rendered the easier.

From many points of view Elizabeth's policy was eminently successful. She avoided the civil wars between Protestants and Catholics which contemporaneously devastated France. The country prospered. The vast majority of the parish clergy, and of their parishioners, accepted the transition from Mary's Romanism to Elizabeth's moderate Protestantism without resistance. But from the first decade of her long reign a growing party, called the Puritans, felt that her reformation was far from thorough, desired the removal of inefficient clergy, the establishment everywhere of an earnest, preaching ministry, the purification of worship by the removal of what it deemed relics of Roman superstition, and the enforcement of rigorous church discipline. These changes Elizabeth resisted as divisive. The Puritans, thus balked, went a step farther, and questioned the rightfulness of an ecclesiastical constitution in which the sovereign and the bishops whom she appointed blocked what the Puritans deemed such needful reforms. The more radical of the party, the "Separatists," ancestors of the Congregationalists, proposed withdrawal from the government church as the only remedy; but the great majority of Puritans believed a national church desirable and thought that the Church of England could be reconstituted on what they held to be a more scriptural model. Calvinists in theology, they found their model of what the church should be largely in the Presbyterianism which had come forth from Geneva. To them the queen showed utmost hostility; but all through her long reign a real religious awakening of the English people was in progress, and when she died, in 1603, religious questions had become the foremost problems in English thought.

It was a turmoiled situation, therefore, that faced the Scottish James I on his accession to the English throne; and his want of skill and evident partisanship but fanned the elements of discord. Religiously, he took the anti-Puritan side. His political policy soon alienated, moreover, the lovers of constitutional liberty. On his death, in 1625, his son, Charles I, but embittered the struggle by attempts to crush Puritanism, to rule without Parliament, and to force episcopacy and the Prayer-Book on stubborn Scotland. In 1642, the great civil war between king and Parliament began, which led soon to the overthrow of episcopacy, and, in 1649, to the execution of Charles himself. An advisory religious assembly, which began its sessions by parliamentary appointment at Westminster in 1643, prepared a strongly Calvinistic Confession of Faith as the creed of England, and established, though very imperfectly, the Presbyterian form of government.

Meanwhile, the surging religious life of England was manifesting other forms. Independency, or Congregationalism, was widespread in the army which Cromwell had led to victory. Baptists, though relatively far fewer, were growing in numbers. The dominant religious type was, however, the Puritan; and with the Puritan, no less than with the Episcopalian of that day, the minister held his office ultimately by appointment by the state. Even Congregationalists accepted many state appointments from the friendly hand of Cromwell. Though generally men of character, these state-made ministers were not always of personal religious experience. The prevailing type of Puritan theology was intensely insistent on the Calvinistic doctrines of election and reprobation; and in its profound reverence for the

Bible taught that God had once for all revealed himself to men through the Scriptures, and no further revelation was to be sought than that contained in the "Word of God."

It was in this situation that George Fox, the founder of the Quakers, began his work. Fox was born in July, 1624, in Fenny Drayton, about in the center of England, the son of a weaver of upright character but poor circumstances.[1] His education was of the slightest, but he grew up a serious-minded youth, who "never wronged man or woman."[2] At twelve, he was apprenticed to a shoemaker who also dealt in cattle and wool. His conversion came about in a simple, though curious, manner. Invited by some friends, who were nominal Christians, to drink with them he consented; but when they proposed that he who should first leave off should pay for all, Fox's conscience awoke at the inconsistency of such drunken practices with the Christian profession and he promptly left them. It was the first ground-note of Fox's religious experience, the conviction that if religion is sincere it must rule the whole life; he became "sensible" that the majority of nominal Christians "did not possess what they professed."[3] As he struggled and prayed, a further experience

[1] The best account of Fox is in his own *Journals*, which have been abridged and published in convenient form by Professor R. M. Jones, *George Fox, an Autobiography* (Philadelphia, 1903).

[2] Jones, *George Fox*, I, 67.

[3] *Ibid.*, I, 68, 69.

came to him. He believed that God spoke directly, though inwardly, to his soul. "At the command of God, the ninth of the seventh month, 1643, I left my relations, and broke off all familiarity or fellowship with young or old."[1] Then followed a period of wandering and of consultation with ministers as to his spiritual state; but to no comfort. Early in 1646, however, as he was approaching the town of Coventry, "the Lord opened to me that if all were believers, then they were all born of God, and passed from death to life; and that none were true believers but such; and though others said they were believers, yet they were not."[2]

Tried by this test, which made Christianity a vital, personal experience, the ministers, from whom he had had so little comfort, seemed to Fox to be wanting; and he came to the further conclusion "that being bred at Oxford or Cambridge was not enough to fit and qualify men to be ministers of Christ."[3] With this radical criticism of the ministry came a dislike for church edifices, or "steeple houses" as Fox called them, since the Lord "did not dwell in these temples . . . . but in people's hearts." The true light of the Christian is the inward revelation of "the pure knowledge of God, and of Christ alone, without the help of any man, book or writing."[4]

[1] Jones, *George Fox*, I, 68, 69.
[2] *Ibid.*, I, 74.
[3] *Ibid.*, I, 75.
[4] *Ibid.*, I, 76, 82.

These doctrines of the "inner light," and of the duty of complete conformity of life to its guidance, whatever the cost might be, were always the really fundamental principles of Fox, and became those of the society to which its critics soon gave the name "Quakers," but which he preferred to call "Friends." With them were associated many relatively minor peculiarities, some of them directly derived from these principles, and others from views which had appeared and reappeared in the Middle Ages and Reformation history, among bodies like the Waldenses, or the Anabaptists. Some of them he may have derived from contact with the early English Baptists, who, in turn, received them from fellow-believers in Holland.[1] Among the direct consequences of his principle of the "inner light," was his conviction that all who were moved by the Spirit of God, whether men or women, were true preachers, and that none not so moved, or who were dependent on appointment in a state church for their credentials of authority, deserved any ministerial recognition whatever. From his conception of the essential equality of all Christians, and his strong hatred of all shams, Fox came to insist that the hat should never be removed as a sign of the inferiority of one man to another, that no merely complimentary titles should

[1] See Robert Barclay, *The Inner Life of the Religious Societies of the Commonwealth* (London, 1879), pp. 221-52, 273, 298, 352, 501, 518.

be used,[1] and that individuals however highly placed, should be addressed as "thou" and "thee" instead of by the plural "you," which then implied a deference to rank which its employment no longer signifies. Since all true religious life is, in his opinion, inward, he rejected all outward sacraments as unnecessary. To his thinking, the Calvinistic division of mankind into the elect and the reprobate is unwarranted, and the Holy Spirit moves effectively on all hearts that will welcome his influence. In sympathy with many earlier religious movements, he understood the New Testament and the "inner light" alike as prohibiting the use of judicial oaths or any appeal to arms or other employment of force.

With these principles and peculiarities, and mastered by a profound consciousness of a divine call, Fox began his mission as a preacher in 1647. Fanatical, extravagant in language, denunciatory, he aroused immense opposition and was met with every insult. Ridicule was heaped upon him. He was beaten, stoned, and set in the stocks. In 1650 and 1651 he spent a year as a prisoner in Derby jail—an experience to be followed by at least seven other imprisonments in various parts of England, the last of which was not ended till 1678. But while Fox encountered hostility from most, his transparent spiritual sincerity, his earnestness, his courage,

[1] Fox did not reject legal titles, such as "king," "protector," "justice," etc.

and the impression that he conveyed of being the bearer of a message not his own, won many converts, mostly, indeed, from the middle and lower classes, but some of wealth and station. Men like Cromwell, who were far from sympathizing with his peculiar views, respected his sincerity and acknowledged his power. Soon others proclaimed his doctrines. By 1654 no less than sixty missionaries of the Quaker faith were traveling throughout England. In 1656 they crossed the Atlantic to Massachusetts, and, before 1660, had borne their testimony in Scotland, Ireland, Germany, France, Switzerland, Italy, Turkey, Palestine, and the West India islands—in many of these lands without any permanent effect. As with Fox, so with his followers, persecution was a frequent experience. At the restoration of the Stuart monarchy, in 1660, no less than 3,170 Quakers were in English jails, and by 1661 four had been hanged in Massachusetts. Undoubtedly these early Quakers did much by fanatical attacks and extravagant conduct to excite hostility; but as the movement grew in age its extremer manifestations rapidly disappeared, to be followed by the sobriety and good order that soon became characteristic of the society.

When freed from prison and till disabled by the infirmities of age, Fox manifested a restless activity. He preached throughout the length and breadth of England. Between 1671 and 1673 he visited Barbadoes and Jamaica, going thence by way of Maryland,

Delaware, New Jersey, and Long Island, to Rhode Island, and, on his return, as far south as North Carolina, everywhere advancing the cause which he had at heart. This long journey through what were slave-holding lands strengthened in him the sense already expressed in 1656 of the evil of human bondage and its essential unrighteousness—a conviction which the Friends were to entertain more deeply and to make more effective than any other Christian body. With less success he visited Holland in 1677 and 1684, the journey on the former occasion being extended to Germany.

On October 27, 1669, Fox married one of his early disciples, who had become a widow, Margaret Fell, possessed of property and position, whose home, Swarthmore Hall, had long been a refuge for the Quakers. A woman of high character and like spirit, she aided and supplemented his work, and survived him by more than a decade. The greatest trophy of the early activities of the Quakers was undoubtedly William Penn. Born in 1644, the son of Admiral Sir William Penn, he enjoyed the best culture and education that England afforded. Always of a mystically religious frame of mind, he came under Quaker influences, and in 1667 threw in his lot wholly with the society, which he defended in vigorous pamphlets, and in common with the humbler members of which he suffered repeated imprisonment. Nevertheless, his political influence was always large. By that influence he was able to bring to a realization a wish that Fox had entertained since 1660, that Quakers should possess some territory in which they might enjoy across the Atlantic a freedom not theirs in England.

After a rather unsatisfying connection with the affairs of New Jersey, beginning in 1674, Penn secured from Charles II in compensation for claims on the English treasury which he had inherited from his father, the charter of Pennsylvania, under date of March 4, 1681. The result was the immediate settlement, under Penn's leadership, of what has become one of the greatest of American commonwealths. Its government, as established by Penn, was of large liberality. Religious freedom in high degree was allowed. Fairness marked its relations with the Indians. Industry and thrift were promoted. The Quaker "experiment" must rank among the most successful of American colonial enterprises, though its course was not without great trials and much political friction, for Penn's colony attracted many who were not Quakers, notably from Germany as well as from the homeland.

It may be remarked that throughout the eighteenth century the Quaker body was the communion of Christians which was perhaps the most widely distributed geographically of any in British America. Numbering perhaps 50,000 by 1760, it was never as large as several other religious communions, but it was broadly scattered throughout the colonies that became the United States.

Fox's last years were full of Christian confidence and peace. He saw his society relieved of most of its civil disabilities by the Toleration Act of 1689. It was never in more flourishing state than when he died, on January 13, 1691, in London. His end was triumphant. To those who stood by his bedside he declared, using the technical language of the piety of his day, "All is well; the Seed of God reigns over all and over death itself."[1] His fame must ever be that of one of the most forceful religious leaders that Anglo-Saxon Christendom has produced. From Fox's death, the Society which he had founded ceased to advance with any rapidity, and soon came sensibly to decline in adherents. But its contributions to human freedom, abolition of slavery, prison reform, and the betterment of social and industrial conditions have been out of all proportion to the relative scantiness of its numbers.

In the judgment of most branches of the Christian church, Fox was far too radical in his rejection of what he deemed the harmful externals of worship and organization. To the thought of most Christians, the church needs an established and educated ministry, an orderly and regular service, and the visible sacraments. But to recognize that he rejected much that long Christian experience has approved

[1] Jones, *op. cit.*, II, 578.

is not to deny the purity of his intentions, or the value of much of his work. He hated all shams and pretenses. He was the enemy of all formalism in worship, however formal his followers have shown themselves in dress, speech, and behavior. He asserted that the life must be the expression of the faith. He declared that all men are capable of accepting the gospel offer. He taught the essential spiritual equality of all believers. But his greatest contribution was his conception of the "inner light." In an age which shut up all divine revelation in the pages of a Book, he maintained that the Holy Spirit speaks directly and revealingly now to the believer; not merely operates on the believer's heart to produce faith as all Protestantism held, but guides, illuminates, and directs. That truth alone, if Fox had made no other contribution to religious thought, is enough to give him place among those to whom Christian life owes much.

QUESTIONS

1. How did the English Reformation differ from that on the Continent? What degree of Protestantism was represented by Henry VIII?

2. What parties were dominant under Edward VI and Mary? Were either representative of England as a whole?

3. What was the religious policy of Elizabeth? In what respects was it successful? Why was it disliked by the Puritans? What was her attitude toward them? Why?

4. What was the religious condition of England under

James I and Charles I? Why the civil wars? What was the attitude of Puritanism toward a state church? Its theological convictions?

5. Describe the early life of George Fox. His conversion? His sense of divine revelations? His criticisms of existing religion?

6. Why did Fox criticize the ministers? Why was not an education sufficient?

7. What was Fox's doctrine of the "inner light"?

8. Describe other peculiarities of Fox's religious belief.

9 What were Fox's qualities as a preacher? How was he treated? His success?

10. What was the early growth of the Quakers? Their missionary zeal? Fox's journeys to America, Holland, and Germany?

11. The value of William Penn to the Quaker cause? Pennsylvania, its foundation and characteristics?

12. Fox's marriage, last days, and death?

13. The limitations and the services of his movement? Its permanent value?

ADDITIONAL READING

Rufus M. Jones, *George Fox: An Autobiography* (Philadelphia, 1903).

Thomas Hodgkin, *George Fox* (London, 1896).

A. C. Thomas and R. H. Thomas, *The History of the Society of Friends in America*, "American Church History" Series (New York, 1894), Vol. XII, 163-308.

ns LUDWIG VON ZINZENDORF
NICOLAUS LUDWIG VON ZINZENDORF

XVII
NICOLAUS LUDWIG VON ZINZENDORF

In all Protestant lands the fresh, creative epoch of the Reformation was followed by a new formalism. The lesser men, who succeeded the great reformers, looked upon their work as essentially complete. The Bible was regarded as the source of truth; but its teachings were viewed as fully and finally garnered into the theological systems of the Reformation age. A new scholasticism arose, as dry as that of the Middle Ages. This was particularly the case in Germany, where it has been well said that for the authority of the mediaeval church was substituted the authority of the new theologians. Great weight was laid on "pure doctrine." Much was made of the church as an institution, of the corporate and official aspects of Christianity, and of the sacraments as of themselves placing their serious-minded receivers in the sure ranks of Christian discipleship. The conscious personal relation to Christ sank into the background, and for it was largely substituted a conception of the Christian life which saw as its essential features orthodoxy of doctrine, faithful attendance on public worship, and employment of the sacraments which the church offered. This condition has sometimes, though not quite justly, been called "dead orthodoxy."

The great reaction from this formal conception of the Christian life was that known in Germany as "Pietism," and it had for its leader Philipp Jakob Spener. Born in 1635, at Rappoltsweiler in Alsace, he grew up under strong religious impressions, which were intensified by acquaintance with the writings of the German ascetic-mystic, Johann Arndt, and translations of the works of English Puritans.[1] Graduation at the University of Strassburg was followed by sojourns in Basel and Geneva and by his settlement, in 1666, as chief pastor in the important Lutheran city of Frankfort. Convinced that the religious life of the city was at a low ebb, Spener, in 1670, gathered a little company of like-minded men and women in his house twice weekly for pious reading and religious conversation. To these meetings the name *Collegia pietatis* was soon given. Five years later, Spener published his *Pia desideria*, in which he recommended the establishment of similar *collegia*, mutual watch, a strenuous, rather ascetic, Christian life, better care of the morals and Christian character of theological students, and simpler and more spiritual preaching. Spener's thought was that a kernel of experiential Christians should be gathered in each congregation which should cultivate

---

[1] The writer owes much to the admirable articles in Hauck's *Realencyklopädie* by Grünberg on "Spener," XVIII, 609–22; by Förster-Halle on "Francke," VI, 150–58; by Mirbt on "Pietism," XV, 774–815; and by Gottschick on "Adiaphora," I, 174–76.

a stricter and warmer Christian life with the hope of ultimately leavening the whole. He felt that only those who had been "born again" by a conscious Christian experience—"conversion"—were fitted for this work or should have a place in the ministry.

Spener's views won friends and aroused opposition, so that, in 1686, he accepted a call to become preacher at the Saxon court in Dresden. Here his troubles were but increased. The theological faculties of the universities of Leipzig and Wittenberg attacked him as unorthodox and as of Puritan strictness in his conception of the Christian life. Though a Lutheran in his own belief, the comparative indifference with which he regarded what seemed to him minor theological divergences so long as "the heart" is right, was regarded by orthodox Lutherans as treason to "pure doctrine." Many supported him, however, and soon German Protestantism was divided into two camps. Plain-spoken pastoral admonitions to the Saxon Elector made his further stay at Dresden uncomfortable, and he was glad to accept a call to Berlin in 1691, where he found greater peace and exercised a large influence till his death in 1705.

Spener's most eminent disciple was August Hermann Francke. Born in Lübeck in 1663, and having lost his father when but seven years old, thoughts of Christian service in the ministry were awakened in him by an elder sister, and, after a course of study in Kiel and Leipzig, he became, in 1685, an instructor in the university of the city last named. Here he labored to advance the study of the Bible. In 1687, in further preparation for the ministry, he went to Lüneburg, and there, as he was writing a sermon on John 20:31, an experience came to him which he ever after regarded as his "conversion." It seemed to him that he had passed from death to spiritual life. A few months later he made a long visit to Spener in Dresden, and began a personal intimacy that was to continue till the latter's death. On the resumption of his teaching in Leipzig, in 1689, he began lecturing with a great following on the Scriptures and was an energetic leader in a warmer spiritual life among the students. Some of the latter, however, in their new-found enthusiasm, began to despise their ordinary studies as worldly and unnecessary; the hostility of Francke's colleagues in the faculty was aroused, and, in 1690, he accepted a pastorate in Erfurt. Opposition followed him thither, and the next year he had to leave this new post. Through Spener's influence he obtained a pastorate, however, in Glaucha, near Halle, and the promise of a professorship in the new university which was opened in 1694, at the place last named, under Prussian auspices. Thanks to Francke and Spener, the University of Halle became the home of Pietism, and Francke continued its most influential professor till his death in 1727.

Francke was a man of many-sided activities as a pastor, a teacher, and a reformer. He built up a great preparatory school, the *Paedagogium*, and a most useful orphan asylum in Halle—a remarkable foundation, established by a multitude of gifts received, so Francke believed, in answer to prayer—and one doing honored work to the present day. With it was soon associated the institution for printing and distributing the Bible, founded by Francke's friend, Baron von Canstein in 1710, and still carrying forward its activities. When King Frederick IV, of Denmark, wished to establish one of the earliest of Protestant missions in India in 1705, it was among Francke's disciples in Halle that he found his first missionaries, and in Francke himself that he had his most earnest supporter.

The pietistic conception of religion, as represented by Francke and his disciples, was thus earnest, consecrated, self-denying, benevolent, and marked by missionary zeal. It was strenuous in its attitude toward amusements, dress, and luxury. Dancing, the theater, and cards, which the older Lutherans largely looked upon as "indifferent matters" regarding which a Christian could do as he pleased, were viewed by the Pietists as hindrances to the Christian life and to be forbidden. So far was this tendency carried that the children in the orphan house in Halle were not allowed to play. Entrance on the Christian life was looked upon as normally by a conscious "conversion." The faults of the Pietists were those which often beset strenuous and earnest reformers.

Convinced of the need of a warmer religious life, they were too much disposed to minimize the value of the church, its services and ordinances, and the real Christianity of those who did not think as they did; but that they did a great and a needed work in Germany there can be no question.

That work in one of its most peculiar and permanent forms is to be seen in the achievements of Nicolaus Ludwig, Count of Zinzendorf, the reorganizer of the Moravians. Grandson of a nobleman who had left Austria for his religious convictions, and son of a trusted servant of the Elector of Saxony, Zinzendorf was born in Dresden on May 26, 1700. Spener was his godfather at his baptism. His father died when the boy was but six months old, his mother married a second time, and his training came into the hands of his grandmother, the earnest, pietistic Baroness of Gersdorf—a correspondent of Spener and Francke. From his earliest childhood Zinzendorf manifested the glowing personal love for Christ—not merely as his Lord but as the truest and nearest of friends, which was to be the prime trait of his religious experience to the end of his life.

When ten years old, the boy was sent to Francke's *Paedagogium* in Halle, where his pietistic tendencies were intensified and he soon became a leader among his youthful companions. He organized little prayer meetings, he became interested in missions, and, when fifteen, established among his schoolmates an

"Order of the Grain of Mustard Seed"[1] for the promotion of the Kingdom of God. Zinzendorf's guardian, an uncle, thinking this zeal unhealthful, sent him, in 1716, to the orthodox Lutheran University of Wittenberg, where he studied law for the next three years. They were a time of growth. His pietistic principles remained firm in essentials; but they were broadened and shorn of many extravagances. Then followed two years of travel, including Holland and France in his route. Amid the corruptions of the French court, then notorious for its profligacy, he maintained his convictions, and he returned to Dresden, in 1721, to enter the service of the Saxon Elector, a man of ripened experience and unshaken religious character.

Political life was begun, however, only to please his relatives, and Zinzendorf would have much preferred the ministry. Most of his life at Dresden was devoted to religious conversation. A meeting for Christian edification was held every Sunday afternoon in his own house. The opportunity soon came in an unexpected way for a much larger service that was to prove his life-work. The remains of the old Hussite movement, the United Brethren (*Unitas Fratrum*),[2] which had flourished exceedingly in Bohemia and Moravia at the time of the Reformation, had been nearly crushed during the Thirty Years' War, and were subject to severe persecution. A revival was in

[1] Matt. 13:31.   [2] See *ante*, p. 212.

progress under a Moravian carpenter, Christian David, and the "Brethren" were casting about for some place of refuge in Protestant lands. This they found on Zinzendorf's estates, and in 1722 David began the establishment of the town of Herrnhut. With them Zinzendorf entered into close association, and soon religious-minded people of all shades of theologic opinion and of most various origins were flocking to this new Christian community. The thought was that here a town could be erected, inhabited only by Christians, separate from the "world," a real "communion of saints." It was a free and social monasticism, without celibacy, but, like monasticism, seeking to live the Christian life under peculiarly favorable conditions and apart from the grosser temptations.

A community of such varied origin could not find its bond in strict doctrinal unity. Zinzendorf sought it in love, and in careful regulation of the life of its members under a constitution of peculiar strenuousness. He wished to remain in as close connection as possible with the Lutheran communion of his birth, but he found it necessary to preserve the old Moravian forms, and, in 1727, the Herrnhut company was organized with bishop, priests, and deacons. In spite of these names, the church organization really depended on the congregation, and in its government laymen had a large share. The affairs of the community were administered by a common board; the widows, maids, and young men were lodged and supervised in separate houses, and with distinctive clothing; an elaborate and in many respects beautiful liturgy soon voiced public worship. From 1727 Zinzendorf was the guiding spirit of the Herrnhut community, and, ten years later, he received formal ordination as bishop in the reorganized Moravian church, or "United Brethren" as the body preferred to style itself, using its historic designation.

Zinzendorf's impulses had always been strongly missionary, and he saw in all who were moved by love to Christ the children of God. He even attempted to influence the Roman and Greek churches. His chief effort within the realm of Protestantism was, however, to found separated "societies," more or less resembling that at Herrnhut, made up of those whom he believed to be real Christians, as judged by his pietistic tests. These he did not deem a separate church, but associations for a warmer Christian life within the various churches. His communion he ever regarded as the true people of God, separated from the world, and largely shielded from its temptations. Soon branch "societies" were formed in various parts of Germany, in Holland, in England, and in Pennsylvania. The noblest work of Moravianism, and that most expressive of Zinzendorf's own character, was that of foreign missions. On a visit to the Danish capital, Copenhagen, to be present at the coronation of King Christian VI, in 1731

Zinzendorf met a negro from the Danish West India Islands, and was impressed with the needs of the race there held in slavery. As a result, the first of the noble army of Moravian missionaries, Leonhard Dober and David Nitschmann, set forth from Herrnhut on their way to St. Thomas, in 1732. The establishment of other missions speedily followed. In 1733 Greenland was entered; in 1734, Lapland; in 1735 efforts were begun among the American Indians in Georgia; in 1737 the African Guinea Coast was reached and work was begun among the Hottentots of South Africa, also; in 1738 South American Guiana was invaded, and labors in Ceylon and Algeria were commenced two years later. The year 1771 saw the establishment, after many failures, of a successful mission in Labrador. These are but part of the regions to which the gospel was carried by indefatigable Moravian zeal; and a glance at their names shows a prime characteristic of these missions. They are prevailingly the hard and neglected fields of the earth. In many of them the Moravians have been conspicuously successful, carrying on their work at marvelously small cost, with unwearied patience and heroic consecration. First of all Protestant bodies the Moravian communion awoke, as a whole, to the importance of missions; and, in proportion to its numbers, its missionary activity to this day far exceeds that of any other branch of the Christian church. Certainly, this one

NICOLAUS LUDWIG VON ZINZENDORF

result of Zinzendorf's work, had he done nothing else, would shed an abiding luster on his name.

From his first connection with the Moravians, Zinzendorf and the communion of which he was the head had to endure bitter criticism, not only from orthodox Lutherans but even from the older Pietists. Much of this was not without considerable foundation. Zinzendorf's basal principle of love found at first too often, even in him, a sentimental expression. The Moravian hymns were objectionable to many earnest Christians by reason of their presentation under very earthly images of the relation of the believer to his Lord. The communion, in 1741, formally chose Christ as its chief elder, and believed his will to be made known by casting lots. It regarded itself as embracing in far too exclusive a sense "the true Children of God." It strove to regulate in a really obnoxious way the most private and sacred relations of family life. As time went on, however, these excrescences were gradually pruned away. The experiences of the Moravians were, in this regard, much the same as those of the early Quakers. The first extravagances gave place to sobriety and order.

Zinzendorf himself had to suffer from this opposition more than mere unpopularity. The Saxon government, probably moved by the complaints of the Austrian authorities that he gave a shelter to persecuted Austrian subjects, banished him in 1736.

This sentence but enlarged the sphere of Zinzendorf's activities. He labored in various parts of Germany, Holland, Switzerland, England, the West India islands, and North America. From December, 1741, to January, 1743, he made his home in Pennsylvania. Here he strove to unite the religious forces of the German settlers of the commonwealth in a spirit of broad Christian charity. He served as pastor of the Lutheran congregation in Philadelphia. He sowed the seeds of Moravian societies in "Bethlehem, Nazareth, Philadelphia, Hebron, Heidelberg, Lancaster, and York in Pennsylvania, and in New York City and on Staten Island."[1] He established a new Herrnhut, at Bethlehem, where American Moravianism still has one of its chief homes. He even attempted to do something, by personal effort, toward spreading the gospel among the Indians of the great Iroquois confederacy, and provided for prosecution of this enterprise in which David Zeisberger was soon to win so fair a name. Much of Zinzendorf's time, during his long exile, was spent in rapid journeyings to superintend and promote the cause he had at heart; and nowhere was his conspicuous talent as an organizer more clearly exhibited than in the results of this restless activity.

A change of sentiment favorable to Zinzendorf was effected in the Saxon government itself. In 1747

[1] J. T. Hamilton, *A History of the Unitas Fratrum*, "American Church History" Series (New York, 1895), VIII, 451.

the sentence of banishment was revoked, and, two years later, primarily to secure greater political security, the Moravian body acknowledged the Augsburg Confession, the basal creed of the Lutheran churches, as the expression of its faith.[1] This act wrought no change in its purpose, aims, or organization. Zinzendorf was now practically freed from all hindrances. He continued his active supervision and his wide-extended travels almost till his death, which occurred in Herrnhut, in the confidence of the Christian faith, on May 9, 1760. Fortunate in his leadership, the Moravian body was equally happy in his successor, August Gottlieb Spangenberg (1704–1792), in no sense a creative genius like Zinzendorf, but a man of conservatism, strong common-sense, and great administrative abilities, who knew how to continue and improve the work of his great predecessor, and to repress its more extravagant features without abating the effectiveness of its zeal.

Zinzendorf's character had its lights and its shadows. Of unbounded enthusiasm, great missionary zeal, and sincerity of consecration, he was yet inclined to what always seems to the Anglo-Saxon temperament a sentimental type of religion, and he would use a scriptural symbol or figurative expression as the basis of an extensive flight of spiritual

[1] The same year the Moravians in England were favored with exemptions (from oaths, jury duty, and certain military services) by act of Parliament, which also declared that their bishops were in apostolical succession.

imagination. But in him positive services to the Kingdom of God far outweighed any shortcomings or defects. He was an organizer of marvelous talent. He devoted position, wealth, above all himself, to his cause, which was that of his Master. He voiced his piety in hymns, some of which, like "Jesus still lead on, till our rest be won," have been beloved of the church universal. Few men have shown such personal devotion to Christ, and he gave the true groundnote of his character in his declaration to his Herrnhut congregation; "I have only one passion. It is He, none but He."

QUESTIONS

1. Did the period succeeding the Reformation maintain the spiritual zeal of that movement? Its characteristics?

2. What was "Pietism"? Outline the life of Spener.

3. How did Spener attempt to advance vital religion? His *collegia?* The type of Christianity which he represented?

4. What was Francke's early religious history? His "conversion"? How did he become a professor in Halle? What importance did Halle have for Pietism?

5. What were Francke's institutions in Halle? Their work?

6. What was the attitude of Pietism toward amusements? What were the merits of Pietism?

7. Describe Zinzendorf's life. Its religious traits? His education? The "Order of the Grain of Mustard Seed"?

8. Who were the Moravians? What did they call themselves? From what ancient movement were they descended? Who was Christian David?

9. How did Zinzendorf come in contact with the Mora-

vians? Their reorganization? Herrnhut? What was its aim and how was it organized?

10. How did Moravian missions begin? Some lands in which they labored? The characteristics of Moravian missions? The missionary zeal of the Moravians?

11. What were some of the criticisms which Zinzendorf and the Moravian movement had to endure? Why?

12. What office did Zinzendorf hold in the Moravian church? His abilities as an organizer? His banishment, its effects? His work in America? Recall to Saxony?

13. Zinzendorf's later life and death? His character?

ADDITIONAL READING

J. T. Hamilton, *The Moravian Church in the United States*, "American Church History" Series (New York, 1895), VIII, 425–508.

A. C. Thompson, *Moravian Missions* (New York), 1895.

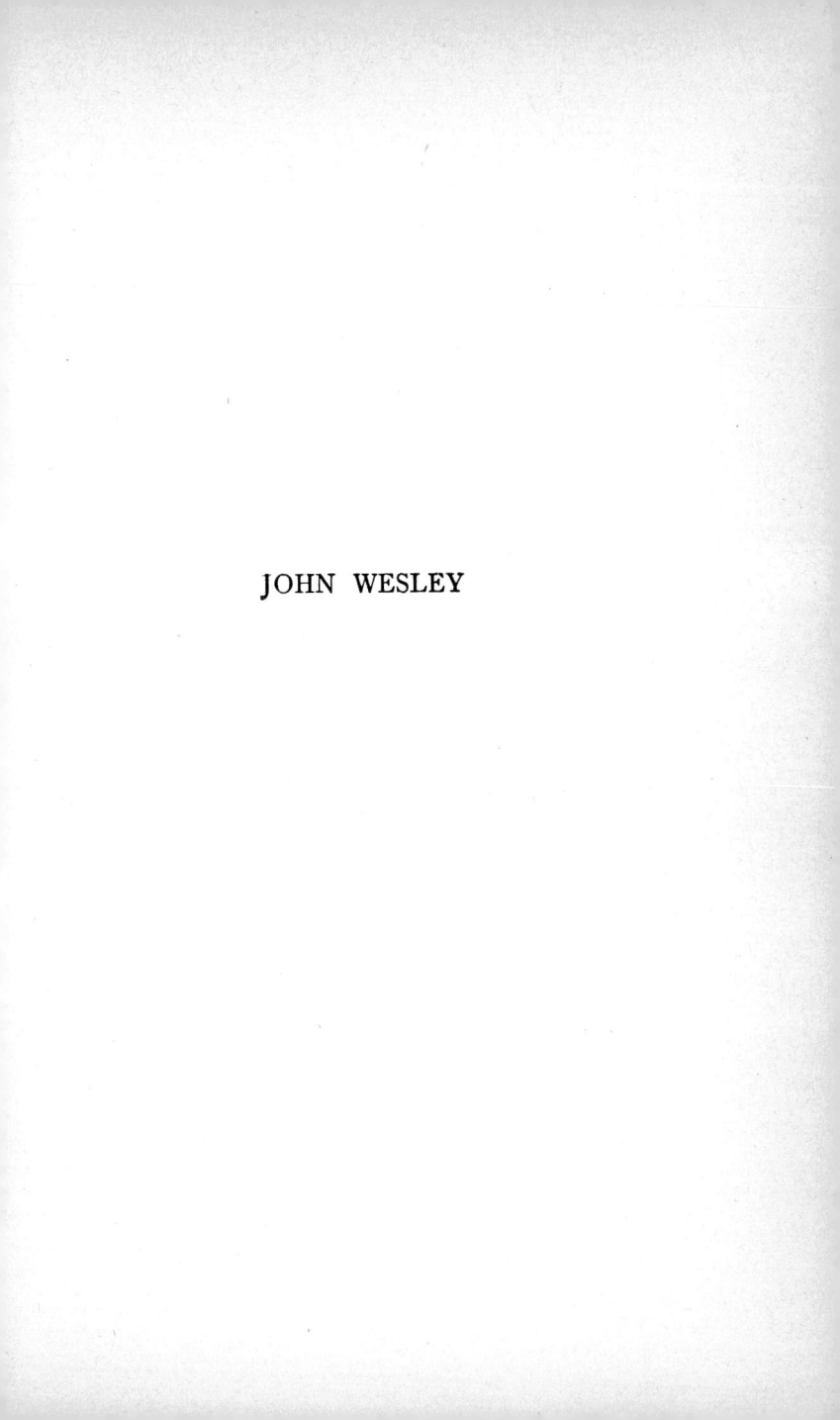

JOHN WESLEY

XVIII
JOHN WESLEY

It is a fact of frequent observation that questions which profoundly arouse the feelings of one age lose their vital interest for its successor. Seemingly of overwhelming importance to one or two generations, they come to be viewed with apathy. Such was the fate of the great religious conflict which convulsed England in the seventeenth century. Long before the *Toleration Act* of 1689 gave a larger, though imperfect, freedom to Dissenters from the national church, the old Puritan fire had burned low. There was little in the England of 1700 to lead one to imagine that it had been the intensely aroused land of 1650. The great struggle had brought, indeed, permanent enlargements of religious and political freedom. The uniformity which Archbishop Laud had desired was as dead an issue as were the ideals of the Stuart monarchy which he had served. The religious condition of the land was, however, one of relative lethargy. Neither among Dissenters nor in the Church of England was a vigorous and out-reaching religious life extensively apparent.

Among the classes of the population distinguished by station or intelligence, the older doctrinal positions were widely regarded as outgrown. The fashionable world had long since scorned everything that savored of Puritanism. Among thinking men the new philosophy just introduced by John Locke, and the new discoveries of science, of which Sir Isaac Newton's law of gravitation was but the most brilliant, were shaking the older theologies, though the leaders mentioned were themselves Christian men. The new conception of the universe as a realm of law thus introduced was demanding adjustment. The result in not a few minds was Deism. That system of thought recognized the world as the work of an all-wise creator, who, however, does not interfere in its ongoing either by revelation or by providence. With many, religion was looked upon as an essentially baseless superstition, which learned men could afford to repudiate privately, but which ought to be maintained because of its police value over the ignorant.

The lower classes, though almost absolutely unaffected by the attitude of mind just noted among their superiors in station, were in a condition of almost unbelievable ignorance, coarseness, and neglect. The administration of law, though ferocious in its severity, was unable to give adequate public security. The jails were sinks of physical and moral rottenness. Drunkenness was frightfully prevalent. The condition of the common people in city and country alike was one of brutality.

There were, indeed, men of character, ability, and

spiritual insight among the ministry of the Establishment and in the dissenting churches. Never perhaps in English history has there been a more brilliant group of intellectual defenders of historic and rational Christianity than in the years that immediately preceded Wesley's activity. The names of Archdeacon Daniel Waterland, Bishop George Berkeley, and Bishop Joseph Butler, to mention no others, must always shine in the story of the earlier decades of the eighteenth century. Nor was earnest piety without its representatives. From the High-churchman, William Law, to the Congregational hymn-writer, Isaac Watts, no section of religious England was without men of warm-hearted religious feeling. But the prevailing type of preaching was that of the passionless essay on moral duties, and the heated controversies of the seventeenth century had led to a widespread reaction which dreaded anything of "enthusiasm," or, as we should say, fanaticism, in the pulpit or in conduct. Preaching was intellectual and unstimulating. Appeals to the fundamental religious feelings were exceedingly rare, and were regarded as scarcely fitting.

It was high time that a new and effective presentation of the gospel should be made, that the neglected emotional nature of men should be roused to religious activity, and the masses outside the churches should be sought. That England was regenerated spiritually and awakened as never before, was, humanly speaking, the work of two men of transcendent abilities, John Wesley, the organizer of Methodism, and George Whitefield, the greatest preacher of the eighteenth century.

John Wesley was born in Epworth, Lincolnshire, where his father, Rev. Samuel Wesley, was rector, on June 17, 1703.[1] His father was a hard-working, earnest head of a rather remote country parish. His mother, Susannah (Annesley), was a woman of unusual talents, intellectual powers, and spiritual gifts, from whom the son drew much of what he afterward became. In a household of nineteen children, even though only ten survived the perils of infancy, the financial problem was always a pressing one; but the brothers and sisters grew up under their mother's instruction, with more than usual cultivation of manner as well as of mind, and in spite of a plainness of speech one toward another which almost savored of bluntness, with great mutual affection. One event of John's boyhood made an indelible impression on his mind. He was rescued, at the last moment, from the fire that destroyed the rectory, and it seemed to him that he was literally "a brand plucked from the burning." A sense of the immediacy of divine providence was characteristic of the boy from his earliest childhood.

When a little more than ten, Wesley entered the

[1] "Old style." In the reformed dating now in use the day would be June 28.

famous Charterhouse School in London, and thence passed, at seventeen, to the University of Oxford. In both he was distinguished for scholarship, but the warm piety of his early home life sank to a low level. Still, it was not extinguished; and in September, 1725, he was ordained to the ministry of the Church of England. He now conscientiously read good books, and was specially impressed by William Law's *Serious Call*,[1] which came into his hands soon after he was chosen a fellow of Lincoln College, Oxford. As Wesley himself said, it convinced him "more than ever of the impossibility of being half a Christian, and [he] determined to be all devoted to God." Law's writings may be called the seed from which early Methodism sprang.

Wesley now entered on the active ministry. From August, 1727, to November, 1729, he served as his father's curate in the parish of his boyhood. In the month last mentioned he returned to Oxford to assume the duties of his fellowship. Meanwhile, in his absence from Oxford, important events had taken place there. Charles Wesley, his younger brother, who was to be the poet of Methodism, then a student in Oxford, had gathered a few like-minded associates into a little club, for the cultivation of the Christian life. They were "High-churchmen" in their sym-

[1] *A Serious Call to a Holy Life*, published in 1728. Dr. Samuel Johnson described it as "the finest piece of hortatory theology in any language."

pathies, and they ordered their lives by strict rule, partaking of the sacraments, visiting prisoners, fasting, and seeking mutual edification. This earnestness and regularity aroused the derision of the student body, and soon led to the nickname, "Methodists."[1] Of this fellowship John Wesley became the leader on his return to Oxford in 1729. George Whitefield joined the little company in 1735.

Though Oxford was thus the cradle of Methodism, none of its leaders was destined to make that seat of learning his home. In 1735, John and Charles Wesley sailed for Georgia, then a colony planned largely on a philanthropic basis by James Edward Oglethorpe. Here John Wesley remained till late in 1737. It was not a pleasant experience. Wesley was a High-churchman. His views were strict and censorious; and his refusal to administer the communion to Miss Sophy Hopkey, after she had become Mrs. Williamson, was unfortunate in view of the courtship that had existed between them before that lady's marriage. Wesley, always a keen judge of men, was not marked by skill in insight into feminine character. His Georgia mission was practically a failure. For his own spiritual development it was, however, of the highest importance. On the voyage out and in Georgia he was thrown much into the company of Moravians, and was convinced that they

[1] The name was not newly invented. See, on its earlier use, Tyerman, *Life and Times of the Rev. John Wesley*, I, 67.

had a depth of religious experience which he had not yet acquired. Returned to London, he immediately sought out the Moravians, and was greatly influenced by one of their leaders in that city, Peter Böhler. He attended the Moravian meetings, and in one of them, on May 24, 1738, had the remarkable experience which he ever after viewed as his "conversion." While Luther's preface to his commentary on the Epistle to the Romans was being read, Wesley records: "I felt my heart strangely warmed. I felt I did trust in Christ, Christ alone, for salvation; and an assurance was given me that he had taken away my sins, even mine."[1] A similar experience had come to Charles Wesley three days before, and to Whitefield a little earlier.

Wesley was a man of prompt action. He would know more of the Moravians, and early in June he started for Germany to meet Zinzendorf and visit Herrnhut. He was greatly impressed with the eager and emotional piety that he witnessed. His debt to Moravian influences was permanent. But Wesley's good sense kept him from sympathy with the more extravagant features of early Moravianism, and, in particular, from the adoption of the Moravian plan of separate towns. Christians should not withdraw from the world, but work in it, where its temptations were the strongest and the powers of evil most firmly intrenched.

[1] *John Wesley's Journal*, abridged edition (Cincinnati, 1903), p. 51.

Wesley's return from Germany was followed by endeavors to preach the gospel as he now understood it, in which Whitefield fully shared. The churches, however, were generally, though not always, closed to them as fanatics by the rectors in charge; and, therefore, in February, 1739, Whitefield began preaching in the fields. Such an innovation distressed Wesley's High-churchmanship; but he felt the gospel must be preached, and, in April following, he adopted the same method of reaching the people. Both were great preachers, but in effective popular address Whitefield was undoubtedly the greater. Such preaching England had not heard for years. Intense, emotional, calling for immediate, conscious conversion, it pressed the message on the attention of men for whom the ordinary discourses of the time had little attraction. It appealed to the heart. It depicted the danger of neglect of Christ and the terrors of the hereafter in lurid vividness; but it urged none the less clearly the forgiving grace of God, and the possibilities of full consecration to his service. Its emotional effectiveness was extreme. In the earlier years both of Whitefield's and of Wesley's preaching, faintings, hysterics, and outcries of distress were not uncommon accompaniments of the sermons; but the number profoundly and permanently awakened to the Christian hope was very great. The preachers encountered ridicule, calumny, and mob violence of all kinds; but they made themselves heard, and it was a ministry largely to the unchurched and neglected that soon won abundant fruitage.

This preaching was notably successful in Bristol and its vicinity, and there, in 1739, Wesley began the erection of the first Methodist place of worship—a task involving great and unanticipated financial responsibilities. The titles of these "chapels," as they were called, since the name "church" was popularly used for the edifices of the English Establishment, were long generally vested in Wesley himself. The same year, 1739, the "Foundry" was made the center of Methodist meetings in London. The chapels soon became very numerous; and a device originally adopted in 1742, as a means of raising the heavy debt on that in Bristol, not only proved financially effective, but was soon made one of the chief spiritual agencies of Methodism. The congregation was composed chiefly of the poor. It was divided into groups of twelve, each member of which was pledged to give a penny a week to a collector. Wesley's keen organizing genius saw at once that the collector might wisely become the spiritual supervisor of his group, and that these bands of associates might aid each other's religious life by testimony as to their experiences and temptations. The result was the "class-meeting," which was at once extended to all Methodism, and has proved one of its most useful features.[1]

[1] *Journal, op. cit.*, pp. 123, 124; Tyerman, I, 377-80.

Wesley had at first built his work largely on the basis of "religious societies," which had existed for at least half a century before his active labors began as voluntary associations for the cultivation of the religious life. These had afforded a ready door for Moravianism; and the society in London with which Wesley was chiefly associated was essentially a Moravian body. But Wesley came to feel justly that English Moravianism was marked by extravagances, while the London Moravians in turn viewed him as not acceptable to themselves. The result was that, on July 23, 1740, the "United Society" met in London as a distinctly Methodist body, and from that event organized Methodism may be dated.[1]

Meanwhile the work was growing with great rapidity, and the groups of disciples required preachers and leaders. Wesley's High-churchmanship revolted against the employment of any but ordained men; but few clergymen were sympathetic, and he soon saw that if his work was to be extended he must use the aid of laymen. Begun in one instance as early as 1739, by 1741 lay preachers had become a regular and greatly employed feature of Methodism. At the first Wesley personally superintended all stations and directed the preachers in them; but the task soon became physically impossible. Unable to go to

[1] *Journal, op. cit.*, p. 100; Tyerman, I, 309, 310. Wesley traced the beginnings of the "United Society" to a rather informal gathering for prayer and conference begun in London in December, 1739. See Tyerman, I, 278.

JOHN WESLEY

them all, he, therefore, in 1744, began the practice of having the preachers come to him. The result was the annual "Conference,"[1] ultimately to become the cornerstone of the governmental system of Methodism. These preachers were uneducated for the most part, and Wesley saw that, though earnest, their usefulness in a field was likely to be speedily exhausted. Many stations also were small, and several could profitably be served in succession by the same speaker. He therefore changed their place of service frequently, and sent the more gifted of them on wide-extended missionary tours. The result was "itinerancy." Neighboring preaching stations were grouped in "circuits," to which these evangelists as well as the abler Methodist leaders ministered in rotation. Thus, by 1746, Wesley had mapped out the main features of Methodism. It was no creation of a moment; but a growth, a marvelous adjustment of means to ends; and the result was such a presentation of the gospel to the common people as England had never before witnessed.

Wesley himself was the most indefatigable of workers. Of middle height, and slender frame, he was of iron endurance. Ordinarily he rose at four in the morning, and his waking hours were filled with restless activities. Without serious home cares, for his marriage in 1751, with a widow, Mrs. Vazeille, was uncongenial and unfortunate, he was able to

[1] Tyerman, I, 441–48.

devote himself wholly to his task. For fifty years he preached on the average of five hundred times annually. In that half-century he rode no less than 250,000 miles on horseback. He supervised all the details of the Methodist movement, appointed preachers, settled disputes, and yet found time to be busy constantly with his pen. His courage was unshakable. No mob-violence affrighted him, no opposition could thwart his purpose. His faults were the defects of such a temperament. He was occasionally over self-reliant. He inclined to be dictatorial. In controversy he was sometimes contemptuous. He was undoubtedly superstitious, holding to the reality of witchcraft, and deciding actions of importance by lot, or by the first verse of Scripture on which his eyes might chance to fall. But his virtues far outweighed his faults. In singleness of aim, sincerity of consecration, and unselfish devotion to his cause he had not a superior in Christian history.

Wesley's humanitarian sympathies were wide. He detested slavery; and described the slave-trade in 1772 as "that execrable sum of all villainies."[1] He favored Sunday schools and endeavored to extend their use. He welcomed the work of John Howard for prison and hospital reform. Wesley was not a constructive theologian; though in middle life he engaged much in theological controversy, especially with Calvinists, whose system he regarded as funda-

[1] Tyerman, III, 114.

mentally immoral. His early companion, Whitefield, was one of those from whom this was a cause of separation for a time. He regarded a conscious "conversion" as the normal means of entrance on the Christian life; and believed Christian perfection obtainable by the disciple, so that, though a man is still liable to ignorance and error and needs Christ's constant forgiveness, yet "no wrong temper remains in the soul, and all thoughts, words, and actions are governed by pure love."[1] In its theology he and his movement were reactionary, reproducing the thoughts of an earlier Protestantism rather than the views which were then beginning to be entertained and which have since profoundly and widely modified conceptions of Christian truth; but in his evangelic and humanitarian enthusiasm he was a leader in the transformation of his age and a prophet of the future.

Wesley had no wish to break with the Church of England, though it is not easy to see how his movement could have been adjusted to it without material alterations in its constitution and worship. He long called his congregations simply "societies," and would suffer none but episcopally ordained men to administer the sacraments. The breach came in 1784, in consequence of the American Revolution. Methodism had been introduced into the American colonies, in New York City, by immigrants under

[1] *Ibid.*, II, 346.

the spiritual leadership of Philip Embury, in 1766. The work grew rapidly. In 1773, the first American Methodist "Conference" was held in Philadelphia. But the American Methodists were without ordained leaders, and the separation of the United States from the mother country made the release of American Methodism from British control desirable. Accordingly, in 1780, Wesley applied to the Bishop of London to ordain a minister for America. The candidate was refused, and, after mature deliberation, four years later, Wesley took the matter into his own hands. In September, 1784, in Bristol, he himself ordained Richard Whatcoat and Thomas Vasey for the American ministry, and consecrated Rev. Thomas Coke, already a priest of the church of England, as "superintendent" for the same work—a title which was soon transformed in America, apparently by Coke himself, into that of "bishop."[1] A year later, in a similar way, Wesley ordained ministers for Scotland; and ultimately for service in England itself. This was a complete breach with the Establishment. Methodism was now provided with its own self-perpetuating ministry.

One further act of 1784 completed the development of Methodism as an independent communion. In that eventful year, by a "Deed of Declaration" executed by Wesley and recorded in the Court of Chancery of Great Britain, the "Conference" was

[1] Tyerman, III, 331-34, 426-41.

given full legal status, its membership defined, and its authority to appoint, control, and expel preachers asserted. In its keeping the determination of the ministers of the Methodist chapels, then three hundred and fifty-nine in number, was placed. This was a resignation, freely made, by Wesley himself, to the representatives of the communion he had founded, of the control over it which he had thus far exercised. It was a wise and far-seeing act. It made Methodism self-governing and self-perpetuating, and it is not the least evidence of Wesley's unselfishness and organizing skill. The master who had created and governed knew when to release his control.

Wesley continued his work in remarkable vigor to the end of his long life. Of his early associates, Whitefield died in 1770, and Charles Wesley in 1788. Till the summer of 1789 he found his strength of body scarcely abated. Till a few days before his death he continued preaching, and his long itinerating journeys lasted almost to the end. He died in London, March 2, 1791, having nearly reached the age of eighty-eight. It was in the fulness of an accomplished work that places him first among English-speaking Christian leaders. No other of his race has been so extensive or so abiding in his influence for good.

At Wesley's death Methodism in Great Britain and the United States numbered 214 circuits, 507 preachers, and 119,735 members. In the period which has since elapsed it has steadily and rapidly advanced, and nowhere so conspicuously as in America. It now counts as of its ministry not less than 50,596 ordained men, besides its host of lay-preachers, and reckons its membership at 8,537,874.

But organized Methodism, great as it was and is, is only a part of the results of the Methodist movement. It revived the religious life of England. It formed the Christianity of a large part of America. It stimulated philanthropy, encouraged missions, and remade the Christian ideals of a large part of the English-speaking peoples. In a measure granted to no other of his nationality and speech Wesley realized his ideal: "I look upon all the world as my parish."

QUESTIONS

1. What was the effect of the decline of the Puritan controversy on the religious life of England? What was Deism? What the state of the higher classes?

2. What was the condition of the lower classes? Were there able men in the ministry? Why was their work relatively inefficient?

3. When and where was Wesley born? What was his parentage and education? What his abilities as a scholar?

4. What books influenced Wesley religiously? How did Methodism begin in Oxford? Who were the leaders of the club? How was it regarded by the students generally?

5. What can be said of Wesley's sojourn in America? Under what influences did he come? Why were they of value to him?

JOHN WESLEY

6. What were the time and circumstances of Wesley's "conversion"? What journey immediately followed it? Why?

7. What were the characteristics of Wesley's and Whitefield's preaching? How was it received?

8. Where did Wesley establish his first "chapels"? What was the origin of the "class-meeting"? How came Wesley to separate from the Moravians?

9. Why did Wesley adopt lay-preaching, itinerancy, and circuits? What was the origin of the "Conference"? What Wesley's authority over the Methodist movement?

10. What were some of Wesley's personal characteristics? His humanitarian zeal? His theology?

11. How did Wesley come to ordain ministers? Significance of the step? When did American Methodism begin?

12. How and when did Wesley resign his authority to the "Conference"? The nature and effects of their action?

13. Wesley's death? The greatness of his work? Its significance?

ADDITIONAL READING

John Wesley's Journal, abridged edition (Cincinnati, 1903).

Caleb T. Winchester, *The Life of John Wesley* (New York, 1906).

W. H. Fitchett, *Wesley and His Century* (London, 1906).

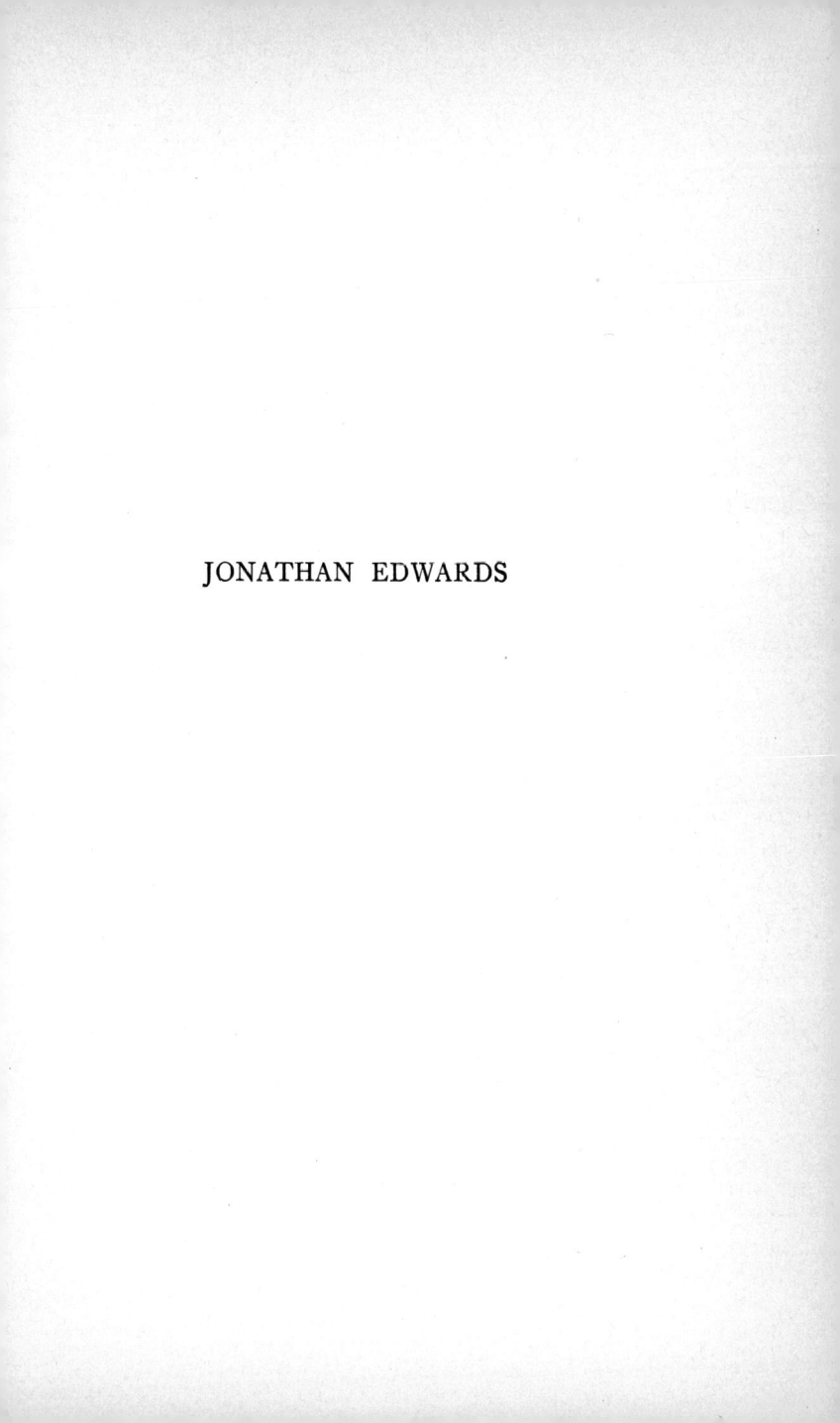

JONATHAN EDWARDS

XIX
JONATHAN EDWARDS

The New England colonies were founded under strong religious impulse. Whatever other factors entered into the determination of their settlers to cross the Atlantic, religion had undoubtedly the first place in forming their decision. To a degree probably unequaled in other European colonization, religion was a universal interest among these immigrants. Their faith, like that of English Puritanism from which they sprang, was of the Calvinistic type, strongly insistent on the sovereignty of God, the duty of entire obedience to his will, the helplessness of man to do right without God's transforming grace, and the natural fruitage of that grace in strong, conscientious character. Like the Puritans generally, they believed that the people should have some share in the government of church and state; and they carried this principle much farther than most Puritans, with resultant congregationalism in church government, and a large degree of democracy in civil institutions.

The intense religious fervor of the immigrants was not inherited, however, in its fulness by their children. In large measure such a result was inevitable. The first generation had been picked men and women in whom religion had been largely the principle of selection. Their children represented more nearly the average type of the English race. Certain special causes contributed, however, to the same decline The isolation of the settlements on the edge of a new continent, the constant struggle with the wilderness, and the presence of savage foes, were factors tending to weaken the ascendency of spiritual interests and to lower the high ideal of life. These were combated, with considerable success, by a devoted ministry and by educational institutions which had their crown in the founding of Harvard in 1636, and of Yale in 1701; but it was nevertheless true that the New England of the first third of the eighteenth century had greatly declined in religious fervor from the New England of the founders a century earlier. From that state of comparative lethargy the land was to be aroused by religious revivals, culminating in the "Great Awakening" of 1740-42, and in those revivals one of the foremost figures was to be that of the man who was also the ablest theologian and most powerful thinker that colonial New England produced, Jonathan Edwards. In him are to be seen the qualities of his age and country in their most characteristic, and at the same time in their noblest, development.

Jonathan Edwards was born in what is now South Windsor, Connecticut, on October 5, 1703, the same year that witnessed the birth of John Wesley. His father, Timothy Edwards, was pastor of the church in that parish, and a man of marked intellectual

JONATHAN EDWARDS

abilities; his mother was a daughter of Solomon Stoddard, the distinguished minister of Northampton, Massachusetts. He was the only son among eleven children. By heredity and training he was a typical representative of that class of conspicuous leadership in colonial New England which sought service in the Christian ministry. His early education was in his father's study; but he developed, even in boyhood, an innate keenness of observation of the ways of nature and a capacity for intelligent reasoning that were prophetic of his maturer powers. When not quite thirteen years old, in 1716, he entered Yale College. That recently founded seat of learning had as yet no certain home, and much of Edwards' course was spent in Wethersfield; but before its close the college had ceased wandering, and in New Haven he graduated, in 1720, at the head of his class. For the next two years he remained at the college engaged in further study. In these student days he not only read such philosophical works as he could procure, but began to formulate ideas of his own which show that had he been later less absorbed in theology, he might have been one of the greatest of the philosophers of the eighteenth century.

Always religious by nature, Edwards, not far from the time of his graduation, had an experience resembling that of Wesley, though even more mystical in form than the latter's "conversion." As he was reading the Pauline ascription: "Now unto the King eternal, immortal, invisible, the only wise God, be honor and glory for ever and ever, Amen,"[1] there came into his soul "a sense of the glory of the Divine Being." He thought: "How excellent a Being that was, and how happy [he] should be if [he] might enjoy that God . . . . and be as it were swallowed up in Him forever."[2] This mystical sense of the presence and reality of God and of the possibility of union of soul with him was to Edwards ever after the guiding principle of his religious life. God was henceforth not merely the most real of beings, but the dearest object of devotion. A Christian life without outgoing affection toward God and cheerful and acquiescent submission to all God's dealings with men was henceforth inconceivable for him. This led him to hearty acceptance of those Calvinistic doctrines of divine sovereignty which had heretofore seemed unpalatable to him; and the Calvinistic system, in its essential features, was to have in him its ablest American exponent.

A few months of preaching in New York City, in 1722 and 1723, ripened the youthful Edwards' spiritual nature by pastoral experience. To this period, when not yet twenty years old, belong his remarkable series of resolutions, of which one of the most characteristic is: "Never to do any manner of

[1] I Tim. 1:17.

[2] Edwards' own narrative, in S. E. Dwight, *The Life of President Edwards* (New York, 1830), p. 60.

thing, whether in soul or body, less or more, but what tends to the glory of God, nor be, nor suffer it, if I can possibly avoid it."[1] His services were now sought by several churches; but, from 1724 to 1726, he filled with much ability a tutorship in Yale College. Probably one inducing cause of his return to New Haven was the residence in that town of the remarkable woman whom he was to marry on July 28, 1727—Sarah Pierpont, a daughter of Rev. James Pierpont, the New Haven pastor from 1685 to 1714. She was indeed well worthy of his regard, and the union thus instituted was to be of the happiest. With unusual susceptibility to deep religious emotion, Mrs. Edwards combined executive force, social charm, and sweet, womanly leadership. A few months prior to this marriage Edwards accepted a call to become colleague pastor with his grandfather, Solomon Stoddard, in the care of the church in Northampton, Massachusetts. To this charge he was ordained on February 15, 1727, and the death of Stoddard two years later left the pastorate wholly to him.

Edwards was at once marked as a preacher of power. As in England before the work of Wesley and Whitefield, the characteristic preaching of the time was unemotional and little calculated to arouse strenuous feeling. Edwards' theologic position and his type of preaching were largely a return to those

[1] In full, Dwight, *op. cit.*, pp. 68–73.

characteristic of the founders of New England. In marked contrast to Wesley, his doctrine was intensely Calvinistic. The intellectual note was more evident than in the discourses of the great English evangelist. But, like Wesley, Edwards appealed powerfully to the emotions, though more by the matter of his message than by its form. In sermons of tremendous logical power, and often of vivid, sometimes lurid, imagery, he set forth God's absolute sovereign right to deal with men either in salvation or damnation, the joys of the Christian life, and the fearful terrors which he held to be the certain lot of the wicked. Such preaching had powerful effect. In December, 1734, a "revival," lasting some months, began in Northampton, that soon attracted public interest not merely in America but in Great Britain.[1]

Naturally one whose own ministry was so evangelistic welcomed George Whitefield when that greatest of English preachers made his meteoric tour of New England in 1740. It seemed as if the successes of his own Northampton ministry were now repeated on a scale commensurate with the English-speaking colonies. Wherever Whitefield went his congregations were as wax in his hands. Men cried out and women fainted. The work thus begun was taken up

[1] At the instance of Rev. Drs. Isaac Watts and John Guyse, Edwards prepared an account, to be found in any edition of his *Works*, and generally known as the *Narrative of Surprising Conversions*

by many evangelists, among whom Edwards himself was conspicuous, and the period of tremendous religious upheaval from 1740 to 1742 is known as the "Great Awakening." To Edwards it seemed at first the dawn of the millennial age. But, intense as it was for the time being, the movement soon spent its force, and it left behind a wake of division and controversy as to its real value. In Edwards the revival had a vigorous defender, though he was not blind to its extravagances; and after it had passed, he wrote, in 1746, in calm retrospect, his noble *Treatise Concerning Religious Affections*, in which he attempted to answer the question, "What is the nature of true religion?" To Edwards' thinking nothing deserves the name of religion that falls short of an absolute change of disposition, wrought by the Holy Spirit, and showing itself in unselfish love for divine things because they are holy, in meekness, tenderness of heart, and a life of Christian conduct toward one's fellow-men.

These experiences produced one change of importance in Edwards' own thinking. The church of which he was pastor had so far departed, under his grandfather's leadership, from original New England practice, as to admit all serious-minded seekers, whether consciously Christians or not, to the Lord's Supper. Edwards was now convinced of the wrongfulness of the custom, and not only refused further admissions on such terms, but wrote powerfully against it in his *Humble Inquiry* of 1749.[1] This change of practice, and certain mismanaged cases of discipline, turned his congregation against him. Great as he was as a thinker and a preacher, Edwards had little skill in handling men. The result was a distressing dispute, issuing in his dismissal from the Northampton pastorate in June, 1750.

Driven from his parish, at the age of forty-seven, with a family of ten children, he ultimately found employment in 1751, in the little frontier village of Stockbridge, Massachusetts, as pastor of its church and as the missionary of the English "Society for Propagating the Gospel in New England" to the Housatonic Indians there settled. To him the change was in many ways an exile, but it gave him the relative leisure and opportunity to write the works on which his fame as a theologian and as a philosopher rests. To Edwards the years in Stockbridge were his intellectual harvest time.

Of Edwards' four treatises, written in this eventful period, that on *Freedom of Will*,[2] published in 1754, is the most famous, though not perhaps the most influential. It was reared as a bulwark in

[1] *An Humble Inquiry into the Rules of the Word of God, Concerning the Qualification Requisite to a Compleat Standing and Full Communion in the Visible Christian Church* (Boston, 1749).

[2] *A Careful and Strict Enquiry into the Modern Prevailing Notions of That Freedom of Will Which Is Supposed to Be Essential to Moral Agency, Vertue and Vice, Reward and Punishment, Praise and Blame* (Boston, 1754).

defense of what Edwards believed a threatened Calvinism, and endeavors to show that man has sufficient freedom to be responsible for his actions, that he is not forced to act counter to his inclination, and yet that that inclination depends on what man deems his highest good. While man has full natural power to serve God—that is, could freely serve God if he had such an inclination—he will not serve God till God reveals himself to man as his highest good and thus renders obedience to God man's strongest motive. Edwards sought thus to maintain God's absolute sovereignty and complete disposal of his creatures, while holding men yet responsible. No keener argument in favor of this cardinal tenet of Calvinism has ever been advanced; yet the work is one so out of sympathy with the prevailing religious thought of the present age that is now largely neglected.

Even less present sympathy is commanded by Edwards' exposition of *Original Sin*,[1] issued in 1758. He affirms the utter corruption of mankind at whatever stage of existence from infancy to old age, and traces that evil state to our share in Adam's sin by a theory more ingenious than convincing. That which makes the individual man the same being today he was yesterday is the constant creative activity of God. In like manner, God, by an "arbitrary constitution," has made all men one with Adam, so that his primal sin is really theirs also.

[1] *The Great Christian Doctrine of Original Sin Defended* (Boston, 1758).

The two works just described were published in Edwards' lifetime; but two further discussions had been completed and were issued seven years after his death. One was *Concerning the End for Which God Created the World*, and had for its purpose to demonstrate that the manifestation of the glory of the creator, and the largest happiness of human beings, far from being incompatible purposes, as had been generally supposed, were "really one and the same thing." The universe in its highest possible state of happiness is the completest exhibition of the divine glory.

Most influential on New England thinking of any of Edwards' writings, though not so famous as his *Freedom of Will*, was the second of these posthumous publications, his *Nature of True Virtue*. In his thinking all virtue may be reduced to a single elemental principle. It is benevolence or love toward intelligent being in proportion to the amount of being which each personality possesses. No love less wide than this can be really good. Judged by this standard, a man must love God and his fellow-men more than he does himself. As interpreted by popular thought, it taught that sin is selfishness and righteousness is disinterested love to God and to one's fellows. No wonder that the earliest American foreign missionaries came from the ranks of Edwards' disciples.

In these works the American mind reached the highest level it attained in the eighteenth century.

They won widespread respect for their author as a man of genius, and they made thousands of theological disciples. It seemed as if Edwards was to have further opportunities to impress his thoughts and character on young men as the head of a school of learning. Princeton College had been founded in 1746, in hearty sympathy with the warm-hearted, revivalistic type of piety in furtherance of which Edwards had done such service. In 1757 he was called to its presidency. He hesitated to accept. Stockbridge afforded him the opportunity of quiet study and leisure for writing. Yet the possibility of influencing men in their formative years which the headship of Princeton would afford was not to be declined. Early in 1758 he removed to the scene of his new work. The small-pox was raging, and as a preventive measure he had himself inoculated. The disease, although usually mild under such circumstances, took an unfavorable turn, and on March 22, 1758, he died.

No man more fittingly symbolizes eighteenth-century New England at its best than Jonathan Edwards. High-minded, upright in all his dealings, learned, a devoted preacher, and a theologian of surpassing power, he represented that love of learning, that carefulness of conduct, and that sense of the primacy of the concerns of the soul, which was characteristic of his people in their noblest development—often, unfortunately, unrealized in the average man of that or any other age. His controversies are now ancient issues from which interest has largely vanished. His theology was molded by the viewpoints of his age, and awakens only a partial response in the present. But one characteristic abides in power and must forever link him with the great men of all Christian history. He had—and in a peculiar degree he made men feel that he had—a consciousness of the reality and presence of God. God was not to him a being remote and obscure. He was the closest of friends, the highest object of his loyalty, his adoration, and his love. That he walked close with God must always be the deepest impression which Edwards makes on those who come to know him and to understand the sources of his power.

QUESTIONS

1. What influences led to the founding of the New England colonies? What was the religious character of the settlers?

2. What causes induced a decline from the religious zeal of the founders?

3. When and where was Jonathan Edwards born? His parentage and early education? His promise as a student?

4. What were the circumstances of Edwards' conversion? What effect did it have on his conceptions of religion?

5. Where did Edwards teach? With what success?

6. Whom did Edwards marry? Her character?

7. Where was Edwards' first pastorate? His character as a preacher? The first revival? What attention did it excite?

8. When did Whitefield come to New England? Effect of his preaching? What was Edwards' relation to the revival?

9. What were the teachings of Edwards' *Treatise Concerning Religious Affections?* What change came over his views of the terms of admission to communion? What effect had this change on his relations to his Northampton church?

10. Where was Edwards next settled? What advantages and disadvantages had the place for him? What was his chief work there?

11. Describe Edwards' *Freedom of Will.* What importance is generally attached to it?

12. Speak of Edwards' *Original Sin.* Is its argument of permanent value?

13. What was the aim of his treatise, *Concerning the End for Which God Created the World?*

14. What was the importance of his *Nature of True Virtue?* Its conception of righteousness?

15. What college presidency did Edwards accept? His death? His character?

ADDITIONAL READING

S. E. Dwight, *The Life of President Edwards* (New York, 1830).

Alexander V. G. Allen, *Jonathan Edwards* (Boston, 1889).

Williston Walker, *Ten New England Leaders* (Boston, 1901), pp. 215-63.

HORACE BUSHNELL

XX
HORACE BUSHNELL

Though the "Great Awakening" of 1740-42 aroused what are now the New England and the middle states more intensely while it lasted than any other revival in their history, its effects speedily passed. As a whole, the eighteenth century was a period of religious decline in American history. The struggle for independence, which was but the severest of several wars in which public interest was profoundly enlisted, and the absorbing discussions which resulted in the formation of the Constitution of the United States, turned men's minds largely from spiritual interests. With the conclusion of these debates, however, a new and protracted period of religious awakening began. Commencing in 1792, and continuing at intervals till 1858, great revivals occurred in New England, the middle and southern states, and the new West of that age which is now the central region of the United States. It was a time of universal quickening. Evangelists, of whom Rev. Charles G. Finney may be mentioned as typical, preached with constant evidence of power to move men. Itinerant missionaries of Methodism, and ministers of Baptist, Presbyterian, Congregational, and other communions carried the gospel message to the new settlers on the ever-extending frontier and organized them into churches. Ministerial training received a great impetus through the establishment of theological seminaries. Foreign missions were inaugurated in 1810. Temperance reform began its beneficent work before the nineteenth century had far advanced. The agitation against slavery more and more enlisted attention from the fourth decade of that century till its settlement in the tremendous struggle between the states. The long period from 1792 to 1865 was, beyond any other in American history, one of religious growth and of quickening of public conscience on questions of moral reform.

In its dominant theological problems, its attitude toward theology in general, and its conception of the Christian life this period still bore the mighty impress of the leaders of the eighteenth century. With Wesley, Whitefield, and Edwards, men felt that the normal method of entrance into the Kingdom of God was by a conscious surrender—a "conversion." To secure such conversions was the object of revival effort. Salvation was emphasized in its individual rather than its social aspects.

The questions with which that period concerned itself in theology were essentially those which Edwards had made prominent; and as with the eighteenth-century thinkers, theology was regarded as capable of as exact, and as fundamentally intellectual, definition as the problems of geometry.

Theology was based on the apprehensions of the understanding rather than on the feelings, and, being so based, was largely in bondage to formalism in logical method and definition. This conception of theology trained a race of giant wrestlers; but it tended to magnify intellectual differences in the apprehension of relatively minor aspects of Christian truth into barriers scarcely to be passed. No period in our religious history has therefore been more prolific in denominational divisions.

Contemporary with this period, however, modifications of a very wide-reaching character were taking place in theology in Germany and England. The nature and work of Christ, the authority of Scripture, and the bases of religious truth were being re-examined. The character of theologic proof was investigated anew. These European discussions were low in influencing American thought, and their effects were scarcely felt in the period just described, though they have since come in as a flood. That when they did come they created no more conflict than actually occurred was due in considerable measure, at least in the northeastern part of the United States, to the work of Horace Bushnell, who with slight knowledge of what was in progress abroad, wrought on similar lines, presented an altered basis for theological conviction, and made their pathway easier for many when the time of transition and restatement arrived.

Horace Bushnell was born on April 14, 1802, in the village of Bantam in the township of Litchfield, Connecticut. His parents were of sturdy, enterprising farming stock. His father had been trained a Methodist; his mother an Episcopalian, but both were devoted members of the Congregational church, which was the only place of worship in New Preston, Connecticut, whither they removed when their son was three years old. In New Preston, Bushnell spent an active, hard-working boyhood; and there he made public profession of his Christian faith when nineteen years old in 1821. Two years later he entered Yale, graduating in due course in 1827.

Bushnell's college course was a time of intellectual questioning and painful doubt. He began to fear that religion could never be demonstrated by the understanding—the only way in which he then knew how to approach Christian truth. In this distressed frame of mind he met with the *Aids to Reflection*, that profoundly influential volume which the English poet-philosopher, Samuel Taylor Coleridge, had published in 1825. It was hard reading but it opened to Bushnell a new world. Coleridge not merely introduced German theology to English readers. To him Christian truth is not so much to be demonstrated by logic as perceived by ethical and spiritual feeling.[1] It derives its evidence "from

[1] The writer has made some use of his address at the celebration of the one-hundreth anniversary of Bushnell's birth by the Connecticut General Association, on June 17, 1902.

within." These thoughts were germinal for Bushnell's later development. They were a radical departure from the type of theological demonstration then characteristic of Anglo-Saxon thinking. They ultimately placed religious certainty for him on a new foundation.

Bushnell's doubts, however, did not immediately vanish. On graduation he tried journalism and next began the study of law. With that employment he combined the discharge of the duties of a tutorship in Yale which he accepted in 1829; and in connection with his labors as instructor a crisis in his faith and in his life-purposes came. The year 1831 was marked by a revival in Yale. Bushnell was distressed by his own want of sympathy with its enthusiasm; but he felt that he must do his duty by his students. He must follow such light as he had. He must "take the principle of right" for his law. It was a turning-point in his experience. A mighty rush of feeling burst the barrier of his intellectual doubts. As he said to his fellow-tutors: "I have a heart as well as a head. My heart wants the Father; my heart wants the Son; my heart wants the Holy Ghost—and one just as much as the other. My heart says the Bible has a Trinity for me, and I mean to hold by my heart." "The whole sky" of his religious firmament became "luminous about him;" and through this gateway of the feelings

Bushnell entered into the freedom and certainty of the Kingdom of God.[1]

Bushnell's new-found faith decided him to enter the ministry, and, from 1831 to 1833, he was a student in the theological department of Yale. On May 22, of the year last mentioned he was ordained to the pastorate of the North Congregational Church in Hartford, Connecticut, and so entered on the service of the city which was to be henceforth his home.

In Hartford Bushnell soon won attention as a preacher and a public-spirited citizen. As a pastor he was greatly beloved. Not an orator in the ordinary sense, his sermons and public addresses were, nevertheless, of impressive power, and continue to command appreciation, in published form, as among the best productions of the American pulpit of the nineteenth century. As a citizen, he was a man of far-reaching vision and inspiring leadership. Hartford owed to him much of the impulse that led to the introduction of public water works, and the beautiful park which bears his name was secured, in 1853 and 1854, entirely by his efforts at a time when the public mind had not generally awakened to the desirability of such improvements. This breadth and vitality of interest were the more remarkable because Bushnell's Hartford ministry was conducted under great physical disabilities. A tendency to pulmonary

[1] Mary Bushnell Cheney, *Life and Letters of Horace Bushnell* (New York, 1880), pp. 56, 59.

affection was evident as early as 1845. In that year and the next he sought health in Europe. Ten years later he went on the same errand to Cuba; most of 1856 was spent in California; but his disabilities so advanced that, in 1859, he had to lay down the burdens of the pastorate, and the remainder of his life he himself aptly described as one of "broken industry." Industrious it always was, and the marvel was that so feeble a frame could serve the active spirit as efficiently as it did.

Bushnell's first considerable doctrinal discussion arose, in 1847, by reason of the publication of two *Discourses on Christian Nurture*.[1] The age, as has been pointed out, was dominated by conceptions of entrance on the Christian life by a conscious, struggling "conversion" which Wesley and Edwards had made prominent. Over against this teaching Bushnell emphasized the value of family training. His argument was "that the child should grow up a Christian," to which he added the further explanation in the second edition of his work, "and never know himself as being otherwise." "He is to open on the world as one that is spiritually renewed, not remembering the time when he went through a technical experience, but seeming rather to have loved what is good from his earliest years."[2] Here,

---

[1] Boston and Hartford. An enlarged and revised edition was published at New York in 1861.

[2] Edition of 1861, p. 10.

then, was a sweeping criticism of what most of his contemporaries in non-prelatical American churches believed to be the only normal mode of entrance on the Christian life; a presentation, moreover, which identified the natural and the supernatural as but different sides of one divine order. Doubtless, its emphasis, like that of the view it opposed, was one-sided. There are many doors into the Kingdom of God. Nathanael came as truly as Paul. But, in the existing state of religious opinion, Bushnell's doctrine encountered strenuous opposition. Yet no theory advocated by him has won so wide acceptance, even if it is still far from meeting universal approval.

A profound religious experience through which Bushnell passed in February, 1848, prepared him for three remarkable addresses of that year, which he gathered together in a volume and published, in 1849, as *God in Christ*.[1] To them he prefaced a "Dissertation on Language" in which he explained, more fully than elsewhere, his convictions as to the nature and limitations of theology. To his thinking, the effort of theologians to define the exact content of religious truth in precise logical formulas was an attempt to achieve the impossible, since language could have no such power. Its words are more or less imperfect symbols of the realities they typify. On the contrary, Christian truth is to be felt rather than logically to be demonstrated. "There is a

[1] Hartford.

perceptive power in spiritual life . . . . , an immediate experimental knowledge of God, by virtue of which, and partly in the degree of which, Christian theology is possible."[1] Bushnell thus voices the appeal of Christianity to the ethical and religious feelings.

Having laid down these principles, Bushnell proceeded to define the Trinity and the Atonement in terms of Christian experience. What God may be in the depths of his infinite existence we may not grasp, but to our finite experience he is known as Father, Son, and Spirit. Christ's work, also, as known by our experience of it, is not a penal satisfaction to God for our sins, nor a governmental expression of God's moral rulership. Its effect is upon us. It is the ultimate expression of God's outreaching love to us, designed to draw us to him and lead us to regard sin and holiness from his point of view.

It is not surprising that a work that controverted then current theology at so many points aroused great dissent, and a demand that Bushnell be subjected to discipline. His own local association, though far from sympathizing in his views, declared him not "justly subjected to a charge of heresy." But another association brought the question before the General Association of Connecticut by appeals in 1849 and 1850, which were repeated in 1852, 1853, and 1854. It was a stormy time; but, in the end, the

[1] *God in Christ*, p. 93.

General Association refused to override the action of the local association of which Bushnell was a member. Thenceforward he was free from the peril of ecclesiastical discipline.

Bushnell's already feeble health was shattered by these labors and struggles; but in his invalidism he labored on the work which cost him most effort and to which he devoted his maturest thought. Published at length in 1858, it bore the title, *Nature and the Supernatural as Together Constituting the One System of God.*[1] Its contention is expressed in its title. The thought of the time separated the realm of nature and that of the supernatural by a great gulf. A miracle was a suspension of the laws of nature, which were for the time being as if they were not. In opposition to these views Bushnell argued that the two realms are in constant contact. Man lives in both. In part of his range of life he is in the sphere of cause and effect—of nature; in part he is free, self-governing or sinning, not under a law of cause and effect, but in the realm of the supernatural, i. e., that which is above the world of nature. Doubtless the growth of the doctrine of evolution has rendered obsolete much of Bushnell's argument; but its general trend is in the direction in which modern theology has moved, that of emphasizing the immanence of God, and of showing that the spiritual and the natural combine in the commonest ongoings

[1] New York, 1858.

of everyday life no less than in the great progress of redemption.

Bushnell's work was by no means accomplished when the volume just described was given to the world, but its more permanently influential part had already been achieved. Two sturdy and carefully wrought treatises, having to do with the Atonement, were to follow—*The Vicarious Sacrifice Grounded in Principles of Universal Obligation*, published in 1866, and *Forgiveness and Law Grounded in Principles Interpreted by Human Analogies*, of 1874. Their argument holds that "love is a principle essentially vicarious in its own nature." All love really worthy of the name, whether in God or man, strives to take on itself in helpful sympathy the sufferings and sins of the object of its affection. So Christ bore our sins in suffering for us, and so he reveals God's love to us. It was not by his interpretation of specific doctrines, however, that Bushnell influenced his age, so much as by his general attitude toward theologic truth, and the basis of its appeal to men. He stood for the rights of the feelings and of Christian experience to be heard rather than for the demonstrations of logic or the formulas which make their appeal primarily to the intellectual faculties. Theology with him is not an external body of truth interpreted to the reason, but a warm, vital Christian life of fellowship with God in Christ finding expression all too inadequately through the imperfect vehicle of language. It is something to be felt before it can fully be known.

With the publication of Bushnell's volume last mentioned his work was about over. His last years had been limited by great physical weakness; but the spirit retained all its eager keenness till it took its flight on February 17, 1876. His was a remarkable example of what may be accomplished amid the varied duties of an exacting pastorate and under the constant burden of disease.

Bushnell was not a theologian in the sense in which that designation may be applied to Edwards. He had no desire to be. He wrought out no close-argued logical system. He believed none possible, and he regarded it as the chief evil of contemporary theology that men had made the endeavor. He founded no school. No party calls itself by his name. But he had a poet's fire of imagination, and a prophet's perception of the reality of God. He strove to reach back beyond the formulas in which his contemporaries believed Christian truth to be absolutely defined to the greater spiritual verities which they and he alike felt, but which he regarded their formulas as merely symbolizing and oftentimes misrepresenting. He sought to make the presentation of Christianity simpler and more natural. In so doing, he made easy for many the transition from the older to the newer conceptions of the Christian faith. His work touched and strengthened and broadened many a mind that has been unable to accept his presentations of truth in their fulness. These are his greatest achievements, and they give him an abiding position in the history of American religious thought.

QUESTIONS

1. Were the effects of the Great Awakening permanent? What was the religious state of America during most of the eighteenth century? What great movement began about 1792?

2. What were some of the results of the new revival period? How long did it last?

3. What was the dominant conception of the mode of entrance on the Christian life? How was theology conceived? What changes were in progress in Europe?

4. When and where was Horace Bushnell born? His parentage? Religious antecedents? His Christian profession? Where did Bushnell go to college?

5. What was the argument of Coleridge's *Aids to Reflection*? What was its influence on Bushnell? What was Bushnell's career immediately after graduation? His religious doubts? How were they overcome?

6. How did Bushnell decide to enter the ministry? His training? His settlement? Character of his preaching? His services as a citizen? His health?

7. What was the view advocated in Bushnell's *Discourses on Christian Nurture*? Why and how did it oppose the current opinion of the time?

8. How came Bushnell to write his *God in Christ*? His theory of the power of language to express religious truth? How is Christian truth to be known?

9. How did Bushnell apply his principles to the doctrines of the Trinity and the Atonement? What efforts were made to discipline him?

10. What was the significance of his *Nature and the Supernatural?* How, in his opinion, are the two realms related?

11. What were Bushnell's later writings? Their purpose? What was the most significant part of his teaching?

12. Bushnell's death? His influence?

ADDITIONAL READING

[Mary Bushnell Cheney] *Life and Letters of Horace Bushnell* (New York, 1880).

Theodore T. Munger, *Horace Bushnell, Preacher and Theologian* (Boston, 1899).

INDEX

INDEX

Abelard, theologian, 178, 179.
Abraham, 13.
Adeodatus, 68, 72.
Ailli, Pierre d', theologian, 210.
Albertus Magnus, theologian, 181, 183.
Albigenses, *see* Cathari.
Alexander, bishop of Alexandria, 51–53.
Alexander II, Pope, 129, 130.
Alexander III, Pope, 162, 167.
Alexander of Hales, 181.
Alexandria, theological school of, 45, 46; Arianism in, 48, 50–60.
Alexios, emperor, 144, 147, 148.
Alypius, 72.
Amator, bishop of Auxerre, 93.
Ambrose, bishop of Milan, 71, 72, 103, 107.
Anabaptists, the, 293.
Anastasius, Roman emperor, 121.
Anselm, theologian, 178.
Anthony, monastic founder, 104.
Antioch, siege of, 148, 149.
Antoninus Pius, Roman emperor, 11.
Aquinas, Thomas, early life, 182; a Dominican, 182, 183; his career, 183, 184; death, 184; his aims, 181, 182; writings, 184; the *Summa*, 184, 185; the bases of truth, 185, 186; sin and grace, 186–88; the sacraments, 188–90; the future state, 191; influence, 191, 192; mentioned, 177, 181, 197, 198.
Arcadius, Roman emperor, 91.
Argyle, the earl of, 260.
Aristotle, influence of, 180, 181, 223.
Arius, theologian, 50–56, 59, 75.
Arles, Synod of, 89.
Arndt, Johann, 304.
Athanasius, early career, 53; purpose, 54, 55; theology, 54; first banishment, 56; second, 57, 58; at Sardica, 57; his great struggle, 58; later exiles, 58, 60; death, 60; character, 61; mentioned, 65, 103, 105, 106.
Augsburg, the Confession of, 231, 315; the Peace of, 231.
Augustine, theologian, early life, 67, 68; temptations, 68, 71; his son, 68, 72; intellectual awakening, 68; dislikes the Bible, 69; a Manichaean, 69, 70; influenced by neo-Platonism, 70, 72; professorship in Milan, 70; influenced by Ambrose, 71, 72; conversion, 71, 72; baptism, 72; return to Africa, 73; the *Confessions*, 67, 68, 73, 80; bishop of Hippo, 73; death, 73; influence, 74; on the church and sacraments, 75, 76, 188; on sin and grace, 76–80, 188; mysticism, 80; his *City of God*, 81; mentioned, 29, 88, 90, 91, 103, 107, 160, 178, 181, 184, 200, 221, 222, 248.
Augustine, missionary, 120.
Augustinians, the, 219, 221, 223.
Awakening, the Great, 342, 346, 347, 357.

Baldwin, crusader, 147, 149, 151.
Baptism, 14, 15, 26, 33, 34, 78, 189, 190, 227.
Bar Cochba, 10.
Basel, Council of, 218.
Basil, the Great, theologian, 60, 106, 107.
Beaton, David, Cardinal, 256, 257.
Beaton, James, Archbishop, 256.
Benedict, monastic reformer, life, 107, 108; his "Rule," 108–12.
Berkeley, George, Bishop, 323.
Bernadone, John, *see* Francis.
Bernadone, Peter, 164–66.
Bernhard, of Clairvaux, theologian, 178, 179, 221.
Bible, translations of the, 161, 162, 204, 219, 229.
Bobadilla, Nicolo, 278.
Böhler, Peter, 327.
Bohemond, crusader, 146, 149, 150.
Boleyn, Anne, 262.
Bonaventura, theologian, 181.
Boniface VIII, Pope, 197.
Boniface, missionary, 120.
Borgia, Francisco, 280, 281.
Bothwell, the earl of, 266.
Bruno, bishop of Toul, 126.
Bucer, Martin, reformer, 238.
Bullinger, Heinrich, reformer, 239.
Bushnell, Horace, religious antecedents, 357–59; early life, 360; spiritual struggles, 360–62; ministry, 362, 363; his *Christian Nurture*, 363; his *God in Christ*, 364; ecclesiastical discipline, 365, 366; later writings, 366, 367; death, 368; influence, 368, 369.

Caelestius, 79, 80.
Cajetan, Cardinal, 225.
Calixtus I, bishop of Rome, 35, 36, 44.
Calixtus II, Pope, 135.
Calpurnius, 90.
Calvin, John, religious antecedents, 239; early life, 239; education, 240, 241; his *Seneca*, 241; conversion, 241–43; the *Institutes*, 243, 248; settlement in Geneva, 244, 245; in Strassburg, 245; marriage, 245; return to Geneva, 245, 246; the *Consistory*, 246; opposition, 246; Servetus, 246; the Academy, 247; his aims and activities, 247, 248; relations to Knox, 255, 259; death, 248; theology, 248–51; mentioned, 258, 277.
Canstein, Baron von, 307.
Cappel, battle of, 239.
Carlos, prince of Spain, 266.
Cassiodorius, 111.
Cathari, the, 160–62, 170, 173.
Catherine de' Medici, 261.
Catholic, origin of name, 23; see, also, Church.
Celestine, Pope, 93, 94.
Chalcedon, Council of, 65.
Charlemagne, emperor, 121–23.
Charles I, king of England, 290.
Charles V, emperor, 228, 229.
Christ, the person of, 6, 13, 36, 48–51, 53–55, 59, 65, 66; imitation of, 159, 160; the work of, 187, 221, 232, 240, 365, 367.
Christian VI, king of Denmark, 311.
Church, the "Old-Catholic," 7, 23, 24, 27, 29, 30; theories of membership, 34–36; Augustine's doctrine, 75; Wiclif and Huss, 201, 210; Luther, 224, 227, 232.
Cicero, 68.
Cisnero, of Manresa, 276.
Clement, of Alexandria, 45.
Clement, of Rome, 119.
Clement III, anti-Pope, 134.
Clement VII, anti-Pope, 205.
Cluny, the monastery and movement, 125–27, 142, 143, 147.
Coke, Thomas, 334.
Coleridge, Samuel Taylor, 360.
Columba, missionary, 98.
Communion, *see* Supper.
Congregationalists, the, 289, 290.
Conrad III, emperor, 152.
Constance, Council of, 205, 211, 212, 218, 226.
Constans, Roman emperor, 56–58.
Constantine, Roman emperor, favors Christianity, 47, 48; in the Arian controversy, 51–53, 55, 56; mentioned, 34, 88, 142, 148.
Constantine II, Roman emperor, 56.
Constantine VI, Roman emperor, 121.
Constantius, Roman emperor, 36–58, 60, 67.
Cop, Nicolas, 241, 242.
Cotta, Ursula, 220.
Councils, see Basel, Chalcedon, Constance, Ephesus, Lateran, Pisa, Sardica.
Cromwell, Oliver, 290, 295.
Crusades, proposed by Hildebrand, 130, 131, 141; causes, 141–43; the First Crusade, 143–51; later crusades, 152; results, 152–54.
Cyprian, bishop of Carthage, 45, 67, 103.

Dante, 191, 198.
Darnley, husband of Mary of Scotland, 266.
David, Christian, 310.
Decius, Roman emperor, 43.
Diocletian, Roman emperor, 43, 74.
Dionysius, bishop of Rome, 49.
Dober, Leonhard, missionary, 312.
Dominicans, the, 181, 182, 198, 224, 275.
Dominick, monastic founder, 164, 275.
Donatists, the, 43, 74, 75.
Dorylaeum, battle of, 148.
Duns Scotus, theologian, 181, 191.
Du Tillet, Louis, 243.

Eck, Johann Maier of, 224–26.
Edward III, king of England, 199, 200.
Edward VI, king of England, 258, 259, 287.
Edwards, Jonathan, religious antecedents, 341, 342; early life, 342, 343; conversion, 343, 344; marriage, 345; ministry in Northampton, 345–48; the *Religious Affections*, 347; the *Humble Inquiry*, 348; at Stockbridge, 348; the *Freedom of Will*, 348, 350; *Original Sin*, 349; *End of Creation*, 350; *True Virtue*, 350; presidency of Princeton, 351; death, 351; character, 351, 352; mentioned, 358, 363, 368.
Edwards, Timothy, 342.
Embury, Philip, 334.
Elias, of Cortona, 171.
Elizabeth, queen of England, 259, 261–63, 267, 282, 288, 289.
Ephesus, Council of, 80.
Erasmus, scholar, 231.
Eusebius, bishop of Nicomedia, 51, 52, 55–59.
Eustace, crusader, 147.

INDEX

Farel, Guillaume, reformer, 244, 245.
Fell, Margaret, 296.
Ferdinand, king of Aragon, 219, 273, 274.
Finney, Charles G., revivalist, 357.
Fox, George, conversion, 291; religious principles, 292-94; preaching, 294; the Quakers, 293-99; sufferings, 294; journeys, 295, 296; marriage, 296; death, 298; his work, 298, 299.
Francis, of Assisi, early life, 164, 165; conversion, 165, 166; his brotherhood, 166-68; missionary labors, 169; disappointments, 170, 171; the stigmata, 172; death, 172; mentioned, 161, 177, 203.
Francis I, king of France, 243.
Francis II, king of France, 261.
Franciscans, the, 166-68, 172, 173, 181, 198, 201, 277.
Francke, August Hermann, 305-8.
Frederick "Barbarossa," 152.
Frederick IV, king of Denmark, 307.
Friedrich, elector of Saxony, 225, 229.

Gelasius I, Pope, 121.
Germanus, bishop of Auxerre, 93-95.
Gersdorf, Baroness of, 308.
Gnosticism, 5-7, 23, 24, 26, 49, 69, 70, 119, 160.
Godfrey, of Bouillon, crusader, early life, 146, 147; the march, 147-50; "Protector of the Holy Sepulcher," 150; death, 151; character, 151; mentioned, 159, 177.
Gregory I, Pope, 120.
Gregory VI, Pope, 127.
Gregory VII, Pope, see Hildebrand.
Gregory IX, Pope, 170.
Gregory X, Pope, 184.
Gregory XI, Pope, 201, 202, 205.
Gregory, of Nazianzen, 60, 106.
Gregory, of Nyssa, 60, 106.

Hamilton, Patrick, 256.
Harvard University, 342.
Henry III, emperor, 123, 126, 127, 130.
Henry IV, emperor, contest with Hildebrand, 130-35; mentioned, 141.
Henry V, emperor, 135.
Henry IV, king of England, 209.
Henry VIII, king of England, 262, 287.
Heraclitus, philosopher, 13.
Hermas, early Christian writer, 5, 104.
Hierakas, ascetic, 104.
Hildebrand, early life, 126, 127; reform in papal elections, 128; chosen pope, 129; his principles, 129, 130, 152; proposes a crusade, 130, 131, 141; contest with Henry IV, 130-35; death, 134; character, 135; mentioned, 121, 144, 147, 159.
Honoratus, monastic founder, 92.
Honorius, Roman emperor, 80, 91.
Honorius III, Pope, 170.
Hopkey, Sophy, 326.
Hosius, bishop of Cordova, 51, 52, 57.
Hospitallers, the, 152.
Howard, John, philanthropist, 320.
Hugo, of St. Victor, theologian, 179.
Huss, John, reformer, 210-13, 218, 222, 226.

Ignatius, of Antioch, 23.
Innocent I, Pope, 79, 120.
Innocent III, Pope, 163, 167.
Inquisition, the, 161.
Irenaeus, bishop of Lyons, 25-27, 66, 119.
Isabella, queen of Castile, 219, 273, 274.

James VI, king of Scotland (I of England), 267, 289.
Jerome, theologian, 106.
Jerusalem, captured by Mohammedans, 142; won by crusaders, 150; Latin kingdom of, 151, 152; captured by Saladin, 152; Loyola in, 277.
Jesuits, see Loyola.
John, the Apostle, 25.
John XII, Pope, 122.
John, king of England, 199.
John, of Gaunt, 202, 207, 209.
Julian, Roman emperor, 59, 60.
Julius, bishop of Rome, 57.
Justin Martyr, early history, 8, 9; conversion, 10, 11; his *Apology*, 11-16; accusations refuted, 12, 13; view of Christ, 13, 14; his *Dialogue*, 9, 14; worship at Rome, 15, 16; martyrdom, 16-19; mentioned, 23, 76.

Kerboga, Turkish sultan, 149.
Knights, of St. John, 152.
Knights Templars, 152.
Knights, Teutonic, 152.
Knox, John, religious antecedents, 255, 256; early life, 256; conversion, 257; at St. Andrews, 257, 258; a prisoner, 258; ministry in England, 258; at Geneva, and Frankfort, 259; in Scotland, 260; pastor in Geneva, 260-62; the *First Blast*, 261; the great struggle in Scotland, 262, 263; Protestantism

established, 263-65; contest with Queen Mary, 265-67; death, 267.
Knox, William, 256.

Lainez, Diego, 278, 280, 281.
Landulf, 182.
Lateran Council, the, 162.
Laud, William, Archbishop, 321.
Law, William, 323, 325.
Le Fèvre, Jacques, 239.
Lefèvre, Pierre, 278.
Leo I, Pope, 65, 120.
Leo III, Pope, 120, 121.
Leo IX, Pope, 126, 127.
Leo X, Pope, 225.
Leo XIII, Pope, 184, 192.
Liberius, bishop of Rome, 58.
Licinius, Roman emperor, 47.
Locke, John, philosopher, 322.
Louis VII, king of France, 152.
Lollards, the, 209; *see, also,* Wiclif.
Loyola, Ignatius, early life, 274; conversion, 275; the *Spiritual Exercises*, 276-78; studies, 277, 278; first disciples, 278; the Society founded, 278; the "Company of Jesus," 279-83; death, 280.
Lucius III, Pope, 163.
Lucius Verus, 11.
Luther, Martin, religious antecedents, 219, 220; early life, 220, 221; spiritual struggles, 220, 221; justification by faith, 77, 179, 221, 222; the *Theses*, 223, 224; the Leipzig Disputation, 225, 226; the great tracts, 226-28; burns the bull, 228; at Worms, 229; in the Wartburg, 229; changing attitude, 230, 231; marriage, 233; death, 231; his work, 232, 233; mentioned, 103, 209, 217, 219, 237-39, 242, 255, 273, 287.

Major, John, theologian, 256.
Mani, religious founder, 69.
Manichaeanism, 69, 70, 74, 160, 161.
Mar, the earl of, 260.
Marburg, Colloquy at, 231, 238.
Marcion, Gnostic, 7, 15, 31.
Marcus Aurelius, Roman emperor, 11.
Marsilius, of Padua, 198.
Martin, bishop of Tours, 107.
Mary, queen of England, 259, 261, 288.
Mary, "Queen of Scots," 260-63, 265-67.
Mary, of Guise, 259, 261-63.
Matilda, of Tuscany, 132.
Mauburnus, of Zwolle, 276.
Maxentius, Roman claimant, 47.
Maximilla, Montanist, 27.

Melanchthon, Philip, reformer, 231, 238, 258.
Methodism, 325-36; name, 326; preaching, 328; organization, 329-31, 333-35; extent, 335, 336.
Ministry, a priesthood, 45; Luther's view of, 232.
Monasticism, rise of, 44, 59, 103; influence on Augustine, 72-74; development of, 103-14; effects, 105, 106, 113, 233.
Monnica, mother of Augustine, 67, 70-72.
Montanism, 27-32, 35-37, 51.
Montanus, religious enthusiast, 27.
Moravians, the, 213, 309-15, 326, 327, 330.
Moray, the earl of, 260, 267.
Moses, religious founder, 13.

Newton, Sir Isaac, 322.
Nicaea, Council of, 51-53, 148; capture of, 148.
Nicholas I, Pope, 121, 123.
Nicholas II, Pope, 128, 130.
Nicolaitanism, 125-27, 135.
Nitschmann, David, missionary, 312.
Novatian, theologian and party leader, 43, 49.

Occam, *see* William of Occam.
Oglethorpe, James Edward, founder, 326.
Oldcastle, Sir John, 209.
Origen, theologian, 45, 46, 103.
Otto I, emperor, 122, 123.
Otto III, emperor, 123.

Pachomius, monastic reformer, 105, 107.
Palladius, 88, 93-95.
Papacy, its growth, 25, 35, 45, 57, 58, 65, 119-36; reform in elections, 128; its claims, 188, 189, 197; the schism, 205; reformatory efforts, 218.
Patricius, father of Augustine, 67.
Patrick, character and writings, 87; early life, 90; name, 90, 94; slavery, 91; conversion, 91; wanderings, 91-93; identical with Palladius? 88, 94, 95; work in Ireland, 93-98; mentioned, 103.
Paul, the Apostle, 3-5, 11, 15, 26, 28, 33, 48, 68, 77, 92, 172, 221, 222, 364.
Paul III, Pope, 279.
Pelagius, theologian, 75-77, 79, 80, 89, 93.
Penn, William, Quaker, 296, 297.
Pennsylvania, 297, 314.
Persecutions, 8, 11, 12, 29, 43, 74.

Peter, the Hermit, crusader, 145, 146.
Peter Lombard, theologian, 179.
Philip I, king of France, 144.
Philip II, king of France, 152.
Philip IV, king of France, 197.
Philip II, king of Spain, 266.
Pierpont, James, 345.
Pierpont, Sarah, 345.
Pietism, 304, 308.
Pippin, the Short, Frankish king, 121.
Pisa, Council of, 218.
Plato, philosopher, 9, 14, 31.
Polycarp, of Smyrna, 25.
Pontitianus, 72.
Possidius, bishop of Calama, 67.
Pothinus, bishop of Lyons, 26.
Potitus, 90.
Poverty, "apostolic," 159, 160, 162, 166, 167, 169, 209.
Praxeas, heretic, 31, 36.
Presbyterianism, 264.
Prierias, controversialist, 224.
Princeton University, 351.
Prisca, Montanist, 27.
Protestant, the name, 231.
Puritans, the, 288–90, 304, 305, 321, 341, 342.

Quakers, see Fox.

Raymond, of Toulouse, 146, 150.
Richard I, king of England, 152.
Richard II, king of England, 207, 209, 210.
Rizzio, David, 266.
Robert, of Normandy, 146.
Rodriguez, Simon, 278.
Rome, early worship in, 15, 16; see, also, Papacy.
Rudolf, of Swabia, 133, 134.
Rusticus, Junius, Roman magistrate, 16–19.

Sabellius, theologian, 49.
Sacraments, the, 75, 76, 188–90, 227, 232, 249, 294, 303.
Saladin, 159.
Salmeron, Alonso, 278.
Sardica, Council of, 57, 58, 119.
Scholasticism, 177, 180, 181, 217, 303.
Scifi, Clara, monastic founder, 168.
Scotus, see Duns.
Separatists, the, 289.
Septimius Severus, Roman emperor, 29.
Servetus, Michel, 246.
Sigismund, emperor, 211.
Simony, 125–27, 130, 135.
Socrates, philosopher, 13.
Spangenberg, August Gottlieb, 315.
Spener, Philipp Jakob, 304–6, 308.

Staupitz, Johann von, 221.
Stephen IX, Pope, 127.
Stephen, of Blois, 146.
Stoddard, Solomon, 343, 345, 347.
Supper, the Lord's, 16, 45, 190, 206, 210, 227, 238, 282, 347, 348.
Sutri, Synod of, 123.
Symmachus, Roman governor, 70.

Tancred, crusader, 146, 182.
Templars, the, 152.
Tertullian, early life, 28; character and conversion, 29, 30; his Montanism, 29–32, 35–37; service to Latin theology, 30, 33; writings, 30, 31; view of Christianity, 31–33; attitude toward "heretics," 32; sense of sin, 32, 33; on forgiveness, 34–36; quarrel with Calixtus, 35, 36; on the Trinity, 36; his style, a quotation, 37–39; mentioned, 44, 46, 49, 68, 103, 119.
Tertullianists, 29.
Tetzel, Johann, 223, 224.
Theodosius, Roman emperor, 60, 71, 91, 119.
Thomas of Bradwardine, theologian. 200.
Totila, King, 108.
Trinity, the doctrine of the, 13, 36, 48–50, 75, 246, 361, 365.
Trypho, Hebrew controversialist, 9, 10, 14.

Ugolino, Cardinal, see Gregory IX.
Universities, 180.
Urban II, Pope, 143–45, 159.
Urban IV, Pope, 183.
Urban VI, Pope, 205.

Valdez, religious leader, 162–64, 166, 167, 203.
Valens, Roman emperor, 60.
Valentinian III, Roman emperor, 120
Valerian, roman emperor, 43.
Valerius, bishop of Hippo, 73.
Vasey, Thomas, Methodist, 334.
Victorinus, rhetorician, 72.

Waldenses, the, 162–64, 167, 170, 173, 212, 293.
Waldo, see Valdez.
Waterland, Daniel, 323.
Watts, Isaac, 323.
Wenzel, king of Bohemia, 211.
Wesley, Charles, 325–27, 335.
Wesley, John, religious antecedents, 321–24; early life, 324; at Oxford, 325, 326; in America, 326; meets Moravians, 326, 327; conversion, 327; preaching, 328; Methodism, or-

ganized, 329-31, 333-35; marriage, 331; characteristics, 331, 332; theology, 332, 333; death, 335; influence, 335, 336; mentioned, 203, 342, 343, 345, 346, 358, 363.
Wesley, Samuel, 324.
Wesley, Susannah, 324.
Westminster Assembly, the, 290.
Whatcoat, Richard, Methodist, 334.
Whitefield, George, evangelist, 324, 326-28, 335, 345, 346, 358.
Wiclif, John, antecedents, 199; early career, 200; theory of "lordship," 201; supported by John of Gaunt, 202; his "poor priests," 203, 204; his translation of the Bible, 204; becomes more radical, 205, 206; the peasant revolt, 207, 208; influence in Bohemia, 210-13; memory condemned, 211; mentioned, 217, 222.
William, the Conqueror, 129, 199.
William, of Occam, 198.
William, the Silent, 282.
William, Thomas, reformer, 257.
Wishart, George, reformer, 257.
Worship, early Christian at Rome, 15, 16; changes in third century 44, 45; monastic, 110; Luther's conception of, 233, 238; Zwingli's, 237, 238; in Scotland, 265.

Xavier, Francisco de, missionary, 278, 280.
Ximenes, Spanish reformer, 219, 274.

Yale University, 342, 343, 345, 360, 361.

Zeisberger, David, missionary, 314.
Zerbolt, of Zütphen, 276.
Zinzendorf, Nicolaus Ludwig von, early life, 308; type of piety, 308, 316; education, 306, 309; the Moravians, 309-11; missionary zeal, 311-13; opposition, 313, 314; in America, 314; last days and character, 315, 316; Wesley visits, 327.
Zosimus, Pope, 79, 80.
Zwingli, Ulrich, reformer, 231, 237-39, 255.